# AMERICANIZATION STUDIES

PATTERSON SMITH REPRINT SERIES IN
CRIMINOLOGY, LAW ENFORCEMENT, AND SOCIAL PROBLEMS

*A listing of publications in the* SERIES *will be found at rear of volume*

# AMERICA VIA THE NEIGHBORHOOD

# AMERICANIZATION STUDIES

### THE ACCULTURATION OF IMMIGRANT GROUPS
### INTO AMERICAN SOCIETY

## WILLIAM S. BERNARD, EDITOR

PUBLICATION NO. 125: PATTERSON SMITH REPRINT SERIES IN
CRIMINOLOGY, LAW ENFORCEMENT, AND SOCIAL PROBLEMS

# AMERICANIZATION STUDIES
The Acculturation of Immigrant Groups
into American Society

REPUBLISHED UNDER THE EDITORSHIP OF
## WILLIAM S. BERNARD

# 2
# America via the Neighborhood

BY
### JOHN DANIELS

WITH A NEW INTRODUCTION BY
FLORENCE G. CASSIDY

INDEX ADDED

MONTCLAIR, NEW JERSEY
## PATTERSON SMITH
1971

SBN 87585–125–8

Library of Congress Catalog Card Number: 73–108242

This book is printed on
three-hundred-year acid-free paper.

# INTRODUCTION
## TO THE REPUBLISHED EDITION

*By Florence G. Cassidy*

*America via the Neighborhood* was published in 1920. It exemplified sanity and objectivity in the midst of the strident voices and confused utterances of the period. It took cognizance of projects which the immigrant had organized on his own behalf and the degree of success achieved. It described the programs which social agencies, trade unions, cooperatives, neighborhood associations, schools, libraries, political organizations, and local units of government had sponsored for his benefit, with and without involving him in finance or policy making. This volume, like other studies in the series, defined Americanization as "the union of native and foreign-born in all the most fundamental relationships and activities of our national life." This was a goal greatly to be desired but difficult to attain in the America of that day.

In fact, it has not yet been fully attained, but wherever and whenever in the past fifty years this underlying philosophy has prevailed and there has been a true working partnership between native born and foreign born, the result has been a richer, fuller, more rewarding life for both partners.

It is the purpose of this preface to indicate the long road we have traveled since 1920, to note fluctuations in public opinion along the way, to point out significant changes in the character of our immigration and in the laws under which the immigrant has been admitted, and especially to call attention to relevant changes in the programs of nationality societies, neighborhood organizations, and social agencies serving immigrants and their children.

The decade which began with 1920 was a period when foreign-born residents of this country, a large number of whom were naturalized citizens of the United States, were frequently referred to collectively as "the immigrant," rather than as persons of various clearly defined national origins or cultural groupings. *America via the Neighborhood,* however, called them by name and spoke specifically of Finns, Poles, and Bohemians. It recognized their historical and cultural differences, and stressed the positive value of using their respective mother tongues and familiar traditions in furthering group solidarity and in building self-directed, democratically controlled ethnic communities. In addition, it described typical civic and educational projects which they themselves had initiated and carried out successfully.

The general public for the most part used the term "the immigrant" indiscriminately to apply to both "old-time immigrants" and relatively recent arrivals, both of whom were experiencing conflicting feelings of self-esteem and satisfaction on the one hand, and of alienation and rejection on the other.

At one moment, the so-called immigrant took pride in identification with the newly independent countries of Europe which had emerged, or regained their freedom, at the close of World War I, a pride which he shows today as he celebrates their fiftieth anniversaries of independence or of restoration to freedom, regardless of whether independence is now a memory or a present reality.

The next moment, he was deeply hurt because of the denunciations of his kinsmen by the adherents of the "Nordic Myth," by the perpetrators of raids on the halls belonging to his mutual benefit societies, and by the proponents of new restrictive legislation, who were constantly pointing the finger of scorn at the alleged social inadequacies of the immigrant, as set forth in the forty-two volumes of the pre-war report of the United States Immigration Commission, then to be found in public libraries throughout our land.

In a very personal way, the immigrant and his family had become "Exhibit A" in the great debate on American immigration policy:

Should immigration to the United States be subject to a definite quantitative limitation in addition to the allegedly qualitative restrictions in the Immigration Act of February 5, 1917?

If some restriction was needed, how much and on what basis?

Should preference be given to immigrants from northern and western Europe as against southern and eastern Europe?

If no restriction, how avoid unfair competition in the labor market?

How forestall economic depressions for which "an unlimited supply of cheap immigrant labor" was held mainly responsible?

Both the "old timers" and the newer arrivals were rejoicing in the fact that immigration figures were going up again. A total of 805,228 immigrants had arrived in the United States during the twelve months ending June 30, 1921, as contrasted with 430,001 the previous year. This was a small number compared with the 1,285,349 who arrived in 1907, the year when immigration to the United States reached its peak, but it was enough to alarm the restrictionists.

The newer arrival, whose family had not been able to join him because of closed frontiers and lack of shipping during the war years, was now planning to send for them, and was dismayed by hostile references to "opening the flood gates to let the new immigrants in." The older immigrant, also, was disturbed by these intemperate attacks, and withdrew more and more into his own organizations where he would not have to listen to raucous denunciations and where he could devote his energy to expanding the programs of his societies and to building new social halls for the use of their members.

Furthermore, the immigrant believed that this was the right time for such expansion, as the 1920 census had revealed that the total foreign-born population of the United States was 13,920,692. It reached 14,204,-149 in 1930, but this upward trend was reversed in 1940. The total foreign white stock (foreign-born plus American-born of foreign parentage) was 36,398,958 in 1920 and attained a high of 39,885,788 in 1930. Obviously, nationality halls built during the previous century were not adequate in number or in size for such a potential membership.

Most of the large mutual aid or beneficial societies, with their combined insurance and sociability features, were organized in a day and age when we had no statutory workmen's compensation in this country, no hospital insurance, very limited private industrial insurance, and very rare labor contracts with pension or insurance provisions. Granted that the "death benefits" paid by these societies were inadequate by present-day standards, the creation of such organizations, nevertheless, marked a step forward, showed the imagination and initiative of immigrant leaders, and gave ample evidence of the readiness of the rank and file to unite in furthering common objectives.

The national organizations themselves were started before 1900 in the main, although the campaign to build "homes" (a term used for social halls for their local lodges, not for residences) was a major activity of the 1920's. The Czechoslovak Society of America was founded in 1854, the Polish Roman Catholic Union in 1873, the Polish National Alliance in 1880, the Croatian Fraternal Union in 1894, and the Ukrainian National Association also in 1894, to cite but a few examples.

Sometimes the local units were organized first, as in the case of the Polish Roman Catholic Union, and the national body linked the individual locals together. In other instances, the national headquarters chartered locals and organized a series of lodges, "nests" (the name used by the Sokols or "Falcons"), chapters, or posts, and took the initiative in forming "councils and circuits," designations used by the Polish

National Alliance for federations of local "groups" formed on a city, regional, or statewide basis.

As time went on, nationality organizations developed various programs which had little to do with insurance, such as the Sokol movement among Czechs, Slovaks, and Poles, with its emphasis on gymnastics, physical fitness, and folk dancing, and the formation of excellent choral societies in Croatian, Finnish, and Ukrainian communities, to name but a few.

In 1920, a large percentage of the naturalized citizens of the United States, like the native born, were thinking more about economic issues and cultural activities than about building up and consolidating their political power. They failed to work out a sophisticated strategy against the extreme nationalists and the fanatical restrictionists of the day who wanted not only to reduce the number of new immigrants to be admitted, but also to add to the categories of aliens among the old immigrants subject to mandatory deportation.

The great debate on American immigration policy, therefore, went on without much effective participation on the part of the opposition and resulted in the passage of a series of acts based on successive new restrictive formulas:

The Quota Law of 1921, limiting the admission of aliens to three percent of the foreign-born of that nationality living in the United States according to the 1910 census.

The Immigration Act of 1924, fixing the immediate annual quota at two percent of the number of persons of that nationality residing in

the United States in 1890, and introducing
The National Origins Quota System to begin
July 1, 1929, which was continued in the
Immigration and Nationality Act of 1952 which
in its main essentials governed our laws and
procedures until the passage of the Act of
October 5, 1965.

There were certain nonquota classifications such
as residents of independent countries of the Western
Hemisphere and the wives, husbands, and minor children of United States citizens; there were also certain
preferences within quotas. In addition special liberal-
izing legislation was enacted, such as the Displaced
Persons Act of 1948 and the Refugee Relief Act of
1953. The general trend, however, was in the direction of restriction.

More serious than the limitations on new immigration was the absence prior to 1940 of discretion
not to deport in hardship cases where deportation
would mean the separation of families.

These were the constantly changing laws which,
together with the social attitudes they reflected, formed
"the invisible environment of the immigrant" from
1920 to 1970. Let us now turn to the varied educational and social work programs organized during
these same years to meet the needs of the foreign-
born and their children and to make the native-born
more aware of immigrant gifts to American life;
whether they were programs actually described in
*America via the Neighborhood,* or social services inspired by this epoch-making study; whether technically organizations serving a specific neighborhood, or

local affiliates of national agencies. What were the changes in the constituency, organizational structure, program content, and major emphases of these organizations during this period?

One of the first organizations to relate its program to the mutual aid societies which had been organized by old-time immigrants was the Foreign Language Information Service, an outgrowth of our government's information service to naturalized citizens and foreign-born residents of the United States during and directly following World War I. In 1921 it was reorganized as an independent private agency and immediately started furnishing releases to the foreign-language press regarding laws primarily of concern to the foreign-born. It also described American institutions and public services readily available to newcomers to America. At the same time, it sent to the English-language press releases about outstanding contributions of foreign-born citizens to our common life. It published a bulletin, *The Interpreter,* and later a magazine, *Common Ground,* both of them publications designed "to interpret America to the immigrant and the immigrant to America." It engaged staff who spoke many languages, cultivated the officers of large nationality organizations, attended the conventions of these bodies, and invited them to suggest topics for releases of special interest to their members. In addition, it issued, and its successors have continued to issue, *Interpreter Releases,* which are technical bulletins about immigration laws and procedures referred to constantly by a great variety of organizations and individual specialists handling cases involving immigration, naturalization, expatriation, suspension of deportation, admission of foreign visitors, student visas, change of status, etc.

The Foreign Language Information Service, which later became the Common Council for American Unity, did not organize neighborhood groups, but gave to organizations working on a neighborhood basis in various ethnic and cultural communities tools that they needed for their own programs of helping the foreign-born become more fully oriented in American society and of making the native-born more aware of the current interests, special needs, and distinctive cultural contributions of various nationality communities. In 1959 the Common Council for American Unity merged with the American Federation of International Institutes, which was an agency definitely in the field of community organization, to form the present American Council for Nationalities Service. Let us now turn to the history of International Institutes.

In the 1920's, International Institutes, like the Foreign Language Information Service and other organizations serving the foreign-born, underwent many changes. When John Daniels was writing *America via the Neighborhood,* International Institutes were branches of the Young Women's Christian Associations, and their initial program consisted largely of visits to the homes of foreign-born women by social workers who spoke their respective languages and knew their traditions. This program, which resulted in the formation of informal, self-directed clubs, was described by Daniels as "a good start."

As time went on, a service bureau was added to

help both recently arrived immigrants and "old time" aliens who were encountering problems under our immigration and naturalization laws, or who needed assistance in filling out complicated government forms which were prerequisites for bringing their relatives to America or becoming United States citizens. Assistance offered also included representing the alien in exclusion and deportation cases where deportation would have meant the separation of families. All these technical services were equally available to men and women.

International Institutes were also increasing their contacts with nationality communities in other ways, particularly through their program of celebrating holy days and holidays dear to the foreign-born, an activity which grew to include the organization of folk art exhibits and the presentation of folk festivals in partnership with nationality leaders, both men and women.

It therefore seemed somewhat illogical for International Institutes to remain branches of a woman's movement. Consequently, with the hearty approval and cordial endorsement of the National Board of the Young Women's Christian Associations, most International Institutes throughout the United States became independent social agencies with boards of directors of men and women, native-born and foreign-born, of many nationalities, races, and faiths—truly representative of their constituencies in corporate structure as well as in program.

Similarly, the Department of Work with Foreign-Born Women separated from the National Board of the Young Women's Christian Association and became the national headquarters of the independent International Institutes and of other local organizations with similar programs but differing names which wished to become affiliated. The resulting national agency at first was called the National Institute of Immigrant Welfare and, later, the American Federation of International Institutes. Still later, it joined with the Common Council for American Unity to form the present American Council for Nationalities Service. The two constituent organizations supplemented each other in program content and in methods of work, the one specializing in the organization of community projects designed to bring native-born and foreign-born together in work for common objectives, the other in the molding of public opinion through the mass media and through special releases to agencies, public and private, serving the foreign-born.

Meanwhile, other organizations, local and national, working with the foreign-born, or the neighborhood, or both, were developing significant programs, some of them on a demonstration or experimental basis.

Whenever neighborhood organizations are mentioned, one at once thinks of social settlements. One of their major activities in 1920 was that of helping mothers' clubs made up of foreign-born women to participate effectively in civic affairs. This was an appropriate year for such an activity, as it was the year in which the Woman Suffrage Amendment became effective nationwide (although women had voted in some states prior to that date).

Many other settlement activities were of deep concern to immigrant communities. Three additional examples may serve to indicate their breadth, variety, and importance:

Leading social settlements, notably Chicago's Hull House, endorsed and supported the findings of Dr. Alice Hamilton's famous studies of the health hazards to which foreign-born industrial workers were exposed. Dr. Hamilton was a resident of Hull House when these studies were initiated; many of the foreign-born living in the neighborhood were employed "in the dangerous trades," to use her phrase; and the creation of a state commission to conduct further investigations was urged by residents, board, and club members alike.

In New York and Cleveland, settlement projects included the sponsorship of neighborhood art theatres which produced plays based on folk material; and in New York, Cleveland, and Detroit, music school settlements gave individual instruction in music and concert opportunities to talented youth among the foreign-born and in the black community.

New York's Henry Street Settlement was a pioneer in establishing a visiting nurse service in immigrant neighborhoods, a type of service which on a greatly expanded scale is now operated by Visiting Nurse Associations throughout the United States.

Research which resulted in new measures to prevent industrial diseases, the provision of enlarged opportunities for self-expression through the arts, and the establishment of a public health nursing service were more truly services of benefit *to* the foreign-born than community programs initiated *by* them. When the people of the neighborhood saw what was being accomplished by these investigations and social demonstrations, they were increasingly interested and gradually became involved more and more in policy making and finance. In other words, they became partners instead of remaining merely clients, pupils, or patients.

The extent of the involvement of individual foreign-born leaders, and of immigrant communities as a whole, in year-around health, recreational and educational services, and the extent to which they united with other organizations in sponsoring city-wide temporary interagency projects varied from year to year and from city to city.

Large-scale recreation programs, when sponsored by social settlements, were usually on a demonstration basis, and were of more interest to the second generation than to immigrants themselves. Most activities of this nature have been taken over by public recreation commissions at the end of their respective demonstration periods. In those cities, however, where park or recreation departments built and maintained a chain of "park centers" or "field houses" suitable for meetings of adult nationality societies or for concerts, as in Chicago, they were used extensively by the foreign-born. Since the park centers were paid for out of tax funds, they were not subject to the objections raised against institutions and organizations

financed mainly by persons living outside the neighborhoods which they served.

Social settlements and some thirty nationality societies cooperated with the New York State Department
of Education and the Board of Education of the City
of New York in sponsoring, planning, and participating in the huge combined homelands exhibit and
festival known as "America's Making Exposition"
held at the 71st Regiment Armory in New York in
1921.

The folk festival movement has continued to grow
ever since, nurtured by International Institutes and
Folk Festival Councils. It reached its high point with
the Folk Festival of the Homelands presented at the
Guild Theatre in New York in 1932. In more recent
years, there has been greater emphasis on general participation in folk dancing than on stage presentations,
and more decentralized, qualitative exhibits of characteristic handicrafts than huge expositions of folk
arts. The expositions, however, were effective in giving recognition and status to nationality communities
at a time when such recognition was greatly needed.

International Institutes in Boston and Buffalo still
emphasize folk dancing and folk music at their international balls; and St. Paul, Milwaukee, Detroit, and
Toledo periodically sponsor homelands exhibits or
folk fairs lasting several days and combining in various proportions features that have long characterized
Old World markets, international pageants, and folk
festivals. They believe that such activities contribute
to the participants' sense of cultural continuity and
emotional security.

The demand for "Black Studies" in our high schools and universities, similarly, is a current example of the ever-present quest for cultural continuity and the need for community recognition. So also is the little theatre movement with the underlying dramatic themes, authors, producers, managers, stage designers, directors, and actors all drawn from the black community. Many of these productions have been inspired by the high standards set by Karamu House in Cleveland, a center founded in 1910 and long distinguished for its music, modern dance, and theatre. (The word "Karamu" comes from East Africa, being the Swahili term for "center of the community" or "place of enjoyment.")

Writers and speakers on the general subject of ethnic communities are apt to couple the phrases "cultural continuity" and "orientation in American society" when outlining a neat twofold program to meet the major needs of immigrants and their children. John Daniels in *America via the Neighborhood,* however, went beyond *orientation* and stressed *"participation* in the affairs of the local community and the larger life of America."

One of the most effective and characteristically American forms of civic participation is involvement in Community Chests and Councils of Social Agencies, or to use present-day terminology, in United Funds and United Community Services. Raising money for causes which they deemed important was not a new activity for the foreign-born, whether naturalized citizens or aliens. As previously indicated, they raised large sums of money for the construction of buildings for their nationality societies. During World War I they participated effectively in Liberty Loan campaigns, particularly in Syracuse, where they were an integral part of the organizational structure of the campaign. In other cities, especially in Cincinnati, Cleveland and Detroit, which were pioneers in the federated giving or Community Chest movement, they took part in and contributed to United War Fund and Patriotic Fund drives. They also participated in varying degrees, the country over, in American Red Cross campaigns.

During World War II, nationality involvement in War Chests, which were combined campaigns for foreign and local needs, was much greater for two reasons:

> Foreign relief appeals for aid to the civilian population in many of their homelands were as much a part of the War Chest as the United Service Organizations (USO) or the local social agencies normally financed by the Community Chest.

> Some War Chests, as in Detroit, had a Nationality Section with its own captains, secretaries and teams drawn from the nationality communities, its own campaign headquarters and featured report days, and provision for its voice to be heard in budget allocations.

From 1937 to 1964, Detroit also had a nationality department in its Council of Social Agencies (later known as United Community Services), whose staff and committee members attended meetings of nationality societies to become familiar with their programs and methods of work and in turn invited them to send representatives to neighborhood councils, sought their views on pending immigration legislation, and worked to secure nationality representation on boards of directors of city-wide agencies belonging to the Council of Social Agencies, often joining with labor leaders to secure adequate labor representation also. All this was in marked contrast to the 1920 picture as painted in *America via the Neighborhood:*

> The deficiency of Community Councils is especially pronounced in immigrant neighborhoods. They seldom include representatives of local immigrant organizations or labor bodies, two vital interests of the foreign-born, and naturally they do not become an organic part of such neighborhoods. [P. 308]

All the successful United Funds today have drawn representatives of organized labor and of nationality communities into their top leadership and into their campaign structure at all levels, including the plant and neighborhood canvass.

The most spectacular change in the past fifty years has been in the character of our immigration, not in the programs of nationality societies, social agencies, or United Funds. Beginning with the refugees from Hitler's Germany, continuing through the years of the Displaced Persons Act of 1948 and the Refugee Relief Act of 1953, on through the coming of the Hungarians in 1956–1957, down to today's Cuban refugees arriving by air in Miami, we have witnessed the arrival of thousands of persons of great talent and high education who normally would never have left their seemingly secure positions at home.

*Refugees in America,* the report of the Committee for the Study of Recent Immigration from Europe, prepared by Professor Maurice R. Davie of Yale University (1947), calls attention to the twelve Nobel Prize winners who came to live in the United States between 1933 and 1947, and points out that 103 refugees were listed in *Who's Who in America, 1944–45,* and 220 in *American Men of Science, 1944.* This study of refugee immigration was sponsored jointly by the American Christian Committee for Refugees, the American Friends Service Committee, the Catholic Committee for Refugees, National Refugee Service and the United States Committee for the Care of European Children. National Refugee Service was merged later with Service to Foreign Born of the National Council of Jewish Women to form United Service to New Americans. This new agency in turn later joined with the Hebrew Sheltering and Immigrant Aid Society and the migration services of the Joint Distribution Committee to form the present United HIAS Service. These were the national agencies that specialized in service to refugees and later, with additions and realignments, in service to displaced persons.

The greatest needs of refugees were for employment at highest skill and assistance in becoming reestablished in the professions, particularly in the removal or overcoming of frustrating barriers based on citizenship and residence, not on medical knowledge, in the licensing requirements for physicians in certain states.

Generally speaking, refugees were not interested in a pattern of organization based on proximity of residence in a given neighborhood in the United States, or on the basis of origin in the same village, city, or region abroad. They preferred organizations established on an "interest basis" such as science, the arts, or membership in the same profession. This is not to say that they were uninterested in civic affairs, but rather to indicate that they were more interested "in the larger life of America" than in the life of the neighborhood.

Following the passage of the Displaced Persons Act, nineteen voluntary agencies were accredited to give "assurances" regarding displaced persons (i.e., assurances of inland transportation, employment, housing, and assurances that the displaced person would not become a public charge). There was also provision for individual assurances endorsed by State Commissions on Displaced Persons. The nineteen voluntary agencies included the five previously active in the resettlement of refugees, but by now the American Christian Committee for Refugees had become part of Church World Service and the Catholic Committee for Refugees had been absorbed by the National Catholic Welfare Conference.

The following nationality organizations were also accredited by the federal Displaced Persons Commission: American Committee for the Resettlement of Polish Displaced Persons, American Hellenic Educational Progressive Association, American National Committee to Aid Homeless Armenians, Serbian National Defense Council of America, Tolstoy Foundation, United Friends of Needy and Displaced People of Yugoslavia, and the United Ukrainian American Relief Committee.

It should be noted also that additional nationality organizations operated within the framework of large religious bodies, as for example, the United Lithuanian Relief Fund of America which was affiliated with the National Catholic Welfare Conference and sent its "assurance" through that organization.

A great many individual sponsors who had never previously worked in cooperation with immigrant communities and who knew very few foreign-born citizens at the outset of the program learned a great deal and derived much pleasure from their involvement in the Displaced Persons Program and their personal contacts with displaced persons, particularly in communities where there were no immigration specialists and where the churches were the sole sponsoring agencies. Americanization seems to have "worked both ways."

The last great change in our basic immigration law was the Act of October 5, 1965, which did away with the National Origins Quota System and provided for quotas to be assigned in the main on a first-come-first-served basis. It is not a wholly satisfactory law to many citizens because immigrants from the Eastern and Western Hemispheres are not subject to identical provisions in the law and the regulations.

Naturalized citizens have now attained a high degree of skill in political activities and many of them wish to join with native-born citizens in working for further improvements in the immigration law. Greater emphasis on America via the ballot may well be an outgrowth of having experienced America via the neighborhood.

Against this background of fifty years of changing immigration laws and experimental community programs to meet varied and changing needs and interests, I invite you to turn to the pages of *America via the Neighborhood* itself, with its emphasis on participation, self-determination and partnership.

### NOTE ON THE CONTRIBUTOR

Florence G. Cassidy, a specialist in social service to the foreign-born, has served as Director of the International Institute of Bridgeport, Field Director of International Migration Service, Director of Adult Education of the National Institute of Immigrant Welfare, Director of the Nationality Department of the Council of Social Agencies of Metropolitan Detroit, and Executive Secretary of the Michigan State Commission on Displaced Persons and Refugees. Currently she is Director of The Peoples of Detroit Project, an interorganizational survey of Detroit's ethnic communities.

## PUBLISHER'S NOTE
## TO THE ORIGINAL EDITION

The material in this volume was gathered by the Division of Neighborhood Agencies and Organization of Studies in Methods of Americanization. Americanization in this study has been considered as the union of native and foreign born in all the most fundamental relationships and activities of our national life. For Americanization is the uniting of new with native-born Americans in fuller common understanding and appreciation to secure by means of self-government the highest welfare of all. Such Americanization should perpetuate no unchangeable political, domestic, and economic régime delivered once for all to the fathers, but a growing and broadening national life, inclusive of the best wherever found. With all our rich heritages, Americanism will develop best through a mutual giving and taking of contributions from both newer and older Americans in the interest of the common weal. This study has followed such an understanding of Americanization.

## FOREWORD TO THE ORIGINAL EDITION

THIS volume is the result of studies in methods of Americanization prepared through funds furnished by the Carnegie Corporation of New York. It arose out of the fact that constant applications were being made to the Corporation for contributions to the work of numerous agencies engaged in various forms of social activity intended to extend among the people of the United States, the knowledge of their government and their obligations to it. The trustees felt that a study which should set forth, not theories of social betterment, but a description of the methods of the various agencies engaged in such work, would be of distinct value to the cause itself and to the public.

The outcome of the study is contained in eleven volumes on the following subjects: Schooling of the Immigrant; The Press; Adjustment of Homes and Family Life; Legal Protection and Correction; Health Standards and Care; Naturalization and Political Life; Industrial and Economic Amalgamation; Treatment of Immigrant Heritages; Neighborhood Agencies and Organization; Rural Developments; and Summary. The entire study has been carried out under the general direction of Mr. Allen T. Burns. Each volume appears in the name of the author who had immediate charge of the particular field it is intended to cover.

Upon the invitation of the Carnegie Corporation a committee consisting of the late Theodore Roosevelt, Prof. John Graham Brooks, Dr. John M. Glenn, and Mr. John A. Voll has acted in an advisory capacity to the director. An editorial committee consisting of Dr. Talcott Williams, Dr. Raymond B. Fosdick, and Dr. Edwin F. Gay has read and criticized the manuscripts. To both of these committees the trustees of the Carnegie Corporation are much indebted.

The purpose of the report is to give as clear a notion as possible of the methods of the agencies actually at work in this field and not to propose theories for dealing with the complicated questions involved.

## ACKNOWLEDGMENT

The author wishes to record, and to express his own appreciation of, the large part which his associates, Miss Elizabeth Roemer and Miss Amy M. Hamburger, have had in gathering at first hand, in the field, the specific facts upon which this book is based.

Grateful acknowledgment is made also of the indis- pensable co-operation of the many persons and organizations who have generously supplied desired information.

J. D.

# TABLE OF CONTENTS

# CONTENTS

# CONTENTS

# CONTENTS

# CONTENTS

# CONTENTS

# ILLUSTRATIONS

# AMERICA

## VIA THE

# NEIGHBORHOOD

## I

### AMERICANIZATION AND THE NEIGHBORHOOD

THE subject of this volume is the Americanization of the immigrant through the medium of the neighborhood.

In order to focus the discussion it is necessary to agree upon the meaning of two of the terms involved—namely, "Americanization" and "neighborhood."

First, what is Americanization?

### CONFORMITY?

One conception of what it is was voiced not long ago by the head of a national organization of women. "We are strangely affected by the clothes we wear," said this lady. "Garments create a mental and social atmosphere. What can be hoped for the Americanism of a man who insists on employing a London tailor? One's very food affects his Americanism. What kind

1

of American consciousness can grow in the atmosphere of sauerkraut and Limburger cheese? Or what can you expect of the Americanism of the man whose breath always reeks with garlic?"

In an editorial which characterizes this view of Americanism as "decidedly the most comprehensive yet proposed," the New York *World* suggests some of its further implications:

If London tailors are to be taboo, by the same token there must be no patronage of Paris modistes. Can a fair American heart beat as loyally under a rue de la Paix frock? The ladies of this patriotic society may well ponder the heroic nature of the sacrifice they will be required to make.

But the great test of perfect Americanization will come in the limitation of diet to native food products. Can a consistently loyal American ever eat a table d'hôte meal? There can, of course, be no French sauces, no French dressing for salads, but in its place the sugar-and-vinegar concoction of the grandmothers. Camembert and Roquefort cheese from Orange County no doubt will be allowable. What will be the rule about tea? Are pork and beans and codfish to breed a more patriotic race? Is sauerkraut to connote treason, but corned beef and cabbage to be the sign of unquestioned loyalty?

This conception of Americanism may be called the *conformity* idea. The newspaper just quoted dismissed it with the comment that "it is hard to take seriously such absurdity." Nevertheless, it is a conception held by a good many people, though not usually expressed in terms so specific. It implies that in order to be truly an American one must dress, eat, talk, behave, and even think according to one prescribed "American" formula. Whoever does not accept and strictly adhere to

2

this formula is, *ipso facto*, not an "American." According to this view, the immigrant's racial inheritance, no matter how much it may mean to him, becomes, upon his arrival in America, a "foreign" impediment which must forthwith be cast away.

The practical application of this conception meets an initial difficulty in the choice of the formula to be prescribed. A perusal of the daily press reports of public addresses and programs put forth in the name of Americanism compels the conclusion that the number of formulæ is about equal to the number of formulators. Though many of the latter are ready to agree that there should be complete conformity, each appears to be insistent upon his own particular prescription. Leaving further questions involved in 100-per-cent American dress and diet to suggest themselves, what, one may ask, shall be the Simon-pure American's manner of speech, as between the Yankee twang and the Southern drawl? How shall this same model American pattern his demeanor as between the soberness of the Puritan and the gayety of the Cavalier? And since among even the fathers of the Republic there arose pronounced differences of opinion on fundamental issues, to what past or present authority shall this made-in-America patriot turn in order to ascertain what opinions he may adopt as absolutely and unquestionably correct?

Even were it possible to get everyone to agree upon one prescription, a second and no less serious difficulty would be encountered in enforcing it.

3

Americans are human; like other human beings, they crave variety and new experience and find conformity even in diet "flat, stale and unprofitable." If it came to a pinch, they would probably be loath to banish such palatable contributions from other lands as sauerkraut and spaghetti —not to mention chop suey! Indeed, how could America follow any prescription which would exclude all the diverse racial elements which have entered into its life? For never will it be possible to "expunge from the records" the historic fact that America is unique among nations as the product of a great variety of racial stocks and cultures.

Americanization conceived in terms of conformity and uniformity is apparently neither possible nor desirable. But while any attempt to formulate American life in specific and rigid terms and to cast it in a fixed mold is futile, is there not an underlying idea here with which everyone would agree—namely, that there are some basic elements in American life of which all who are Americans must partake?

### INJECTION?

A second conception of Americanization, and the one which is probably most prevalent, confines the term largely to teaching immigrants English and civics. Most of the so-called "Americanization work" of schools and other public and private agencies proves to be limited to such merely instructional efforts, and many of the persons connected with such agencies appear to regard "Americanization" as a job order which is practically completed when the immigrant has been run through the mill of the classroom.

One man, from whom information was sought as to the situation in his community, expressed this view naïvely:

We used to have an Americanization problem [he said], but we haven't got one any longer. Several years ago we got all the foreigners in our town into some English and civics classes and in two or three months we Americanized 'em all.

As distinguished from the concept of Americanization first mentioned, this one may be called that of *injection*. It attaches prime importance to classes, lectures, and the distribution of educational and uplifting "literature," and implies that if enough of such instruction and information can be injected into the immigrant he is thereby automatically Americanized.

That English and civics are necessary aids is unquestionable, but to hold that they are all there is to Americanization hardly measures up to the larger implication of the term. Indeed, the facts indicate that English and civics are not even the beginnings of Americanization.

Is it not true, however, that this concept of Americanization has the same underlying idea as the one previously considered—that is, the idea of sharing certain essential elements of American life? English is to be learned by the immigrant in order to be used, and to be used in order to bring him into fuller intercourse and mutual understanding with native Americans. Civics is to be studied by him in order that he may become a citizen, and citizenship is to be acquired so that he may discharge his obligations and exercise his privileges as a member of the body politic of America. Does not the degree of Americanization involved depend, then, not on the mere possession of these two instruments— English and civics—but on the actual use to which they are put, or, in other words, upon the responsible share which the immigrant thereby takes in promoting the welfare of the community?

The conception of Americanization as conformity confuses certain superficial and variable signs of the reality with the reality itself. The injection idea confuses with the larger result in view the particular and partial methods of obtaining that result.

## THE PRACTICAL VIEW

A third conception of Americanism is frequently voiced by people of a characteristically practical outlook, who may not have thought much in any formal terms of "Americanization," but who have had a good deal of actual experience with immigrants.

People of this sort usually refer by way of example to individuals they have known personally at close range.

"Well, now, there's Pete Bolinski. He's been here twenty years, worked hard, got ahead, bought a nice little home down in the Polish district, and takes good care of his family. I've known Pete a long while, always found him as square as they're made, and would trust him in anything. I don't know just what you mean by Americanization, but if what you're after is good Americans, give me men like Pete."

"Does he speak English?"

"Well, English isn't Pete's long suit. He's been too busy working to spend much time in learning it. He can talk just about enough English to get along on, and he manages to do that pretty well."

"Is he naturalized?"

"Now that you ask me, I'm not sure that I know. I guess he must be, or if he isn't, there's some good reason why, for Pete's not a fellow that tries to shirk his responsibilities. He's loyal, all right, and his heart's in the right place."

This may be called the *practical* idea of Americanization. It is concerned mainly with the individual immigrant's integrity and responsibility, and regards his Americanism as depending not so much upon his conforming to some prescribed American type or upon any rigid tests as upon his whole character and daily life. The question of most importance is that of the immigrant's practical contribution to the welfare of the community. Is he doing a fair share? If he is, then for all practical purposes he is an American.

### CONSTRUCTIVE PARTICIPATION

More or less variant conceptions of Americanization could be multiplied indefinitely, but the three which have been cited will serve to represent the chief outstanding points of view. It appears, however, that these three concepts are animated by the same inner motive of enlisting the immigrant in the common life of America. One proposes to accomplish this result in one way, another in another way, but all have it as their goal. No matter how many other viewpoints were considered, would not this central idea be inherent in them all? Is it not self-evident that the essential objective in any program of Americanization is *constructive participation* in the life of America? However widely programs may differ as to the method of bringing this about and as to the channels for its expression, is it not logically inevitable that such actual participation must in every case be the ultimate aim? Is not what all desire simply this--that each individual shall enter effectively into America's well-being and upbuilding?

If this is accepted as an adequate understanding of Americanization, it next becomes necessary to determine the essential characteristics of American life, in which participation is to be enlisted. The futility of trying to identify Americanism with specific and rigid conformities has already been pointed out. Nor would an end ever be reached if one attempted to describe the multitudinous aspects and details that go to make up the totality of American life. But may not general agreement be secured regarding two elements which underlie and include all the others?

### A POSITIVE LOYALTY

The first of these is loyalty to America. That is indispensable. But it is necessary to avoid

8

confusing loyalty itself with any partisan contention as to what loyalty involves and what expression it should take. Nothing is commoner, in
the conflict of opinion and prejudice, than for the
contending parties to accuse each other of disloyalty, when as a matter of fact the crime of
which each is guilty is simply that of disagreement. Only a slight acquaintance with human
nature and the facts of history is needed to foretell
that any attempt to enforce purely partisan
conceptions of loyalty must result either in solidi-
fying and perpetuating the alleged disloyalty or in
arousing a smoldering resentment which sooner
or later will burst into a full flame of revolt.

There are, of course, specific tests of loyalty in
its negative aspect of disloyalty. These are
chiefly the committing of any act of treason or
sedition, or the use of violence or the deliberate
incitement to violence in opposing or attempting
to overthrow the government. But a merely
passive loyalty is far from adequate. What is
desired is a positive and constructive loyalty,
which not only refrains from doing something
bad, but actually does something good. Such
loyalty must spring from downright devotion to
the American ideal, and implies carrying that
ideal into action. The American ideal is the
*ideal of democracy,* and democracy is the second
essential of American life.

The quest for democracy in the worship of God
brought many of the first Colonists from the Old
World to America. Insistence on democracy in
government and taxation led the Colonies to

declare their independence and establish the American nation. Determination not to allow democracy to be restricted by lines of race and color engulfed America in the Civil War and brought reunion, with slavery abolished. To make the whole world "safe for democracy" was the motive which at length impelled America to play her decisive part in the great World War. America was born in democracy and has always lived by democracy.

## THE DEMOCRATIC IDEAL

What is democracy? Volumes have been written to answer this question, but is not the substance of them all epitomized in Abraham Lincoln's historic words, "government of the people, by the people, and for the people"? Lincoln was speaking of political democracy. But the term is not limited to the political field; it extends to the whole range of human relations. In its broadest scope the democracy of America is all the social activity of America, including formal government, which is "*of* the people, *by* the people, and *for* the people."

Participation in American life, therefore, involves loyalty to America, devotion to this American ideal of democracy, and a responsible share in the activity through which this ideal is measurably realized in practice and present fact. Such participation is the very essence of Americanism.

It was this outstanding fact which, above all others, impressed that early student and interpreter of American institutions, de Tocqueville. In his classic work on *Democracy in America*, written about fifty years after the Declaration of Independence, de Tocqueville pointed to democracy as the young nation's most striking characteristic.

Many important observations suggest themselves [he wrote], but there is one which takes precedence of all the rest. The social condition of the Americans is eminently democratic; this was its character at the foundation of the Colonies, and is still more strongly marked at the present day.[1]

As a result of the Revolution, he continues:

Society was shaken to its center; the people, in whose name the struggle had taken place, conceived the desire of exercising the authority which it had acquired; its democratic tendencies were awakened; and having thrown off the yoke of the motherland, it aspired to independence of every kind.

In America the principle of the sovereignty of the people ... is recognized by the customs and proclaimed by the laws; it spreads freely, and arrives without impediment as its most remote consequences . . . . At the present day the principle ... has acquired in the United States all the practical developments which the imagination can conceive . . . and it appears in every possible form according to the exigency of the occasion.[2]

### AMERICANIZATION NEVER ENDS

If Americanization consists of democratic participation in the life of America, then manifestly it is a process which begins as soon as any

---

[1] De Tocqueville, *Democracy in America*, part i, chap. iii.
[2] *Ibid.*, chap. iv.

such participation begins, but which never reaches an end. It may be divided into stages, such as before or after naturalization, and perhaps a sort of average Americanization, based on "the average American" may be struck. But in no case is Americanization something which, once achieved, thereafter remains forever fixed and secure. On the contrary, it is a continuous process, which increases or diminishes in degree as one's activity in the community increases or diminishes.

American life has many channels, through any or all of which one may work. There may be participation in politics and government, in industry, in education, in social service, in religious activity, in recreation, in art, in science, and in any number of subdivisions of these major fields. One person's participation may be very extensive, touching many fields, but comparatively superficial in them all. Another's may be of narrower scope, but greater intensity. The sum of anyone's Americanism cannot be judged exclusively from any one angle. All the elements involved in his activity must be taken into account, and a sort of composite total arrived at in this way. Only thus can one person's Americanism be fairly and adequately compared with another's. Ideally, of course, it is desirable that everyone's participation in the life of America should steadily expand, and it is to outstanding individuals whose lives exhibit such constant growth in activity and usefulness that we are wont to point as embodiments of the American ideal.

## THE NEIGHBORHOOD

Thus conceived, Americanization is not something which corresponds with the molding of clay into a certain static form. On the contrary, it models the life of America into forms ever new and more adequate. It is dynamic. It makes American life to-day different from what it was yesterday, and to-morrow different still. It never rests, but moves ever onward. It is not simply imitative. It is creative.

### APPLICATION TO ALL

Americanization thus understood cannot be restricted to the foreign born. It applies to everyone. There are no exceptions. There is no one who can say, with truth: "My own Americanism is now fully achieved. In no respect can it be increased or improved. It is perfect." On the contrary, everyone must recognize that his own Americanization is going either forward or backward.

Every baby born in America, no matter how long his ancestors have been here, must be Americanized. He is himself a little immigrant who upon his arrival knows even less about America than the adult immigrant from other portions of the planet. He cannot speak English. He takes slight interest in civics. By nature he is a combination of autocrat and anarchist. His induction into the life of America must take place gradually and somewhat painfully for himself and others, and must be accomplished more by his taking part in that life himself, in proportion to his years, than by learning book lessons about it. Twenty-one years must elapse before this native-born candidate for Americanization may participate in political and governmental affairs as a voter. How much of an American he eventually becomes depends on the part which he takes in American life. His Americanism may, in fact, be minus, for have there not been traitors of American birth? It may be feeble and stagnant, for are there not specimens of native descent who could hardly be held up as models for general emulation? It cannot be assumed that because a person happened to be born in America he is by virtue of that single fact a better American than the foreign-born immigrant. Which of the two is really the better American depends upon which makes the more substantial contribution to the well-being of the community.

### PARTNERSHIP OF NATIVE AND FOREIGN BORN

Thus Americanization is a problem which applies to native born as well as foreign born. The immigrant has certain peculiar needs, including English and naturalization, but otherwise his Americanization and that of the native born are of one piece. The immigrant, like the person of native birth, cannot be Americanized and brought to take his share in the democracy of America merely by being taught to read textbook lessons about it or being told in lectures what a wonderful thing it is. He, too, must learn what this democracy is from actual experience in partaking of it and practicing it. This means that native Americans in dealing with the immigrant must avoid a policy of paternalism, dictation or repression, and adopt an attitude which is truly democratic. In short, since Americanization is the business in which both are engaged, native Americans should take the immigrant into a genuine partnership.

At the same time they must recognize the responsibility which rests upon them as the senior partners to set an adequate example. They must realize that if Americanization means taking part in American life, then they can hardly expect the immigrant's Americanization to rise above the standards which they themselves set. If, for example, they themselves are indifferent to the political affairs of the community, as many native Americans are, or employ corrupt methods in politics, as some do, they should scarcely complain if the immigrant is sometimes indifferent or open to graft. If they exploit the immigrant as a laborer, they should not be surprised if the immigrant is not altogether averse to exploiting his employer. They must bear constantly in mind that the Americanization of the immigrant is necessarily conditioned by the extent and quality of their own Americanization, and that his devotion to the American ideal of democracy will be roughly commensurate with the degree in which he finds this ideal expressed in present realities.

Furthermore, if the immigrant's part in American life is to be of the greatest possible value, it must include his cultural contributions. He represents lands and peoples which were old in history and in ripened culture centuries before the American nation came to birth, and he comes to America bringing rich gifts. Taking the immigrant into partnership involves the privilege and the obligation of making these gifts an integral part of our life and culture, which are thereby colored and enriched. It is through the medium of his own culture, indeed, that the immigrant most naturally and effectively unites with the land of his adoption.

### THE MEANING OF NEIGHBORHOOD

The second term which needs to be defined is "Neighborhood."

In common speech this term is used loosely, practically as a synonym for locality. Even when it is more definitely applied, as when some local social-service agency speaks of the "neighborhood" in which it works, it usually has reference to a small locality within specified and mostly arbitrary boundaries. Such use of the word views the neighborhood from the outside. But when the neighborhood is felt from the inside, any merely geographic conception of it gives place to one which is essentially social, and in which physical boundaries are of secondary importance compared with the human factors involved.

In the scale of human relations "neighbor" comes next after "friend." A "neighborhood"

16

is a local group of people the members of which enjoy this comparatively intimate relationship with one another. An isolated village, with a homogeneous and stable population, provides such a situation. Under conditions of modern city life, however, it is seldom that a group of people as small in number, as homogeneous in kind, and as stable in residence as those of such a village are isolated in anything like the same degree. On the contrary, congestion of population means that a much larger number of people are living within an equal area. Racial, religious, and class differences interfere with homogeneity. Constant moving in and out disturbs stability. Ease of communication and of access between different localities subtracts from local separateness. All the people in a given small area do not know one another. In many instances natural differences retard the development of an inclination for general acquaintance and the large numbers involved make this physically impossible. Frequently people living next door to each other or in the same tenement are not acquainted.

### EFFECT OF CITY CONDITIONS

Indeed, it might seem at first that the neighborhood had become completely disrupted and lost in the hurly-burly of city life. Observation confirms, however, what further reflection would suggest to be inevitable—the normal human instinct for association, combined with the natural economy of finding associates as near at hand

17

as possible, usually results in a spontaneous growth of neighborhood even under adverse conditions. But it is neighborhood of a sort much more complex than that of the simple village. Association develops along lines of race, religion, and class rather than on the basis of contiguity alone, and the social and overlapping groups which thus arise may be far more coherent and responsive than the geographic group which includes them all. Nevertheless, there is a tendency in the direction of general neighborhood unity growing out of common locality of residence; not a unity in which all natural differences disappear, but one in which they become subordinate to community of interest and action. Immigrant neighborhoods from their very nature often include the forces of both social and local unity.

## IMMIGRANT NEIGHBORHOODS

There are three types of neighborhoods in which immigrants are found. The first and by far the commonest, owing to natural causes, is the urban colony, in which immigrants of one race are settled more or less compactly together in one section of a city. There are also some separate immigrant towns which may be regarded as ultracolonies. Such conditions, even when the colony is situated in the midst of a large city, correspond with those of the village as respects homogeneity. All the members of the colony neighborhood are of one race. Most of them, as a rule, are of the same religious faith. Differ-

18

ences in economic-social status have not become pronounced among them. Their common experience as immigrants and their common motives as pioneers bind them closely together. It might very reasonably be presumed that, under such conditions, immigrant colonies would prove to be rich in the real substance of neighborhood life. It is believed that the facts to be presented will confirm this presumption. Inasmuch as the great mass of immigrants are found in colonies, it is with this type of neighborhood that the present volume will chiefly deal.

The second kind of neighborhood in which immigrants are found may be called the cosmopolitan type, and is composed of people of different races. Among the foreign born the tendency toward racial colonization is so strong that such cosmopolitan neighborhoods are comparatively rare. Even in districts which contain overlapping or intermixed colonies of different races, each race tends to cohere. Under such conditions, however, especially when the different racial groups are not large enough to form well-developed colonies of their own, a loose sort of cosmopolitan neighborhood arises. Such neighborhoods come into existence also in localities settled by American-born young people of different races, who are accompanied or followed in their migration from the colonies by their foreign-born parents. Here association among the foreign born still follows racial lines in the main, the inability of many to speak and read English being an ordinary obstacle in the way of complete community between the different races. On the other hand, the American-born element, varying from a small minority to a large majority in different localities, and the proportionate use of English as a medium, serve to a greater or less degree as solvents.

The third type of neighborhood involved is one which is predominantly American, with a small admixture of immigrants. This situation also is comparatively rare. It occurs most frequently in smaller cities where there are not many immigrants and no serious social or financial obstacles to prevent their living in different localities. It also arises when prosperous immigrants, most of whom have learned to speak English, move out of the colonies and buy homes in American neighborhoods.

### SCOPE OF INQUIRY

In its content, the neighborhood is a local cross section of nearly the whole field of American life. For that reason this volume is necessarily a cross section of the subject matter of the other volumes of this study, each of which is confined to one particular field of activity, such as education or industry. Here it will be necessary, for example, to discuss the school, the labor union, the political club, and various agencies of social service. Such discussion will not duplicate the consideration of these agencies and activities in the other volumes. It will consider them only from the point of view of their interrelationships with the neighborhoods in which they are situated. ⹁ For instance, this volume will not discuss, except incidentally, the school's standardized activities, which operate in substantially the same form and manner from one locality to another. All that is covered in another volume on the schooling of the immigrant. The present volume will take up only such connecting links between the particular school and its own neighborhood as parents' associations and social centers, and will consider these only in relation to specific neighborhood problems. Certain agencies which are presumed to be concerned primarily with the neighborhoods in which they are situated, such as social settlements and community councils, of course fall mainly within the present volume's scope.

Inquiries conducted over a period of about fifteen months, either by personal investigation on the ground or through correspondence, have extended into twenty-six states, from the Atlantic to the Pacific coast and from the far South to points near the Canadian border. Intensive study has not been confined to any one part of the country. A great many cities, neighborhoods, and agencies have been included. Since the purpose in view, however, has been to discover the most effective *methods* of Americanization rather than to single out particular agencies for either commendation or criticism, and inasmuch, also, as it is not desired to embarrass anyone who is quoted as making criticisms, it has appeared advisable, in presenting the facts, to omit in the main identifications of agencies, and thus to focus attention upon methods and principles, which as a rule are not identified exclusively with particular auspices, but which take shape and emerge out of the sum of experience.

### ATTENTION FOCUSED ON THE FOREIGN-BORN ADULT

The term "immigrant" is used here as applying strictly to the foreign born. Though Americanization includes everyone, whether native born or foreign born, within its proper scope, the present volume, as was stated at the outset, is concerned with the Americanization of the immigrant. The American-born offspring of immigrants are no less properly subjects of Americanization, and indeed present peculiar and exceedingly important problems of their own. But they are not the foreign born; they are not the immigrants; and they enter into the present discussion only in so far as their Americanization bears upon and promotes the Americanization of the foreign born.

Many native Americans take the attitude that Americanizing the foreign-born adult is a hopeless problem, and that effort should be limited to the first generation of American birth. The discussion which follows, on the contrary, will focus attention upon these very foreign-born adults, and will face squarely the question of whether and by what means they can be Americanized.

Pains have been taken to find out what the immigrant people are doing in a democratic neighborhood way which works for their own Americanization and relates them with American life on their own motion. Indeed, since this was found to be a field little explored by native Americans, it was taken as the starting point of the whole inquiry.

### REACHING THE INDIVIDUAL THROUGH THE GROUP

When the 1910 census was taken, the number of foreign-born people in the United States had reached the vast total of thirteen millions.[1] As already noted, the great majority of these immigrants are found in colony or community neighborhoods of their own.

Even assuming that the Americanization of these immigrants could be accomplished by working directly upon each individual, it is manifest that the agencies and resources required to perform such a gigantic task are not available. It follows that if these foreign-born millions are to be Americanized on an adequate scale, the individual immigrant must be reached indirectly, through the medium of his neighborhood group. In other words, Americanization must proceed by extensive as well as intensive methods. Americanizing influences must be brought to bear not upon the individual alone, but upon the immigrant group as a whole. If this can be done successfully, thousands will be affected in the time that direct individual attempts would reach only a scattered few hundred.

### AN ORGANIC PROBLEM

But the problem here presented is not merely one of economy of effort. A fundamental organic

---

[1] The 1920 census findings are not yet published.

problem is also involved. It is this. Since Americanization is understood as actual participation in the activities of the community, is it possible for the individual to be Americanized otherwise than in connection with his community group? In the case of the average immigrant, living among people of his own race, must not such participation in community affairs take place through the medium of his own colony neighborhood?

The fundamental character of the principle which this question involves and which underlies the whole problem of integrating the immigrant with the life of America may be more deeply appreciated if we look back in our country's history to the time when the nation was still in the process of being firmly established.

### THE EARLY COLONISTS

It is not undesignedly that I begin this subject [wrote de Tocqueville] with the township. The village or township is the only association which is so perfectly natural that wherever a number of men are collected it seems to constitute itself.[1]

The township to which de Tocqueville here refers as the nucleus of our democracy was, in fact, the first neighborhood in America. It typified exactly those village conditions which have already been suggested as constituting a neighborhood in its most rudimentary state. Indeed, it would be difficult to devise a better

[1] De Tocqueville, *Democracy in America*, part i, chap. v.

definition of neighborhood than that contained
in the words which de Tocqueville applies to the
township, an "association which is so perfectly
natural that . . . it seems to constitute itself."
Here is the significant observation which de
Tocqueville goes on to make:

The native of New England is attached to his township
because it is independent and free; his co-operation in its
affairs insures his attachment to its interest; the well-being
it affords him secures his affection; and its welfare is the aim
of his ambition and of his future exertions; he takes a part
in every occurrence in the place; he practices the art of
government in the small sphere within his reach; he accustoms himself to those forms which can alone insure the
steady progress of liberty; he imbibes their spirit, he acquires
a taste for order, comprehends the union or the balance of
powers, and collects clear, practical notions on the nature
of his duties and the extent of his rights.

The township serves as a center for the desire of public
esteem, the want of exciting interests, and the taste for
authority and popularity, in the midst of the ordinary relations of life; and the passions which commonly embroil
society change their character when they find a vent so near
the domestic hearth and family circle.

In the United States the inhabitants were thrown but
as yesterday upon the soil they now occupy . . . the
instinctive love of their country can scarcely exist in their
minds; but everyone takes as zealous an interest in the
affairs of his township, his county, and of the whole state as
though they were his own, because everyone, in his sphere,
takes an active part in the government of society.[1]

## THE COLONISTS OF TO-DAY

Turning to the immigrant colonists of the
present day, let us see whether there is any cor-

[1] De Tocqueville, *Democracy in America*, part i, chap. xiv.

respondence between their neighborhood life and the part it plays in binding them to America, and the vital part which the township neighborhood played in making democratic Americans of the Colonists of New England. Does the colony neighborhood of the immigrants of to-day serve them and America likewise as the nucleus and practice school of American democracy?

# II

IN a community which is geographically separate and which is composed of immigrants of one race, so that the racial character of the neighborhood is as pronounced as possible, it is obvious that whatever forces are inherent in the racial group, making either for or against Americanization, must operate most freely. If, as is generally believed, the natural bent of a racial group, left to itself, is to remain foreign, to shut itself off from American life in spirit and in fact, then certainly this propensity should reveal itself in such a community. If, however, the group moves toward Americanization, even under such conditions of geographical separation, then with equal certainty it may be concluded that the forces inherent in the group tend in that direction.

Except for rural settlements, like those of Scandinavian and German farmers in the Northwest, separate communities of immigrants are relatively uncommon, compared with the generally prevalent urban colony. But a sufficient number of them are scattered here and there over the country to make their outworkings in terms of Americanization very significant.

In order to put this question to the test of facts, observation was made of three such one-race communities. One is Bohemian, one Dutch, and the third Jewish. All three are small enough to be taken practically as single neighborhoods, and thus to serve as excellent subjects for neighborhood study. Two of them, the Bohemian and Dutch communities, are situated on Long Island within a few miles of each other and near New York City. The third is a Jewish community in New Jersey.

It was not known beforehand what the situation in these communities would prove to be. Here are the facts as they came to light:

## A BOHEMIAN COMMUNITY

This is one of the oldest Bohemian settlements in America and had its beginning in 1855. A land agent persuaded three Bohemian families, who had just arrived in the United States, to buy lots there, telling them about the riches of the country. When they arrived they found the locality thickly wooded. There were no roads, the nearest Americans were three miles away on a farm, and these Bohemian settlers had to set to and establish themselves as pioneers. Some ten years later they persuaded another small group of Bohemian immigrants to join them.

Although these first settlers are all dead, many of their children are still living in the village, which by gradual increase now numbers about five hundred people. Many of the present resi-

**LANDMARKS OF THE BOHEMIAN VILLAGE**

The hall of the C. S. P. S. free-thinking society is the center of community life.
The monument to Jan Hus stands for love of liberty.

dents are middle-aged people who have gone
there from New York City. They were influenced mainly by the desire to be among people
of their own race, in an atmosphere of mutual
understanding. Some years ago there were a
few Irish and German families living there, but
when the parents died the children moved away,
and now the village is entirely Bohemian. To-day
about a third of the residents are of foreign birth.
The rest were born in America.

At first the men found employment on the
surrounding farms and estates, while the women
helped to clear the land. About 1870, however,
a strike in the cigar factories of New York City
led the manufacturers to place some of their work
in the surrounding small towns, among them our
settlement. Ten years later a cigar factory was
started in the village itself, under the management of a Bohemian Jew. Since then this industry has been the mainstay of the settlement.
Three-fourths of the workers in the local factory
are women. Some of the girls work in mills in
another town, riding back and forth on bicycles,
and the few who take domestic-service positions
on estates during the summer often go with their
employers when the latter return to the city.
Most of the men work either on surrounding
estates, in the near-by town as plumbers, brick-
layers, carpenters, and the like, on the railroad,
or in some shipyards not far away.

The little village presents an unusually attractive appearance. Most of the houses are white,
built of wood. They are clean and well kept,

with Red Cross signs showing cheerily in the windows. There is no rubbish about and there are no run-down buildings. With the exception of four families all own their homes, and as each has from five to ten acres of ground about it, there is plenty of open space. In summer the residents take great pride in their green lawns and abounding flowers and vines. Though the village grew up without any set plan, roadways being petitioned for as they were needed, the streets are wide and the sidewalks well paved.

At one end of the village is the Bohemian Hall, a spacious two-story structure. At the other end is the cigar factory. In the center stands the public school, and beside this a monument to Jan Hus, the Bohemian national hero. The hook-and-ladder company occupies a neat white building. Besides these landmarks there is a hotel with bowling alleys, the union cemetery, a small Catholic church with separate cemetery, an Episcopal chapel, two village stores, one of which contains the post office, a barber shop with adjoining ice-cream parlor, and a bicycle-repair shop. There is no drug store, no doctor nor midwife, and no constable in the village. During the day there is little activity anywhere except in the factory, but toward evening, after the day's labors are over, the community "wakes up."

### ORGANIZATIONS

These Bohemians are mostly "freethinkers." Originally Protestant, Bohemia was compelled

to accept Roman Catholicism when conquered
by Austria, and still remains nominally a Roman
Catholic country. But in protest against this
enforced observance there grew up in Bohemia
a partially concealed freethinking movement, the
spirit of which became inbred in the people. As
soon as Bohemian immigrants reach America, the
"land of freedom," most of them fling aside even
nominal affiliation with the church. The village
under consideration is predominantly a freethinking community. Though the venerable
minister of the Episcopal chapel is deeply respected and loved, and though out of deference
to public opinion weddings and christenings are
usually solemnized by him, only children attend
the services. "They go to Sunday school because
they like the parties that are given." The Catholic contingent is comparatively small and keeps
somewhat to itself. A young Bohemian priest
has recently taken charge and hopes to increase
his following. "My father used to be foreman
in a cigar factory near here," said he. "The
people all know me and will take to me because
I am one of them."

The center of community life is the local chapter of the Česko-Slovansky Podporujici Spolek
(Benevolent Society), a nation-wide Bohemian
mutual insurance association. This local chapter
was started in 1887, and for some years met at
the hotel. In 1905 a building containing a gymnasium and various meeting rooms, which had
been put up by the local *sokol*, was taken over by
the chapter and rebuilt, serving thenceforth as

its headquarters, though the *sokol* still continues to meet there. The *sokol*, or gymnastic society, corresponding to the German *turn verein*, is the Bohemian organization under cover of which the freethinking and freedom-seeking movement flourished.

The C. S. P. S. is primarily a mutual insurance society, which pays sickness and death benefits to its members. In general the local chapters have stuck closely to this practical object. This particular chapter, however, has risen to the larger demands and opportunities of the local situation. Besides conducting a so-called Bohemian school, supplementing the public school, where Bohemian language and history and the principles of freethinking are taught to the children, the society holds entertainments, lectures, and community gatherings of various kinds. Its members say:

It is our church. Here the young and old come together in common interest. We still talk Bohemian here, but we tell the young people, who often object, that this is on account of the old people who cannot understand English very well. We are leaving it to the young people, to do what they think best after we are dead.

The women are separately organized in a mutual insurance society—a branch of the national Jednota Českych Dam (United Bohemian Women).

There is also a branch of the Bohemian National Alliance, with a membership of both sexes. In the past the purpose of this organization has been to promote Bohemian independence, and the local chapter has sent to Bohemia contributions of money which seem large for so small a community. "We are trying to help our brothers on the other side," said the secretary, "but we are not taking any further part in their struggle, for America is our country."

## SELF-GOVERNMENT

The Bohemians are enthusiastic supporters of the public school, which all the children of this village attend. The first school was built in 1856, and started with eight children in its one room. As late as 1890 as many as fifty children were meeting in this same room. In 1904 a foreign-born leader was instrumental in obtaining the present two-story building, having four classrooms and a large playground, where a hundred and twenty children are now in attendance. Half a dozen older children are attending high school in the near-by town.

In government, the village is semi-independent. It supplies its own fire protection, through the local hook-and-ladder company, a voluntary organization made up of some of the younger men. The building was erected by voluntary contributions and funds secured through entertainments. Lately a chemical fire engine, of which the people are very proud, has been installed. Current expenses are met by voluntary taxation. If a fire breaks out during the day when the men are working, the women go to the rescue. "You should see us work," said the postmistress. "We are just as good firemen as the men."

This village and another about two miles distant form one election district. Voting takes place in the hook-and-ladder company building. The community is about half Democratic and half Republican. There are only one or two Socialists. A Socialist in an adjoining town said that some years ago he spent a great deal of time trying to get the people of the village to join the Socialist party. As most of them were free-thinkers, he took it for granted they would be responsive to his persuasions. In this he was disappointed, for, although one year he managed to get out twenty votes, he found that interest died down as soon as he let up on his propaganda.

With only two exceptions, the men in the village are either fully naturalized or are now in process of naturalization. One of these two is an old man who has never been able to learn enough English to answer the questions in court, though he has been up for examination several times. The C. S. P. S. actively promotes naturalization, and the by-laws of the *sokol* require that all members must pledge their intention of becoming citizens. Any newcomer in the community is immediately approached on this subject, and "if he is not an American citizen already, public opinion forces him to become one." There are one hundred and eighty registered voters. Residents of the village have served on several township boards, and one has been elected recently to the board of auditors.

# INHERENT FORCES

For school support, this village is combined with another in a joint school district and joint board. The district as a whole is mostly American, and takes in some of the large estates, the owners of which, however, have few children, or, at least, few who attend public school. The school board numbers five—at present there are three Bohemian men and two American women representing the other village. The school building of the Bohemian village is used as a voting place in the annual elections.

## AMERICANISM

If the question is whether Bohemians are good Americans [said one of the local leaders], the interest they took in the war and the help they gave in Red Cross, Liberty Loan and other war-time drives would be proof enough. First of all we sent twenty-six boys to the war, of whom only three were drafted. Twenty-three voluntarily enlisted. We subscribed over $32,000 to the Liberty Loans, and bought a large amount of War Saving Stamps. Is not this a satisfactory showing?

A local Red Cross workroom was conducted in the hook-and-ladder building. The C. S. P. S. and the women's society explained the aim and object of the Red Cross to the older people, and secured understanding and whole-hearted co-operation from the whole village. On Decoration Day the village made a demonstration of its Americanism in a parade which was part of a general celebration in the near-by town. It was significant that in this parade only one small Bohemian flag was displayed, while American flags abounded.

35

# AMERICA VIA THE NEIGHBORHOOD

Why shouldn't we be interested in the war? [said a resident]. We are Bohemians by descent, but we are Americans in allegiance. This is our country and we are fighting for democracy.

I am very proud of this village [said the elderly man, himself an immigrant, who has done more than anyone else to promote its welfare]. We are all Bohemians, but we are as good Americans as anyone.

I don't think you will find any better anywhere in the United States. The Bohemian strength is in freedom, and the Bohemians come here because they want freedom and want to live in the American republic. I am 100-per-cent American myself and so are most of our people. But I believe that our Bohemian traditions and language should be passed on to our children. Of course the language will gradually be forgotten as new generations grow up, but I hope the spirit of our ancestors will never die out.

Their own estimate of their Americanism is confirmed by that of the Episcopal minister, an American of Anglo-Saxon stock, who lives in the near-by town, but has held Sunday-school services in the Bohemian community for many years, and knows it thoroughly.

There are no better American citizens anywhere than right here [he said]. I have been coming here for nearly fifty years. I built the chapel and have officiated at the weddings of most of the people. We are the best of friends, though we do not agree about religion and the adults do not come to my church. Some of them let their children come to have a good time. They are hard-working, moral, honest, and healthy people, who respect law and order. Their home life is very wonderful; we Americans could learn a good deal from them.

Then, referring to their Americanization, he added, with a look of reminiscent sadness:

But life has changed here since I first came. The people are getting Americanized fast and forgetting some of their fine old customs. For instance, their weddings used to last three days; the most wonderful meals were served and there was an abundance of everything. But the last time I married a couple we had only lemonade, ice cream, and cake.

As to the Americanizing influence of such a separate community as this, compared with that of the usual city colony, there is significance in a remark made by the secretary of the local branch of the Bohemian National Alliance, who formerly lived in a large city himself.

The people are much more Americanized here than in the city [he said]. The reason is that this is a freer and better life, where there is really more chance to get in touch with Americans. In the city we stick together. Here we mix more. For instance, we have to go to the near-by town to buy everything. The people who work on the estates have to learn to speak English. This is a small place and there is more chance to get into things. I know that more people speak English here than in the city.

Though the remark quoted may sound paradoxical, referring as it does to an all-Bohemian community, it is borne out by the facts. There is a good deal of contact in work and sociability between the people of the village and the native Americans of the town. The young people go there to attend the movies and dances and to take part in baseball games, and some of the men belong to American lodges. Townspeople often come to entertainments at the village in an informal, friendly way.

With the exception of some of the older people,

everyone can speak English, though some of the older generation have difficulty in reading and writing it.

They come to me for advice [said a leader]. I have to make out their papers, read their letters when children write in English to their old parents, and sometimes I have to write letters for them.

On the other hand, a few of the young people cannot speak Bohemian, or at least profess ignorance of it when associating with "Americans." This latter attitude, however, is not general, as a conscious effort is being made to preserve the Bohemian language and respect for the old customs and traditions.

There were two men who found fault with the community. One was the principal of the school. He does not live in the village and is not in close touch with its life.

These Bohemian peoples have no ambition [he said]. They want their children to leave school as soon as possible and go to work. Another difficulty here is the English. The children speak Bohemian at home and their English is very poor. Some of the small children do not understand any English when they first come to school.

The other complainant was the Bohemian Jew who is manager of the cigar factory. There is usually little or no ill feeling between Bohemian Jews and Christians. But between this particular individual and the community there is slight friendliness. It is intimated that he got himself elected to the school board so that he might influence the parents to put their children to work in the factory as soon as possible. The school principal says that pressure to this end has been brought to bear on him. It is also reported that the factory manager was evicted from the house he formerly occupied, because he kept it in such a filthy condition.

I don't live here because I want to [he said]. I failed, and have to live where I can find a living. My wife does not like it here, either. I do not belong to any society. I am a Bohemian, you understand, but I am an American first and I do not like the Bohemian way that the society does business. The American government is too lenient with these foreigners. They should be forced to speak English and not allowed to hold meetings in their own language. I do not agree about their Bohemian school. Why should the children learn Bohemian? They are Americans, and English is good enough for them.

In numbers, the community is just about holding its own and perhaps gaining a little, but its recruits come mainly from middle-aged and older people. It is significant that the younger people are inclined to leave. The local resources for work do not satisfy them and they are constantly looking for better opportunities.

Then, too [as one of the elders said], life is too slow for them here. They want to see something of the world. It is not exciting enough for them. My son is working on the railroad, but now he wants to get married and move to a big city. He is Americanized and he does not think there is enough chance for him down here.

### A DUTCH COMMUNITY

This community, as compared with the Bohemian community, which is only a few miles distant, presents some very interesting differences and likenesses. It is a village situated on a bay. It had its beginning a few years earlier than the other. In 1850 a few Dutch families settled there, attracted by the sea and the opportunity for oyster gathering. Thenceforth its numbers slowly increased, and reinforcements from Holland were still coming as recently as six or seven years ago, when a group of ten families arrived. Most of the immigrants knew one another in the old country and came from the same fishing villages. Many who had gone inland when they first came to America were later attracted to this community.

We Hollanders follow the sea [said one], and anyone born by the sea has to get back to it, if there is any chance at all.

A few Germans and Bohemians have married into the village, and one native American family simply happened to come there and is now fully identified with its life. But the other residents are all Dutch. Here, again, about a third to-day are of foreign birth. Of the remainder, approximately half were born and reared in the village itself.

We have not tried to keep other races out [a resident remarked], but we Dutch people are clannish and have our own way of doing things, and that is why you find only Dutch people here.

To-day the population of the village is about eleven hundred. Seafaring and oyster packing are still the main support of its people. Some of

DISTINGUISHING FEATURES OF THE DUTCH VILLAGE

These immigrants are a church-going people.
Oyster packing is their main support.

the men follow trades in the near-by town and some work on the surrounding estates. Some of the girls work in the lace mills in another town, but in marked contrast to the Bohemian village, where most of the women work, practically all the married women in the Dutch village stay at home.

It has not always been that way [said one of the men], for they used to work in the oyster shanties during the sorting. It is not so many years ago that they used to come to the shanties in their big wooden shoes, but since they have become "Americanized" they object to the cold and draught and prefer to stay home and keep themselves busy scrubbing and polishing so that everything shines.

At least three-fourths of the families own their homes.

They are thrifty people [a tradesman stated], and there are but few families who do not have a savings account in the bank. Besides, they always have cash on hand and do not carry anything on account. For instance, the milkman is always paid in cash and has no trouble in collecting his money here, but in the near-by town his American customers are always running bills and he often has a hard time to collect what is due him.

This village is given a distinctly maritime setting by the water front, the oyster-packing shanties, and the boats and ships in the offing. Otherwise it presents much the same neat and prosperous appearance as the Bohemian village. Everything is immaculately clean. Here, too, the settlement grew up without any definite plan, and the houses have anywhere from half an acre to five acres of ground about them. Rising in

41

the center of the village are two churches, one the Christian Reformed and the other the Dutch Reformed, the latter a modern-looking building with meeting rooms for social purposes in the basement. In addition there is the summer hotel, the neat white building of the hook-and-ladder company, the post office, three village stores, two ice-cream parlors, a garage, and a bicycle-repair shop. There is no school building, as the village is situated so near the town that the children go to school there.

THE CHURCH AS A MEDIUM

In striking contrast to the Bohemian community of freethinkers, this is a churchly group and the churches are the center and chief dynamic force of its life. Practically everyone belongs to one of the two churches, which represent different stages of adjustment to New World conditions. The Christian Reformed church is similar to the All Netherland church of Holland, and it is this church which most of the immigrants join first and to which most of the older people still belong. Its services are in Dutch, with the exception of a Sunday-afternoon service in English. Sunday school is prohibited on the ground that religious teaching is too holy for any layman to undertake, but the children and young people receive instruction twice a week in the old Dutch catechism. There is little or no activity not strictly religious.

As the younger people come into closer relation

with American life and begin to speak English they tend to leave this church and go over to the Dutch Reformed.

According to the pastor of the latter, who is American born of Dutch parentage, this church has realized that if it is to keep its hold on the young people it must adapt itself to new and changing conditions and make itself the assimilating and Americanizing force in the community.

It is understood [said the pastor], that if the church is to keep its place as an all-pervading influence among the people, it must adapt itself to the different ways of living over here and represent the best interests of the community as an American community and an integral part of this country.

All services are held in English, with the exception of the Sunday-afternoon service, which is conducted in Dutch for the convenience of the old people. Every week-day evening there is some meeting or other in the basement. Some of these are held by the Ladies' Aid Society, which is for the older women, others by the Christian Endeavor, which is made up of middle-aged people, and still others by the Missionary Society for the young people. Besides, there are two Bible classes, one for men and the other for women. The pastor, a very energetic man, exercises a great deal of influence in all the affairs of the community.

Although the two church groups stand out distinctly in the general as well as denominational affairs of the community, the common ties insure unity when occasion demands; as, for example, in the Liberty Loans and Red Cross drives, when the two churches worked hand in hand.

Unlike the Bohemian village, this one has no mutual insurance or national societies which are independent of the church. The Dutch churches in Holland and America have, as a rule, disapproved of purely secular organizations, and Dutch people are in general unaffiliated with societies of that sort. To meet the practical need which a mutual insurance society fills, the Dutch Reformed pastor formed such a society in connection with the church, to which practically all the members of his flock belong.

## INTERRELATIONSHIPS

The children, it has been said, attend school in the near-by town. Until recently the village people wanted a local school, but now they are beginning to feel that the present arrangement makes for closer contact and association with "Americans" and promotes mutual friendliness and better understanding. Like the Bohemians, these Dutch people are strong supporters of the public school.

This is a refined community [said one]. The Dutch believe in education and do not want to send their children to work right away. About ten young people are attending a technical school in New York, several young men are in college in Michigan, and one is studying for the ministry in Grand Rapids. Some of the girls are preparing to become teachers and some are taking up nursing.

According to the principal of the grammar and high school in the town, about one hundred and thirty children from the Dutch village are in school. So regular is the attendance that the truant officer has had to visit the community only once. The children are bright, and many of them continue through the first or second year of high school.

All the children in my school are alike to me [said the principal], and I don't know whether they are Dutch or American.

The organization of this community for purposes of local government is about the same as that of the Bohemian village. There is the same sort of hook-and-ladder company, established by voluntary contribution. This village and another nearby form one election district, and voting takes place in the fire building. The people are almost solidly Republican, with but a few Democrats and only one Socialist, reported to be an individual "who has a grievance against society." With the exception of a few old men, all are American citizens.

The first thing a Hollander does when he comes to this country [said a resident] is to take out his citizenship papers. This is done largely for the practical reason that many of the Dutch people take to the sea, and they are liable to have a good deal of trouble with the marine law unless they are naturalized.

The village takes an active interest in voting, especially when there is an election for the town

board, on which it is usually represented. For
purposes of school government the village is consolidated with the near-by town. Of the eight
members of the school board, two, both of whom
are sons of pioneer settlers, represent the Dutch
community.

Though a few of the old people have never
learned to speak English, in general English is
the language of common use, both at work and
in the home. There is no school for teaching the
Dutch language, and no organized effort is being
made to perpetuate it except through church
services and instruction in the Dutch catechism.

While this community did not have the special
interest in the war that the Bohemians had, in
view of the prospect of Bohemian independence,
its response to the Liberty Loans was substantial.
Red Cross work was organized by the pastor of
the Dutch Reformed church and a local workroom was conducted under the chairmanship of
the only woman of native American stock in the
village. She says that all the women knit and
sewed, and co-operated heartily in providing
Thanksgiving dinners for the men at a near-by
camp. Practically everyone in the village joined
the Red Cross.

The migration of the younger generation has
not become a serious problem here, mainly
because seafaring satisfies the youthful zest for
adventure. But the boys and girls go to the
near-by town a good deal, especially to attend
movies and dances. The dogma of the church
is against dancing, but this prohibition is not

strictly enforced, for the attitude of the young people has compelled some concession.

## A JEWISH COMMUNITY

This community, Woodbine, New Jersey, was founded by the Baron de Hirsch fund through a special organization incorporated as a "Land and Improvement Company." It was intended to be an agricultural settlement. In 1891 a site of some 5,000 acres of flat, uncleared land was purchased. Divided into fifteen-acre plots, on which some dwellings and outbuildings were erected, this was sold on easy terms to Jewish families. Most of the colonists were recent immigrants from Russia who had no farming experience and had been employed previously as "tailors" in the sweatshops of New York.

Almost immediately it became necessary to make a departure from the proposed agricultural plan. Pending clearing and fertilizing, the land was so unproductive that in order to keep the prospective farmers there at all some means of temporary livelihood had to be supplied. So a factory building was erected by the company, and its use, rent free, together with additional subsidies, was granted to a cloak-making concern. This was the beginning of an industrial development which soon predominated over agriculture. The Jewish young people took more kindly to the factory than to the farm, and it soon became evident that only a few of them could be counted

47

upon to till the land. Soon a village was laid out about the factory, and grew rapidly. Half a dozen more small factory buildings were put up, and the new industries attracted additional settlers. Fifteen years ago the village and a surrounding farming area, not including all of the original tract, was incorporated as a borough, or township.

The present population of the community is estimated at about 1,800, of which at least 95 per cent is Jewish. The residue of 5 per cent is composed of Italian, Polish, and Rumanian immigrants, most of whom are on the farms and make better farmers than the Jews, and some half-dozen families of American descent. Although the number of people here is considerably larger than in the case of either of the communities previously described, the racial solidarity combined with the geographical separateness of this Jewish community is such that it may be regarded as one neighborhood.

The village occupies an area about a mile square, and is flat throughout, but trees, which were planted early along the sides of the streets and are now well grown, somewhat relieve the monotonous expanse. A railway cuts through the middle, dividing the village into northern and southern halves. On one side of the tracks stands the group of factory buildings. On the other side is the borough hall, which is a good-looking two-story building, and the one-story concrete office of the company. The rest of the village is built up with dwellings, the majority frame houses, but a goodly number of cement or brick. Most of the residents own or are buying their homes. One side of the village is less developed and less well kept than the other. A frame school building, for children of the primary grades living in that section, stands at one corner. On the other side there are some twenty-five small stores and business places of various kinds, including a hotel and a little motion-picture theater. Buildings of community character include a recently erected high school and adjoining grammar school, two synagogues, a small building used for the Hebrew school and occasional gatherings, another belonging to the Workmen's Circle, and at one corner a school building no longer in use. The village, as a whole, presents a fairly good appearance, but many of the frame buildings are run down and much patched, the premises about many of them are unkempt and a good many of the houses are vacant.

### A TOWN THAT RUNS ITSELF

Outside the usual obligations to the county, state, and Federal governments, this Jewish community is self-directing. As a borough it elects its own officers and manages its own affairs. The company bulks large in the situation as a promoting agent and, if so disposed, could doubtless be a controlling factor, inasmuch as it owns practically all the undeveloped land and some of the improved, holds many mortgages, and pays about half the taxes. Borough buildings and improvements are usually financed and maintained from three co-operating sources—subsidies from the company, taxation, and voluntary individual contributions.

At the head of the borough government is a mayor and council. There is an elected school board and certain other elected officials. A board of health is appointed by the mayor and council, and there are some minor appointees. The fire department is a voluntary organization. There are no police or courts, recourse being had to the county court when necessary.

Elections are by ballot on appointed days. Borough meetings (*i.e.*, town meetings) are held from time to time as required, and are said to be very well attended, not only by voters, but by some men not yet naturalized, and some women, although woman suffrage has not yet been adopted in New Jersey. A good majority of the Jewish men are fully naturalized, or have taken out their first papers. Elections are not usually conducted on national party lines, but are determined by local issues and the personal standing of candidates.

### THE SCHOOL SYSTEM

While the center of the Bohemian community was seen to be the freethinking society, and that of the Dutch community the church, in the case of this Jewish community the center is the public school. A supervising principal is in general administrative charge. The present incumbent has held this position some twelve years. Although himself a Christian, he is thoroughly interested in and identified with the community, as are the members of his family.

## INHERENT FORCES

School attendance is excellent, and there is little absence, except on the part of non-Jewish children, in whose case regulations are not strictly enforced. There are a few children of the local native American stock, who are unprogressive and deficient both physically and mentally. Only about 10 per cent of the Jewish children leave to go to work before completing the eighth grade; of those who remain, close to 90 per cent go to high school; and of these, in turn, nearly half finish the high-school course. The percentage, it is said, would be still larger were it not for the financial necessities of some of the parents. Well over half of those who complete high school go on to normal schools and colleges, chiefly to the University of Pennsylvania, Cornell, and the Carnegie Institute. The local high school is certified by the state educational authorities, and its graduates are admitted to the above-mentioned institutions without examination.

The grade building has a large assembly room, equipped with platform and stereopticon. Activities outside the classroom consist chiefly of a literary society, debating, and baseball. The school baseball team plays in a district league, some of the games being held there, and others in neighboring towns. One year the local team won first place, and another year it tied for first. The value of such contests in giving the local young people broader participation in American life is fully appreciated by the principal. The writer overheard a young fellow talking with him about the choice of an umpire for a game with a visiting team. The ethical aspect of the matter was carefully discussed.

The school is brought actively to bear upon the life of the community. Home visiting by the teachers is encouraged. Visiting of the school by the parents is also promoted. During the last state "visit the school week" this school had probably the largest number of visitors of any in the county. The chief link between school and community is a parents' and teachers' association, which meets about once every six weeks in the assembly room. General educational questions are discussed, and also local problems, such as tardiness, sanitation, and co-operation with the teachers. There are usually local speakers, often including one who speaks in Yiddish for the benefit of the older people, followed by discussion from the floor, in both English and Yiddish, in which the Jewish mothers take an active part. During the winter an evening school for adults is conducted, with classes in English and civics, combined with practical assistance in naturalization. Besides Jews, a few Poles and Italians have attended. The assembly room is used frequently for various community meetings and stereopticon lectures.

The writer went through all the rooms in the grammar school and met all the teachers, of whom several were Christians. This was true of the majority, it was said, in earlier years. All were alert and efficient, the discipline was good without being rigid, and most of the children were neatly dressed and of bright appearance. Especially striking was the variety of features and the comparative absence of pronounced Jewish types. In answering a number of questions, the children, with few exceptions, spoke English as well as any children of their age. A few were born in Europe, a larger number elsewhere in America, but the majority in the local community. Very significant, however, was the fact that only a scattering few said they intended to live there after they grew up. Nearly all of them, on the contrary, proclaimed most decidedly that they expected to go "to the city."

The people are proud of their public-school system, which ranks as the best in the county. The several boards of education in the county meet together once or twice a year, for mutual consultation, and on these occasions the attainments of this Jewish community are frequently held up as examples.

Of the other general borough activities, suffice to mention the fire department, the personnel of which is a group of young volunteers. Recently an Italian and a Pole joined the force. The latter was especially welcomed, as one of the Jewish members said, with a smile, because he could put his brawn to good use in cranking the auto-wagon, which the less husky Jews regarded as a pretty stiff proposition.

## PRIVATE INITIATIVE

The community fairly swarms with voluntary organizations of many kinds. Besides two synagogues, and a Hebrew school for instruction in the language and religion, all the leading Jewish mutual insurance societies are represented either by local branches or by individual members. Though the older men predominate in these, most of the younger men join one or more of them when they marry. The Workmen's Circle, a mutual insurance society with social and educational features, owns a small building, the first floor of which is rented as a store, while the second is used for activities which include a library, lectures, and assistance in naturalization. There is an enthusiastic Zionist society, which, however, includes few of the younger people. According to the president, none of the local people would go to a Zionist state themselves, and in fact such a state is not intended for American Jews, but for the oppressed and homeless Jews of Europe and Asia. For the latter, he thinks such an all-Jewish state would work out in much the same helpful way as does an all-Jewish community in America.

A board of trade and a building and loan association have promoted the town's economic development. The only labor union is a branch of the Amalgamated Clothing Workers of America, which, because of the spirit of co-operation pervading the community, has never had to resort to strikes. Indeed, opposition between "capital" and "labor" is not much in evidence. One of the most interesting organizations is an industrial copartnership, recently organized to tide over a slack period, in which the copartners are at once capitalists and laborers. They consist of some twenty clothing workers, including two Italians who were taken in because they were the particular kind of workers needed to complete the functional scheme. To provide working capital, each man contributed from savings an equal share, amounting to several hundred dollars. Besides the copartners, who work themselves, there are about the same numbers of employees. Copartners and employees alike are paid on a straight wage basis, but any profits or losses fall to the former. The writer saw all the men at work, and talked with several of the leaders. All spoke English well, and were very intelligent and earnest about the undertaking. All of them have lived in the community a good while, some having come there as young boys, but none were born there. The president is head of the local Socialist group. One of the others is a member of the borough council, another is president of the Zionist organization and treasurer of the labor union. Altogether, the enterprise is an unusual example of democratic industrial organization.

The women are no less active than the men in organization. Besides a mutual insurance and a charitable society, there is a woman-suffrage club, and a large Red Cross chapter which took charge of the local canvass for the Victory Loan.

The American point of view of the community is indicated by the fact that the streets have been named after great Americans—Washington, Adams, Clay, Franklin, Longfellow. English

is the prevailing medium of speech. Wherever
the writer went, he heard mainly English spoken,
and, with the exception of one Rumanian farmer,
everyone he met spoke English. The people
and the place have an American look. When,
going deeper, the community's Americanization is measured by its constructive participation in American life, certainly the facts
show that such participation is present in large
degree.

### EFFECTIVE PARTICIPATION

Most of the Jewish people of this community
lived for a time in New York City, in the Ghetto
of the lower East Side. The writer asked a number of them how the Americanizing influence of
the two situations compared, in their own experience. Their replies were significant. They
emphasized the political side. In the city, they
said, they were swamped and lost. Everything
was so big and vague and the issues so complex
and far removed that they were hard to grasp.
They did not feel that they had or could have any
active part in affairs. Under such circumstances,
naturalization did not seem important and there
was not much incentive to voting or political
interest. But in this village of their own everybody knew everybody else, issues and candidates
were familiar, the community ran itself, so the
people naturally wanted to take part, and most
of them did take an active part, in local affairs.

Significant also in this connection was a remark
made by the leading Socialist. He had said that

his group never included more than twenty members and never had been active. Asked why such was the case, when, as a rule, Socialism flourished among the Jews, he answered:

Well, I've been trying to puzzle that out myself, and I've concluded that it's because the community is so small that everyone knows what's going on. Concrete local issues and personalities are the deciding factors instead of abstract principles.

Between the Jews and the other immigrant elements a very natural community of interests has developed. This is evidenced in a plan to provide these other groups, all of whom are Roman Catholics, with a church of their own, in response to a wish they have frequently expressed. It is now proposed to give them the use of an abandoned schoolhouse on the edge of the village, which they can maintain in common, each race holding separate services in its own language if it so desires.

But what of the half-dozen native American families, to whom earlier reference was made? Alas! no program of Americanization could "point with pride" to them as its models. Two of these families are self-respecting and respected, but the others are a sorry, run-down lot, who are known chiefly for their promiscuous relations and their general shiftlessness.

This Jewish community has a problem which it has never solved, and on account of which it now faces an uncertain future. This is the exodus of the young people as soon as they complete their education and begin life for themselves. This exodus has been going on ever since the beginning of the community.

The explanation generally given is in the form of a question, "Well, what is there to keep them?" Some of the older people think this failure to hold the young is due to the lack of industries with high wages, providing clerical as well as mechanical employment. Others say that it is because there are not adequate recreational opportunities, and that a well-equipped community clubhouse might be a solution. The majority, however, feel that it is neither this thing nor that, but simply that the young people are too ambitious, too imbued with the love of adventure that goes with youth, too desirous of direct contact with the general life of America, to remain in this little Jewish community.

### APPARENT SEPARATENESS, BUT REAL UNION

When these particular communities were selected for study it was not known what situations would be brought to light. But when the inquiries were completed and the actual facts ascertained these facts appeared to speak so clearly for themselves that they have been presented simply as they stand, with little comment or interpretation. If Americanization is constructive participation in American life, is it not self-evident that, although composed almost entirely of one race and geographically set apart, these communities have not cut themselves off from America, but have, on the contrary, largely Americanized themselves?

A little further analysis will indicate the factors which have brought about a result that seems so paradoxical.

In each of the three communities described the following conditions have been present. First, practically all the people have been of a single race. Second, by their geographical separateness they have been left comparatively free to work out their own destiny. Third, each of them has been small enough to be virtually a single neighborhood. Fourth, they have had placed upon them a substantial measure—in the case of the Jewish community, a very full measure—of responsibility for their self-direction. Fifth, they have been included, for broader governmental functions, with the township, county, state, and national organization, and have necessarily had economic, political, educational, and social relations with the surrounding American population.

Such appears to be the five-cornered foundation upon which the seeming paradox has been built. Being all of one race, the people of each community have understood each other's traditions, aspirations, abilities, and problems. Though most of them have eventually learned English, all have meanwhile had their native tongue as a medium of communication. Common bonds of race, language, and, for the most part, of religious belief, have made for close association and cohesive organization. Geographical separateness has permitted these natural tendencies to work themselves out along the lines of least resistance. Confinement within a single neighborhood has made it possible for everyone to know everyone else, to comprehend the local situation, and to take an active part in community affairs. The obligations of community self-government have developed responsibility and constructive initiative. Governmental and other interrelations and interresponsibilities have inevitably bound these racial communities up with the American community at large. In short, the conditions and their outworkings correspond very closely to those of the township neighborhood of New England which de Tocqueville described.

Except in so far as these communities are reinforced by fresh immigrants, they are working toward their own dissolution, by graduating their native-born young people into the general current of American life. Separate racial communities, as previously noted, are uncommon in comparison with the generally prevalent immigrant colonies in the midst of larger cities, which are to be dealt with later. One factor alone—the necessity for finding immediate employment—would account for the flocking of the great mass of immigrants to the larger cities with their varied industrial opportunities. From this point of view, the separate racial community is neither natural nor practicable. The writer is not advocating the general establishment of such communities, or any general policy of leaving immigrant groups solely to their own resources. He wishes it clearly understood that these communities have been examined, not as patterns to be followed in their outward form, but as specimens through which to observe the process of Americanization under conditions where the racial factors involved are most pronounced.

It is not maintained that all such communities in the United States, without exception, are substantially Americanized, or on the way to Americanization. There may be exceptions, where the situation is un-American or anti-American. Nor is it maintained that this self-Americanizing process always takes place at the same rate. In fact, the rate appears to vary a great deal in accordance with many elements involved, and in some cases the process may be proceeding very slowly. It is maintained, however, that in general under such conditions a process of gradual self-Americanization does take place, and that *inherent* forces operating within the immigrant group itself tend eventually to make such separate communities an integral part of the American nation. The communities here described are loyal to America. In high degree they exemplify the characteristically American qualities of self-reliance, self-help, and initiative, and thus they are putting into actual practice America's democratic ideal of activity which is "of the people, by the people, and for the people." Through the medium of their own neighborhood life they have been brought into essential union with the life of America.

# III

## UNION THROUGH RACIAL COHERENCE

EVEN when immigrant groups are colonized in
the midst of American cities and surrounded by
a population of native Americans, they often
show a degree of group solidarity equal to that
which exists in geographically separate communities. Indeed, there is usually an approxima-
tion to such solidarity in urban immigrant
colonies.

Of all the immigrant groups in America, the
Finns, and especially one element among the
Finns, have gone farthest in intensive development on the basis of such solidarity. In fact,
the Finns are ordinarily regarded as "clannish"
to an extreme, as sticking exclusively to one
another and their own affairs. Some critics
would say that the city-dwelling Finns have
deliberately separated themselves from other
elements of the population more fully than have
other immigrants in isolated communities. In
the latter case, these critics would say, the immigrants, though geographically set apart, are
reaching out to relate themselves to American
life; but the Finns, instead of looking outward
and affiliating with the Americans immediately
about them, choose to look inward, to organize

by themselves, and thus to shut themselves off from American life.

Just as in the preceding chapter the question of the outworkings of Americanization in separate immigrant communities was submitted to the test of the actual facts, so this Finnish group has been selected to show the results, in terms of Americanization, of an extreme group solidarity.

Do the neighborhood activities of the Finns in fact tend to keep this group of immigrants permanently alien to the life and interests of America or do these activities actually work toward Americanization? In order to distinguish between superficial or immediate appearances and the realities beneath, it is necessary to keep in mind that the essence of Americanization is constructive participation in America's well-being.

## FINNISH BACKGROUND

So little is generally known about the Finns, because of the comparative recency of their immigration and their comparatively small numbers, that it is advisable to sketch a general background for the account which follows.

Finland lies at the northwestern corner of what was once Russia, across the Gulf of Bothnia from Sweden, facing the Baltic Sea on the south and the Arctic Ocean on the north. Though thus bordering Slavic and Scandinavian peoples, the Finns are in race and language an isolated group, supposedly descended from the Tatars who at one time swept over Europe from the east. In the modern period, Finland was a part of Sweden till 1863, when it was seized by Russia and became an autonomous Russian province. Now Finland is one of the "small nations" which have achieved their independence as a result of the World War.

Though not large in area, it has figured prominently in several world-wide movements. In Finland, women were fully enfranchised as early as 1906. The Finnish parliament was the first in which the Socialist party attained a majority. Finland is also one of the countries in which the co-operative movement is most advanced. In point of literacy, Finnish immigrants stand next to the top of all the racial groups who come to America.

The first Finnish immigrants came in the seventeenth century, when Sweden was trying to colonize Delaware, but so completely has this early infusion of Finnish stock been absorbed that hardly a trace of it can be found to-day. It was not till 1890, or thereabouts, that Finns began to come here in considerable numbers. Many of them left Finland because of the attempted complete Russification of that country, an attempt that proved impossible of accomplishment.

At first most of the Finnish immigrants were peasants and settled chiefly in the mining regions of northern Michigan and in Oregon, spreading westward and eastward from those regions. Since 1890 the immigrants have come increasingly from industrial districts of Finland and have been better educated and generally more progressive. They have settled chiefly in the Eastern and Central states, as well as in the other zones. To-day the number of Finns in the United States is approximately 250,000.

In describing certain group activities of Finnish immigrants reference will be made chiefly to one of the oldest Finnish settlements in this country, in which a general scheme of group action has been most fully developed. This city is Fitchburg, Massachusetts. The account will be rounded out by reference to other localities.

### THE FINNS IN FITCHBURG

Fitchburg has a population of about **41,000,** of which about a third is of foreign birth. Besides the Finns, the immigrant element includes Italians, French-Canadians, Jews, Armenians, Germans, Lithuanians, Swedes, Norwegians, Spanish, Turks, and doubtless others, but the Finns are the largest single group. They began coming about 1890, and to-day number approximately 5,000. Most of them are workers in the principal industries of the city—paper mills, textile factories, and machine shops.

The Finns are not segregated in one district, but all except a small minority live in one major colony and several outlying colonies within easy reach. Both in area covered and in numbers the Finnish settlement as a whole is too large to be regarded as a single neighborhood. Here, as in most of their settlements, there are several subdivisions among the Finns, each of which forms a distinct neighborhood in itself.

Racially, there is a division between the Finns proper and the Swedish Finns. The latter are descended from the Swedes who migrated into Finland when it was a part of Sweden. Although many of them speak Finnish, just as many Finns speak Swedish, and although there is considerable social intercourse between the two elements, in the main the Swedish Finns keep to themselves and affiliate more with Swedes, if any are at hand, than with Finns. They form a minor percentage of the total immigration from Finland.

Among the Finns proper there are three divisions—the church, the temperance, and the Socialist groups. The church contingent, consisting of Protestants of several denominations, is the most conservative. The temperance element occupies a middle position between the pronounced conservatives and the Socialists.

In Fitchburg there are four Finnish churches—Lutheran, National, Congregational, and Baptist. Two of these were without pastors when this study was made. One of the other pastors stated that his congregation was decreasing and that it was hard to hold the young people. For the latter he had two church societies, a choir, and a confirmation class. This church and another had together conducted summer classes to teach the Finnish language, history, and literature.

The temperance group maintains a small center in the same building used by the National church.

This contains a hall for meetings and plays, a library of Finnish books, a kitchen where light refreshments are prepared, and a smoking room. Twice a month there are programs of lectures, music, and dramatics. As the building is rather run down, the members wished to buy an old residence which they could remodel; but this happened to be in an American district, and some of the residents circumvented the Finns by buying the house themselves, saying that its use by the Finns would disturb the neighborhood.

## THE SOCIALIST GROUP

The third and most active group, which is a little larger than the other two combined, is composed mainly of Socialists. The Socialists, both in Fitchburg and elsewhere, have accomplished most along lines of group action and in working out the remarkable scheme of organization to which the remainder of this chapter will be devoted. Though there is a small ultraradical element among the Finns, especially in some of the Western states, the great majority of Finnish Socialists belong to the moderate or evolutionary group, which adheres to orderly political procedure and discountenances resort to violent revolutionary tactics. The Finnish Socialists remained with the moderate Socialist party when it was split in 1919 by the secession of the revolutionary Communist and Communist Labor factions. The Finnish Socialists of Fitchburg, some of whose activities will now be described, are of the main evolutionary group—the Socialist party proper. The writer wishes to have it understood at the outset that he is not dealing with the political beliefs of the Socialists, nor arguing for or against their theories. He is simply reporting certain facts which are significant from the point of view of Americanization through neighborhood activity.

### WORKERS' EDUCATIONAL ASSOCIATION

The neighborhood center of these Finnish Socialists is the Finnish Workers' Educational Association. This organization is made up of men and women on an equal footing and is entirely supported by the members. It owns a good-sized building which houses most of its varied activities, the majority of which combine recreation and education. Chief among them is dramatics, of which the Finns as a race are extremely fond. The building contains a large theater hall with a well-equipped stage. A dramatic director is employed on full time. Plays are presented every week, all the actors being members of the association. The quality and appeal of these performances are such that they are attended by many of the younger generation of the temperance group and even by some of the church followers.

Music is another interest, and a musical director also is employed on full time. There are several choruses, an orchestra, and a band. Dances are held nearly every week, and every other week there are general entertainments, which often include educational motion pictures. A regular lecture course is conducted, and a "Sunday school" where young people especially are instructed in the principles of Socialism. The building contains a library, and various rooms where subsidiary groups, as, for instance, a ladies' sewing circle, hold their meetings.

The association conducted classes in English and citizenship before these were started by the public schools. Now the schools have assumed this responsibility, and the association encourages its members to attend the classes thus supplied. Assistance in naturalization, however, is still provided.

Two other activities are carried on outside the association building. One is gymnastics. Several classes, for men, women, and children, use the gymnasium in a much larger building, which was erected jointly by all the Finnish associations of the Eastern states. The other outside activity is a farm-park, situated within easy reach of the city by street car, which is owned and operated by the association. It contains a running track, an outdoor theater, a swimming pool, and a dancing pavilion. All this equipment was installed voluntarily by the members themselves, who gave their spare time without payment till the work was completed. The park is used chiefly in the summer, and often as many as a thousand people gather there for Sunday picnics. The dances are open to the public, and according to the Finns these are sometimes attended by "Americans."

# AMERICA VIA THE NEIGHBORHOOD

The Finnish Workers' Educational Association was established [one of its oldest members stated] for the purpose of helping the Finnish people of Fitchburg to become good American citizens. Its members have done things in a social and democratic way. As a result of continued education, every member is now an intelligent unit who can think and act for himself. Furthermore, our members are an orderly element in the community, and not for many years has there been even a single arrest among them.

The building erected and owned by all the Finnish Workers' Educational Associations of the East is a handsome four-story brick edifice, the location of which is significant. Standing in a central square of the city, close to the post office, the courthouse, the library, and an armory, it seems silently but strikingly to proclaim that the Finns are not an alien group, but an integral part of the community. This proclamation is borne out by the fact that this building is the meeting place of all the labor unions in the city, including the Central Labor Federation, in which the Finns form only a minor element. The Finnish Socialists are strong supporters of unions, and in general are opposed to separate Finnish unions, looking upon membership in American unions as one of the best means of connecting themselves with American life and promoting closer relations with native Americans.

In this building also is conducted a training course for Finnish community workers, who come there from other parts of the East to equip themselves to carry on in the Finnish neighborhoods of their own communities such activities

FITCHBURG'S SYMBOL OF AMERICAN UNITY

The publishing building of the Finnish Workers' Educational Associations (No. 1, right foreground) stands as one of a civic group which includes (2) the Post Office, (3) the Armory, (4) the Public Library, and (5) the Court House.

as those here described. Most of the space of the building is occupied by the Finnish Socialist Publication Society, which publishes two papers of national circulation, one in Finnish and the other in English, prints translations of standard literature, and carries on an active campaign of educational propaganda throughout the Eastern part of the country.

## THE CO—OPERATIVES

Next in the Finnish scheme of group action are the co-operatives—that is, certain primarily economic undertakings conducted on the basis of what is known technically as "co-operation." Though these co-operatives are not nominally identified with the Socialist party, nor their membership composed wholly of Socialists, as a matter of fact Socialists as individuals have had most to do with their successful development and the Socialist group has given them moral support and constant assistance in the way of educational propaganda.

The In-to Co-operative Association has a three-story brick building on the main street of the city. On the first floor and in the basement it conducts a meat and grocery store, a furnishing store, a bakery, and a dairy. The second floor is occupied by a co-operative boarding house, separately organized, and the third floor consists of apartments which are rented to Finnish families. Located in outlying sections are four branch groceries.

Though the purely business aspect of this enter-

71

prise is not important in the present connection, the democratic form of organization is directly pertinent. Shares at five dollars each may be bought by anyone up to the limit of five shares for one person, but only one vote goes to each shareholder, irrespective of the number of shares he holds. Goods are sold to members and non-members at the prices generally current, but the members receive interest on their shares, and dividends (that is, a division of profits) prorated according to the purchases made by each individual. Dividends of lesser amount are rebated to all customers, as an extension of the benefits of the co-operative plan. A good many women are members. The clerks in the various stores are all members, though this is not required and they join through their own interest. The whole body of shareholders elects a board of directors and a treasurer, and this board then elects a president and a manager. Besides the regular shareholders' meetings, social meetings are held every few months, at which educational discussion of the principles of co-operation often takes place.

In neatness and attractiveness of display the central Finnish store can stand comparison with any in the city. A third or more of the trade of this store and its four branches is with the general public other than Finns. All the clerks, most of whom are American-born Finns, speak English as well as Finnish.

Four or five years ago [said the manager] only one or two of our clerks were able to talk English, but now ability to speak English is made one of the conditions of employment.

72

A FINNISH CO-OPERATIVE CENTER

This building, erected in Fitchburg by the Finns themselves, contains a grocery store, meat market, boot-and-shoe shop, bakery, milk-distributing plant, restaurant, and living apartments.

The co-operative boarding house, which occupies part of the store building, is similarly organized. Some sixty Finnish mill hands, who did not like the poor and sloppy food of the available cheap restaurants, got together and started this boarding house in a two-room flat. The number of boarders increased so rapidly that soon it became necessary to have more room. When the co-operative store building was erected its second floor was rented for this purpose. Anyone may join the boarding house by depositing five dollars, which is returned to him if he moves away. The prices charged are sufficient to cover the actual cost of food, service, and rent. As far as possible, supplies are bought from the co-operative store. The tables are usually crowded. The boarders include many women and some whole families. Fathers and mothers meet there after the day's work in the mills, bringing the children with them. Part of the floor space is set aside as a reading and smoking room. Besides Finns, a considerable number of other mill hands take advantage of the good food, low prices, and wholesome sociability thus provided. The prices and regulations as to membership and orderliness are posted in both Finnish and English.

The third, and financially the most ambitious of the Finnish co-operative undertakings is a credit union. This is practically a bank, but there is one important difference between its organization and that of the ordinary bank. Every depositor must become a shareholder, and just as in the case of the stores, these depositor-shareholders, having one vote each, irrespective of the number of their shares or the amount of their deposits, elect and control the board of directors. The capital supplied by deposits at present amounts to something over $100,000. In its loans the bank especially favors the development of co-operative undertakings, either locally or elsewhere. Its operations have, in fact, extended as far as New York City.

## NEIGHBORHOOD SIGNIFICANCE

The several co-operatives which have been outlined, including the Workers' Educational Association as co-operative in substance though not in form, may now be considered together from the viewpoint of their neighborhood significance.

They bind a large part of the local Finnish community in a close economic bond. So practical is their appeal that, although individual members of the Socialist group have been most active in their promotion, the number of non-Socialists associated with them has gradually increased till now it amounts to something like a third of the total. On the other hand, some Socialists who opposed these undertakings in the beginning, as not being sufficiently radical, have yielded to their practical value and success. The co-operatives now have the approval of all except a few ultraradicals, who contend that by improving the worker's lot they make him less revolutionary, whereas conditions should be allowed to become so intolerable that complete revolution will be the only way out.

Thus the co-operatives have struck deeper than the lines dividing the Finnish community into three differing groups, and have provided a common basis of neighborhood interest and action among them. The spirit which animates the co-operatives, and which they have more or less instilled into the Finnish community, is suggested by the first word in the name of their store society—the *In-to* Co-operative Association. Asked what this word meant, the manager of the store replied that there was no exact equivalent in English, but that it was a sort of combination of "enthusiasm" and "loyalty."

The co-operatives have also worked toward closer relations with the American community. Membership is open to Americans, and a few have joined. An obvious deterrent is the fact that Finnish is spoken at the meetings, but the Finns say they would welcome Americans, and they hope, as the generation of English-speaking Finns increases in proportion, to get more Americans in. Most of the co-operators are members of English-speaking labor unions, and so have an opportunity to interest their fellow members in the co-operative idea. As previously noted, about a third of the customers of the stores and many of the patrons of the boarding house are non-Finns, including other immigrants and native Americans.

### LITTLE HELP FROM AMERICANS

The attitude of the American community toward the Finns appears to be one of ignorance and

indifference in the main, with more or less outright hostility toward the Socialist element. The
chairman of the Americanization committee of
the leading women's club said that people had
assumed that the Finns wanted to stay by themselves and that nobody had taken the trouble to
approach them.

The present secretary of the Y. M. C. A. said
that before he came no attempt whatever had been
made to reach them. He himself formed some
English classes for them two years ago. These
classes opened auspiciously in the council chamber
in the city hall, but within a few weeks the attendance fell to zero. According to a Socialist inform-
ant, the trouble was that the instructor, doubtless
not knowing that most of his pupils were Socialists,
made some remarks criticizing Socialist principles
and the Workers' Educational Association. The
Finns in the class did not speak English well
enough to defend themselves, but naturally they
were offended and dropped out. Better success
attended a naturalization class which the same
Y. M. C. A. secretary started on a different tack,
in one of the buildings belonging to the Finns.
About a hundred and twenty-five Finns belong to
the Y. M. C. A., forming a tenth of its total membership of twelve hundred. Most of these Finnish
members, however, are American-born young men
of the church and temperance groups. The Socialists regard the Y. M. C. A. as "patronizing."

The librarian of the public library seemed
more interested in arranging his books than in
reaching the Finns. He said he had about a

hundred Finnish books. He did not know that
the Finns had two good-sized libraries of their
own. The women's club included no "foreign"
women, but a less formal women's league had
taken a few Finnish women into membership.
The labor unions have welcomed the Finns more
heartily than any other American organization,
and, as previously mentioned, accept the hospitality of one of the Finnish buildings for their
meetings. Finnish union members say that it
is chiefly at union meetings that they learn to
speak English. But except for the friendliness
of the unions, it looks as though the Finns are
doing more for Fitchburg than the rest of Fitchburg is doing for the Finns.

### GROWING INTO THE COMMUNITY

Gradually the Finns are relating themselves to
the various activities of the community. They
serve as clerks in stores and banks, and a few are
in the professions. In political affairs they are
just beginning to figure. One alderman is the
only representative they have had in the city
government in the past. A year or so ago the
Finnish Socialists persuaded the English-speaking
and Lithuanian Socialists to unite with them on
one candidate who, however, was not elected.
Recently a Finnish woman ran for the school
board, but also failed of election.

Great hope is placed in the rising American-
born generation. The children attend the public
schools, speak English as well as any, and mingle

with the other children in school affairs. Among the Socialists, the children are organized as a Young People's League.

> They are a wonderful group [said a young Finn]. They have been drilled in the fundamentals of co-operation. In a few years they will become the leaders in our activities. All of them speak English, and gradually English will be substituted for Finnish.

There are two forms of co-operative activity on the part of the Finns which are not yet developed in Fitchburg, but some description of which is necessary to round out the general scheme.

### DOMESTICS CREATE OWN NEIGHBORHOOD

On an avenue in New York City stands a four-story stone building called the Finnish Women's Co-operative Home. Briefly, this is its story:

About ten years ago a little group of Finnish servant girls, who met somewhere every week or so for sociability, began to talk of how good it would be to have a place of their own. By way of experiment, they raised about one hundred and fifty dollars among themselves, enough to furnish several rooms and to pay their rent for a month. The idea "took" so well that the enterprise was put on a regular co-operative basis. Shares at five dollars each were sold to a larger body of girls, and an entire house was rented and equipped. Not long thereafter the adjoining house was added, and a few years ago they moved to their present four-story building.

The original plan of a sociable meeting place

has greatly expanded. The Home to-day is primarily a place where Finnish servant girls may live between jobs, or, in the case of green immigrant girls, while they are getting their bearings. They may also stay there overnight after attending late parties. Formerly, when on their "day out" girls stayed in town at dances or entertainments, which lasted after midnight, they did not like to go back at such an hour to the households where they worked, and, if these were in the suburbs, often they could not make train connections; so, having no other safe place to go, they used to spend the night riding back and forth on the subway with their escorts. When not working, they had to live in rooming houses of the usual type.

The building they now have can accommodate about forty girls. Besides dormitory space and a few private rooms, it has a general living room, where the girls may receive men friends, and which contains a small library (mostly light fiction in English), newspapers, and a graphophone. For recreation and education these girls, most of whom are Socialists, depend on the local Workers' Educational Association, which has a large building not far away. At the Home itself there is a sewing club which meets one evening a week, for which music and lectures are provided by outside friends, and every little while special parties are held. The dining room is open to the public as a restaurant, especially at the mid-afternoon coffee hour. There is an employment bureau which is kept busy by housewives in search of domestic workers.

Without exception, all the co-operators who conduct this Home are servant girls, mainly specialized workers, such as cooks and waitresses, who now get good wages. Altogether there are some four hundred shareholders. The majority of these are scattered over the country. Those who are near enough to attend the general shareholders' meetings elect from among themselves a board of directors, which in turn elects a president, a housekeeper, and a clerk for the employment bureau. Everything is done by these Finnish servant girls themselves. They are not satisfied with their present quarters, which they rent, but plan to build or buy a still better building. Besides paying all running expenses, with no philanthropic or outside assistance whatever, they have already set aside over a thousand dollars toward a building fund. The seed from which all this has grown was a handful of girls, a hundred and fifty dollars, and the simple principle of co-operation.

The neighborhood aspect of this particular enterprise is suggestive in connection with the present domestic-service situation in the United States. These girls are scattered in their work over a wide area. They have little real neighborhood life in the localities where they are employed. Usually they are not accepted as part of the family by their employers, and they have opportunity for only the most casual association with other domestics—to whom, as a rule, these Finnish workers are superior. But instead of drifting about aimlessly and more or less deviously, as many domestics do, they have set to and built up through their co-operative Home a centripetal neighborhood of their own. Through it they have established morale and a self-respecting status. The writer, in visiting the Home, saw many of the girls moving about. They looked neat and intelligent, and had an air, not of the "independence" which is supposed to characterize the typical domestic, but of substantial self-dependence. Most of the girls have had a grammar-school course. They have learned more or less English from working for English-speaking people, and have quickly adapted themselves to American dress and customs. One special contribution they have made has been to translate into Finnish recipes which they have found to be favorites in American homes. These are published in Finnish for the assistance of domestics who cannot read English and are not yet so well initiated. Many of the girls, it was said, bought Liberty Bonds and subscribed to the Red Cross.

### SOLVING THE HOUSING PROBLEM

In another part of New York—a Brooklyn district—are two Finnish co-operative apartment houses which have established a remarkable neighborhood nucleus of family life. The first of these apartments was built some four years ago. Discussion of the proposal started in the Socialist hall—that is, the local Workers' Educational Association. Members of that organization had found it increasingly difficult to rent, at figures within their means, apartments or houses which were well built and not too small. They could not afford to buy homes individually; so sixteen families got together, formed a committee, engaged a Finnish architect to draft plans, bought land, and put up an apartment house costing $45,000. Each of the sixteen families paid in $500, thus providing $8,000. A first mortgage of $25,000 was placed with an American bank, a second mortgage of $5,000 with the Finnish Credit Union of Fitchburg, previously mentioned, and the balance of $7,000 was lent by the shareholders in various amounts, from their savings. The second building was erected a year and a half later, at a cost, owing to rise of prices, of $55,000, of which $25,000 was supplied on first mortgage by the Credit Union, and the balance, over and above capital from sale of shares, lent entirely by the shareholders themselves.

The initial payment of $500 from each family figures as purchase capital, and each family thereby becomes the virtual owner of its particular apartment, but the property as a whole is held jointly. The individual shareholders may sell or sublease their own apartments, subject to approval of their successors by the governing committee. Every month each family pays an equal allotment sufficient to cover upkeep, taxes, insurance, sinking fund on mortgages, and service. The only paid worker is the janitor, who is himself a shareholder. This monthly payment now stands at approximately $28 for a thoroughly modern five-room apartment with bath and hot-water heat. No where else in the vicinity is there an apartment house which compares with this one in quality of construction, and inferior apartments of the same size rent for about twice the amount which the co-operators pay.

The general supervision of each apartment house is vested in a committee, the president of which serves as manager, without salary, collecting the monthly payments and attending to general repairs. Small repairs are made by members of the committee free of charge, but larger ones are paid for or let out. Repairs in single apartments are taken care of by the respective owners, who are also left free to decorate their rooms as they wish, the result being an interesting variety. Any shareholder can bring up questions at any time, and besides the regular shareholders' meetings special meetings are frequently called, either in one of the apartments or in the near-by Socialist hall. Four times a year the apartment houses hold a joint meeting at this hall, to which others, including non-Finns, are invited, and where the principles of co-operation are discussed.

The families who came together in this way, though all Finns and all Socialists, had not known one another intimately before. Skeptics prophesied that it was impossible for sixteen "landlords" to live together in harmony. A speculator in the vicinity counted on buying the house cheap within a year. On the contrary, a strong neighborhood life has developed. Instead of feeling like a comparatively irresponsible tenant, each family has a sense of ownership and responsibility, not alone for its own apartment, but for the whole property with which its own is inextricably tied up. This common responsibility has furthered voluntary co-operation in matters of upkeep, and has led to much normal sociability.

It is so different from where I used to live [said one of the women]. There I did not know even my next-door neighbor. But here we visit back and forth all the time, and scarcely a week goes by without a coffee party taking place in one of the apartments.

Other races and Americans would be welcomed if they cared to come in as shareholders or subtenants, but as yet none have done so. There is one subtenant family of the Finnish church group.

We Socialists do not object to the church people [said one of the co-operators], but most of them will not have much to do with us.

Nevertheless, a group of Swedish Finns of the church contingent, impressed by this practical demonstration, are going in for a similar apartment of their own not far away.

In many sections of New York City so-called tenants' strikes have broken out. Landlords profiteer and expel tenants. Tenants execrate, vandalize, and well-nigh assassinate landlords. Both are haled into court and summoned to "hearings." As yet nothing much has come of all the fuss. But in the midst of all this furor these Finnish co-operators have provided a concrete, constructive, and successful demonstration of one way in which the harassing housing problem may be solved.

## DEMOCRATIC ACHIEVEMENT

Most of the undertakings which have been described are not the only ones of their kind. With the exception of the credit unions, the co-operative home, and the apartments, which represent the most recent developments, they are paralleled in many parts of the country.

Wherever Finns are settled in considerable numbers they have their Workers' Educational Association. Over two hundred buildings, ranging from those of modest proportions up to a four-story marble and granite structure on upper Fifth Avenue in New York City, are maintained by these individual associations, which function also as the local party organizations of the Finnish Socialists. The different associations are combined in three regional divisions, including, respectively, the Eastern, Central and Western states. The regional headquarters, in conjunction with the national headquarters of the Socialist party in Chicago, conduct an unremitting campaign of education, publication, and practical organization.

The Finnish Socialists have particularly fostered co-operatives and are usually the most active element in them. There are several hundred Finnish co-operatives of many kinds, including stores, dairies, and boarding houses, distributed over the country. These co-operatives are combined in a number of regional organizations for concerted self-help. Systematic education in the underlying principles of co-operation is carried on as a necessary prerequisite to its success in practice, and a part of the annual earnings of each local society is set aside for the educational fund. The Finnish co-operatives are an integral part of the general co-operative movement in America, and are usually held up by that movement as models.

The most remarkable fact about all these extensive and effective activities [writes a Finnish editor] is that they have been developed by the workers themselves almost without any use of so-called trained intellectual elements, which is a splendid proof of the great natural constructive abilities of the average Finnish workingman. Out of the 15,000 members of the Finnish Socialist Federation there are, by actual count, only six men who ever had any college education or other academic training. The hundreds of functionaries in the co-operative stores and in the publishing companies, the music leaders, the writers, the editors, the lecturers, the actors are almost without exception plain workingmen and women who during their childhood had no or very little school education, but who through persistent self-study and co-operation with their fellow workers acquire admirable abilities in all branches of social activity.

### CONTRIBUTION TO AMERICA

In the light of the evidence which has been presented, what answer shall be made to the question whether the solidarity of the Finns as an immigrant group, or more particularly that of the Socialist element within this group, tends to keep them out of the common life of America or to bring them in to it? Here again, as in the case of the separate immigrant communities considered in the previous chapter, there is a paradox. The inner substance of what is taking place proves to be different from its outward appearance.

That these Finns are "clannish," in the sense that they have organized closely among themselves, is obvious. But that either the purpose or the result of such intensive organization is to exclude American influence and keep the Finns an alien group is plainly contradicted by the facts. The Finns have organized among themselves for the simple reason that common race and language are the most natural and practicable bases of organization. But in so doing their purpose is positively to adjust themselves to American conditions. Their "clannishness" is of a sort which works out constructively, not alone for themselves, but for America. Not only are they educating themselves, not only are they meeting their own needs and developing those qualities of self-dependence and enterprise which are fundamental in American life; they are participating in the common life of America by making positive and constructive contributions. They are providing a remarkable demonstration of what can be accomplished by people working democratically together. In the midst of the clash and confusion of economic and social struggle, they are showing America how the principle of co-operation may be brought to bear on the solution of some of her most vital problems.

### COHERING TO COALESCE

The Finnish group has been selected in order to test the outworkings, in terms of Americanization, of immigrant group solidarity. This group represents such solidarity in an extreme degree. In view of the results which have been reported here, it is reasonable to assume that similar solidarity on the part of other immigrant groups has similar results; and that, like the Finns, other immigrant groups also *cohere* among themselves the better to *coalesce* with the life of America.

# IV

COLONY PIONEERING

THE great mass of immigrants who come to America settle first in urban "colonies" of their own race. The chief reason, even though they have been peasants in the old country, why they cast their lot in a city when they land in America is because they know that there they can find variety of employment and good wages. As distinguished from the occasional immigrant towns which are largely self-governing entities, colonies are compact settlements of immigrants included within the boundaries of American cities to whose general governmental operation they are subject. So far as formal government and the direction of local civic affairs is concerned, therefore, the city colony provides less opportunity than the separate town for the immigrant group to express itself. On the other hand, it brings that group into closer geographical contact with American influences and activities.

In size such colonies range from little clusters up to aggregations which are themselves as large as a city. In point of numbers and in area covered they often extend far beyond the proportions of a single neighborhood. But in view of their racial homogeneity, such larger colonies may be regarded as a number of neighborhoods which overlap one another and are essentially similar in character.

The outward and picturesque features of such colonies, under their popular nicknames of the "Ghetto," "Polish Town," "Little Italy," and the like, are now generally known. As a rule, however, they are looked upon as "foreign" quarters, which cut the immigrant off from American influences and thus constitute a serious menace to the community. There is slight acquaintance with their inner workings and little comprehension of their real significance.

The development of immigrant colonies is in the first place altogether natural; so natural, indeed, as to be inevitable. Why this is so will readily be appreciated if the reader will imagine himself an immigrant in some foreign land. Under such circumstances, would he go to a locality all the other residents of which were natives of that foreign country but to him "foreigners," or would he seek out other Americans who had gone before him, and from whom he could get such information and help as he needed?

Most of the immigrants who come to America are laboring people of little education. There is, of course, no considerable similar emigration from America to foreign countries. Americans who find it necessary for business reasons to live in other countries are mostly persons of means and education, who often acquire some knowledge of the language and customs of the country before they go.  It is indicative of the naturalness of racial colonies that even such Americans react to their foreign environment much as foreign immigrants do to their American environment.  That such is the case appears in the following quotations from the letters of Americans resident in other countries.

Here is a letter from Mexico:

Americans in Mexico, when in cities, "flock together"; they have their own organization and fraternities; they cling to the use of English, many of them even after years here being unable to express themselves in Spanish; in the past few years very few, if any, Americans have become naturalized citizens of Mexico.  I know of no Americans who have taken an active part in the politics of this country.

This correspondent adds, however, that:

Many of them, with a realization of the necessity for it, do study and become quite proficient in Spanish. . . . Many years ago, as shown by the records, when an American colony came here, most of them became naturalized Mexican citizens; I had occasion to look this up.

A second report from Mexico goes into more detail:

I have resided in this republic for more than twenty-one years, during which time I have occasionally returned to the United States, and have maintained an office in New York, keeping on hand a passport from our State Department in which my intention to eventually return to the United States is reiterated.  I mention the foregoing in order that you may understand that, born and bred, as I have been, in New York, my residence here and the liking all Americans that have lived in Mexico have for this country have not caused me to in any way lose contact with our country.

Most Americans that I have known in Mexico have been hard-working, and, while respectful of the laws here, have not, as a rule, amalgamated with the citizens of this republic, as have many colonists of other nationalities, such as the Germans, French, Italians, and Spanish. I ascribe this in part to the difference of language, but mainly to our nearness to the United States, to occasional visits there, to the reading of American newspapers, keeping in touch with the old home, and, in late years, to the necessity for constant contact with one another, owing to the disturbed conditions in Mexico. We have an American Club, and within the last year and a half have organized an American Chamber of Commerce.

Few Americans become naturalized here, though many remain in this republic for years. These observations should be qualified by the fact that, owing to the repeated calls of President Wilson, a large majority of former American residents in this republic have returned to the United States, most of whom, I think, have not again come to Mexico, the number of Americans now in the republic being perhaps one-fifth of what it was in 1910.

While my observations have not been extended to precisely the American laboring class, of which there are but few in this republic, since wages have always been lower than in the United States, and perhaps my conclusions will not be of much value for your purposes, I think I can say that most Americans that live here have a working knowledge of Spanish, and the educated men, naturally, have learned the language of the country, as such men would do wherever they might habitually reside.

Another correspondent writes from the Argentine:

The Americans resident in the River Plate region are now numerous. They are of the middle-class type—commercial representatives, packing-house men, and business managers. They are decidedly clannish and their business as well as social relations are confined as closely as possible to their own colonies. They are bad colonists in the strict sense of the word, since they do not allow for the defects of a new country and are always ready to make unfavorable comparisons with "God's country." The number of Americans married to Argentine women is very limited indeed.

## This general statement is thus supplemented:

A couple of generations back, when the colony was less numerous, a large percentage of the early arrivals married here and have now become assimilated as Argentine families; so much so that North American antecedents are not taken into account as being of "foreign" origin. After two generations the Englishman is an Englishman, but the American descendants speak of North America as a matter of course, just as if it were a province or state of this country.

## A second letter from the Argentine is somewhat fuller as regards the tendency toward assimilation:

Until of recent years few Americans came to stay in this country, those who took up their residence permanently being connected with established commercial enterprises.

Of the laboring classes the arrivals have been so limited that they cannot be taken into account.

With the increased business relations resulting from the establishing of American banks, and due, also, in a good measure, to the war, which has obliged merchants to look to the United States for the supplies which they had previously obtained from Europe, there has been a considerable arrival of Americans representing firms in the United States that have been or are doing business or are seeking same.

Therefore in answering your inquiry there are two sections of Americans to refer to, *viz.*

(a)   The settlers from some time back representing the
        minority.
(b)   The younger generation of later arrivals, during the
        last decade, representing the majority of residents.

Of the former (a) it may be said that they have identified
themselves with the business community of the country and
have acquired the language by long association, but nevertheless have retained their nationality and customs, and
as soon as opportunity offered have constituted associations
for concerted action.   However, many of the descendants
of these, being native born, have associated with and married
natives.

Of the latter (b), while keeping together socially (with the
older residents) and having their own organizations, it may
be said that there is a tendency to fraternize with the natives,
and in the desire to acquire the language many young
Americans take up their residence with native families.

With regard to naturalization, few Americans have become naturalized citizens.

The attitude of the Americans toward the people of the
country is one of friendship, esteem, and respect, and this
attitude is reciprocated here.

## A letter from Brazil indicates a similar situation there:

Practically all of the Americans in Brazil are business
men, financiers, and professional men.   A few have been
here from twenty to forty years and are thoroughly
Brazilian in manner, customs, and speech.   There are
many American ranch and plantation owners and over-
seers in the interior who have been here for many years,
have married Brazilian women, and who are Brazilians
to every intent and purpose.

The American business representatives naturally learn the
language at once as a matter of business.   The Americans
in Rio de Janeiro have the American Chamber of Commerce,
the Country Club, the Athletic Club and several other
distinctly American organizations.   They observe the Amer-

ican holidays and practically all return to the United States at certain intervals.

The Americans who have their families with them reside chiefly in one of the new sections of the city. Those here alone reside in all parts of the city. Scores of Americans here are greatly attached to Brazil as a place of residence and will probably continue to reside here all of their lives. The great majority, however, will continue to be American citizens — although they easily absorb the Brazilian customs in large measure.

Most of the American and English children here go to private English-speaking schools where Portuguese is taught, but where the lessons are taught in English.

There are a few instances where Americans have become naturalized Brazilians and many of the old American residents here are very strong defenders of things Brazilian. There was an American scientist who worked many years here and aspired to become curator of the Museo Nacional. He became a naturalized Brazilian in order to win the position, but later events prevented him from securing the post. There are a few Americans who are members of the Brazilian bar and several here are members of Brazilian academic and other societies.

The foregoing quotations are suggestive in many ways which may well be kept in mind as the discussion proceeds, but what they show particularly is that American residents in foreign lands stick together in about the same way that immigrants do in America. The chief difference is that most of these Americans are transients, whose interest in the foreign country is subordinate to their continued attachment to the United States, whither they eventually return. They do not cast their lot with the country in which they are living. The average immigrant to America, on the other hand, stays here, and, though retaining a natural interest in his native land, does cast his lot, for better or for worse, in the land of his adoption.

### THE COLONY'S CONSTRUCTIVE FUNCTIONS

For the average immigrant a colony of his own race is the most natural route to the life of America. When he lands he is unable to speak or read any English. If he were to go at once into an American neighborhood, how in the world could he get first aid in information? Obviously, he must depend for such information upon his fellow countrymen who have preceded him, and these he finds in the colony. He must have shelter for himself and his family. Even assuming that he would be admitted to an American neighborhood forthwith, he cannot pay the price of admission. The only living quarters within reach of his savings (a recent report of the United States Department of Labor states that the average amount which an immigrant brings with him is $112) are those of the humblest type, such as the immigrant colony offers. He needs food, and craves the kind to which he has been accustomed and which he can get only in the colony. He must have work at once, and where so readily as in the colony will he find assistance in getting it—preferably in a place where some of his countrymen are employed, from whom he can learn as he goes along?

These are some of the material reasons why immigrant colonies are not only natural, but necessary. But there are others, of vital importance to the immigrant and to America. If the immigrant is to have his mind free to get a foothold in America, he must feel "at home" as soon as possible. He must have sympathy, understanding, encouragement, and friendly help in many ways. He must have some recognized place in a human group and not be merely an isolated atom knocked about in a strange world. All these vital needs are satisfied in the colony, and, for most newly arrived immigrants, nowhere else.

Furthermore, if the immigrant is to escape demoralization by the sudden and complete change from his former life, he must have, during the adjustment to his new environment, some moral support and control, of a kind which he will recognize and understand. This function the colony performs. There are the immigrant's fellow countrymen who are familiar with his former habits and standards. They share his life experience and point of view. They uphold him in loyalty to inherited standards, which, unless better ones are substituted, are his moral anchors and safeguards. They condemn him for recreancy to these standards. They interpret to him, in terms which he can understand, the different standards of America, and help him to absorb them gradually and substantially.

The colony is thus a neighborhood in the truest and most human sense of the term, whose function is to serve as the normal medium for the immigrant's induction into the life of America.

This function is in part carried out informally and casually, through the general process of colony life—in the give and take of ordinary conversation, the going and coming on the street, gathering in the café, trading in the shops, attending the omnipresent "movies," and reading the foreign-language press. In these and similar informal ways information about America is acquired and exchanged by the immigrants of whom the colony is composed, and thus their adjustment to American conditions and their general participation in American life are continually furthered.

In more specific ways, however, the colony's Americanizing function is effected through certain inner organizations. Reference is made here not to the public and private agencies, such as the school and the social settlement, which are established in the colony under native American auspices, but to organizations originating among and maintained by the immigrants themselves. The latter, though as yet but little explored by native Americans, are numerous and rich in variety.

### BENEFIT SOCIETIES THE BASIC TYPE

The commonest type of immigrant organization is the mutual insurance or benefit society. Nearly every immigrant colony of nearly every race contains societies of this kind. The exceptions are a few racial groups of whom other forms of organization are characteristic, and some, as for example, the Mexicans, who are still so new to America that they have not yet reached the

**AN IMMIGRANT NEIGHBORHOOD GATHERING**

Over two thousand Bohemian newcomers assembled in the Harrison Technical High School, Chicago, to witness an entertainment and consider local improvements. (see p. 270)

stage of definite organization. In the great majority of racial groups, the benefit society is the basic and most prevalent type.

The specific purpose of these societies is to insure their members in case of sickness and death. Some pay death benefits only, some sickness only, but a majority include both. The fund from which these benefits are provided is created by regular dues and special assessments, which are paid in by the members of the society. The dues are usually graduated according to age and payable in monthly installments, and the minimum is set so low that any immigrant who is not actually poverty-stricken can afford to join. The benefits, while correspondingly modest, are substantial in relation to the income of the members. Those who so desire may pay larger dues entitling them to increased benefits.

The majority of these societies are confined to men, as the economically responsible heads of families, or admit women in auxiliaries only. Some include men and women on an equal footing, the proportion which admit both sexes differing considerably between one racial group and another, in accordance with the woman's traditional status. In most groups, however, there are separate societies of women. Some societies have provision for insuring the whole family—father, mother, and children—although only the father may figure as a voting member. Many societies employ or have working agreements with a physician, for examination and necessary treatment.

99

These mutual insurance societies, though patterned after European models, represent co-operative initiative on the part of immigrants in meeting a serious problem which confronts them as soon as they reach America—namely, the possibility of calamity through the sickness or death of the wage earner. Family protection is the chief motive in their formation, but the maintenance of self-respect by safeguarding against charity is also a leading consideration. Such societies constitute the immigrant's first organized constructive contribution to America. Through them he relieves America of such public or private outlay on his account as would otherwise ensue, and at the same time expresses and further develops a quality which is regarded as fundamental in Americanism—the quality of thriftiness and self-help.

The natural way in which local societies of this kind come into being is illustrated in the following simple account, given by a member of one which was organized by a group of Italians in Birmingham:

We have been here about thirty years. At first we did not have any society. We used to sit around in stores and talk about things. When any of our friends got sick or had bad luck we used to go down into our pockets and help them. Then we decided to form a society to help one another. To-day this society has nearly three hundred members.

As a rule, immigrant colonies contain not one or a few, but many such societies. Some are identified with churches, but in most racial groups these are a small minority, and at this point reference is made especially to societies which are wholly secular. Individual membership ranges from a mere handful, in little societies which are constantly springing up but which are not strong enough to last long, up to well toward a thousand in the best established. The average is about a hundred and twenty-five. The great majority of adult male immigrants belong to one or more such societies, and most immigrant families are represented in them through their wage-earning heads at least. It is plain, therefore, that these societies have an extensive place in the self-organization of immigrant colonies.

### THE FIRST RALLYING CENTERS

They are, as a rule, the immigrant's first rallying centers for general social purposes. Even in racial groups whose life is supposed to focus in the church, benefit societies often precede the founding of a church, and colonies which are not large enough to have a church of their own usually have societies of this character.

Sometimes such a society will be composed, at least in the beginning, of people who come from a single province, or even a single village, in the old country. A group of compatriots may come over on the same ship, and on landing in America may seek accommodations in the same locality and band together to preserve their native ties. This occurs most frequently among the Italians, particularly the Sicilians. Under these circumstances the society has an intensely neighborhood character.  Two illustrations may be cited as typical.

In one case about seventy-five Italian families, all hailing from the same town, settled in a little cluster by themselves on the outskirts of a large Italian colony in New York City.  They have a men's benefit society of some seventy members. This was organized eight years ago, but until recently it regarded itself almost as a branch of the old country community, and shared in the annual celebration in honor of its patron saint by sending donations.  Meanwhile the American environment was having its effect, and two years ago this society published its declaration of independence by holding its own saint's-day celebration over here.  Since then it has been still further Americanized.  Besides taking part in the various war drives, it has affiliated somewhat with a social settlement in the neighborhood and has become a branch of an Italian federation which is undertaking a general program of Americanization.[1]

In the second case, a group of immigrants from another Italian town settled not far away from the group above mentioned.  Their society, likewise composed of men, was organized nearly twenty years ago.  It also kept up active communication with the old-country community, but instead of regarding itself as the branch it organized a branch over there.  The latter was supplied with the same constitution and by-laws and its members were initiated by the same rites as those

[1] Sons of Italy.

of the parent body in America, into which such members as came over later automatically graduated. This society, too, has gradually become Americanized. It responded generously, according to its means, to war-time demands; it has contributed to a hospital and made a donation of a hundred dollars toward a community clubhouse fostered by a settlement in the neighborhood.

In both these instances the membership now includes others in the locality who do not hail from the two parent towns. That is, the old-country neighborhood of the past has gradually been replaced by the new American neighborhood of the present. As a rule, benefit societies have their origin in the American neighborhood. They are formed by people of the same race who find themselves living in the same locality and feel a need for such organization. As individual members move away for various reasons and the colony gradually dissolves, these societies tend to lose their local identity, but as long as the colony remains compact they are distinctly neighborhood affairs.

### BROADER INTERESTS

In addition to their specific benefit features, these societies very naturally develop broader functions. In this respect they fall into several groups. The majority have not as yet gone much beyond their primary object. A goodly proportion have enlarged their interests in various ways which indicate the possible scope of organizations of this type. A few have gone a long way toward realizing such possibilities. Certain functions other than insurance are common to all benefit societies, but in the case of the majority these are exercised only in a rudimentary way.

One function is to visit sick members, especially those who are in hospitals. Immigrants have a dread of hospitals, which may readily be understood. It is bad enough to be sick, but to be sick in a place where there is usually no one who speaks your language and can understand you is nothing less than terrible. Such hospital visiting not only allays this feeling, but arouses an interest that sometimes takes the substantial form of donations from the immigrant society. Though these are usually humble in amount, they represent the establishment of active cooperative relations between the immigrant group and the American agency.

Benefit societies are centers for exchange of information about America and the local community. This exchange is not a part of the formal order of business, nor does it appear in the minutes. It takes place in informal chattings at the meetings and in casual intercourse between the members outside. Two topics of special interest are how to learn English and how to become citizens. Not a few immigrants are in this way referred to the nearest public evening school, and to people who can help them in their naturalization. Many societies stipulate in their by-laws that all members on admission shall signify their intention of taking out citizenship papers, and only such as are citizens may be elected as officers and delegates to conventions.

Besides routine meetings, limited to the members, most benefit societies hold one or two big social events every year—a picnic in the summer and a ball or entertainment in the winter. These are open to the neighborhood. "American" friends are usually invited and addresses on subjects of general interest are often made by local politicians and others. Such gatherings tend further to broaden the neighborhood character of the societies and their interest in the larger community.

The majority of benefit societies are not very active outside their routine channel of insurance. Except when officers are to be elected, the meetings consist chiefly of the treasurer's being on hand to receive dues, and members dropping in to pay, chat a little while and then go out. But even under such circumstances the broader functions suggested above are present as a sort of germ plasm, out of which more advanced forms of activity may naturally be developed.

### CULTURAL AND ADAPTIVE ORGANIZATIONS

The second and third groups of benefit societies —that is, the more ambitious—can hardly be considered apart from societies of other kinds which have similar activities. To the immigrant, benefit features in a society are a matter of course, like bread with one's meals. Educational or athletic societies, and in fact the great majority of immigrant organizations of all varieties, have such features. It is sometimes difficult to say whether a given organization is a benefit society which has developed educational activities, or an educational society which includes benefits. Sometimes one function is more specifically in view when the society is formed, sometimes the other, or again they may figure equally. As sufficient note has already been taken of benefit societies as such, consideration will now be extended to the whole range of immigrant neighborhood organizations.

These fall into two general divisions, according to whether they originate in Old World inheritances or New World conditions. One division consists of the cultural organizations, whose primary function is to conserve the immigrant group's traditional culture. The other comprises what may be termed, in distinction, adaptive organizations, whose primary function is to adapt the immigrant group to its new environment. These two purposes are not mutually exclusive, and in fact most immigrant organizations partake of both; the line of distinction is drawn according to the predominant motive.

The mingled feeling of an immigrant toward the things of the old country and those of America was thus expressed by an Italian:

The immigrant's love for his native land is like that of a son for his mother. His love for America is like that of a husband for his wife. You would not want the son, when he married, to forget the mother who bore and reared him, and to uproot all the habits and standards which she implanted in him. Why, then, ask the immigrant to forget his mother country and cast off all that he owes to her? Just as love for a mother and love for a wife, each in its place, go most happily together, so will the immigrant and America form the happiest union if the love which the immigrant feels for the land of his birth is harmonized with love for the land of his adoption.

The popular notion of "Americanization," when it recognizes at all the self-Americanizing activities of the immigrants, sees little value in their cultural societies, regarding them as obstacles in the way of assimilation. What, however, are the actual results of such cultural organizations, so far as they are a factor in the immigrant's neighborhood life?

The most important organizations of distinctly cultural character are nationalistic associations, the church, foreign-language schools, libraries, and temperance, athletic, gymnastic, singing, and dramatic societies.

### NATIONALISTIC ASSOCIATIONS

The term "nationalistic" is used here to apply to an organization whose object relates directly to the old country. In the case of immigrants who represent subject races, this object has usually been that of fostering revolution in the native land. In other cases it has been to promote the welfare of the native land in one way or another, as, for example, by contributing to educational movements there.

Comparatively few local organizations, however, have this as their primary purpose. As a rule, such nationalistic activities are carried on through central bodies, such as the Bohemian National Alliance, to which local societies contribute, thus sharing in the nationalistic cause while devoting themselves to their local functions. Sometimes, however, a local organization deals directly with the old country. This occurs oftenest in the early years of an immigrant group, while the memory of the homeland is still vivid and acquaintance with America is only beginning. Among Armenian and Syrian immigrants, for example, there are local societies chiefly concerned with relieving the hardships of their brothers in Asia. This is also true of a more recent Oriental group, the Koreans.

An official of the Korean National Association of North America writes that the objects of this body, of which there are now "eighteen local organizations in various places in the United States and Mexico," are as follows:

To help the Koreans liberate themselves from the yoke of Japan.

To preserve the Korean culture and civilization.

To encourage the Koreans for education to be better men as well as to understand the Americanism and American institutions.

To aid and encourage them to pursue the right kind of vocation.

To do the charity work, particularly among the Koreans.

To lead them in living up to the standard of the real American life in every sense, etc. . . . .

Our activities are fully in accordance with our objects

mentioned above [he adds]. And also we publish newspapers three times a week and have branch organizations wherever the Koreans are throughout the country, to carry out our plans. We have debating societies and lecture system to discuss political, social, and religious questions.

This Korean program is a fair sample of the scope of most nationalistic societies. Though nominally it gives first place to Old World objects, actually it is more a program of Americanization than many things that are called by that name. First of all, such societies serve as an outlet for pent-up nationalistic feelings. They provide immigrants from oppressed lands with the first channel for self-expression and a sense of establishment in America. Thereby they promote appreciation of the freedom of America, and in the end, though they may keep up their nationalistic propaganda till their people in the old country are free, they themselves become wedded to America.

How this works out is illustrated in the case of a local society of Polish Falcons in Buffalo. This organization was formed to give near-military training to Polish immigrants in America, so that they might serve Poland as soldiers, if needed, in the winning of her independence. When the war came, however, nearly all the members of this society chose to enter the American army, serving America first and Poland through America. This particular society has for many years maintained a social center of its own, and is now planning a much larger building and increased activities. It has turned its face from Poland to America. Most of the nationalistic associations whose Old World objectives have been attained as a result of the war have done the same.

## SCHOOLS AND LIBRARIES

Parochial schools, conducted in connection with racial churches by some immigrant groups, parallel the public schools, and are subject to inspection and regulation by public authorities in some states. In addition to special religious instruction given in the foreign language they are expected to follow the same curriculum as the public schools and to use English as the medium of instruction. The serious educational problem which is connected with such schools is taken up in another volume of this series.[1] At this point it suffices to note that the religious instruction they provide is auxiliary to that of the church.

There is another type of school which most immigrant groups maintain in one form or another. This school is intended not to parallel, but to supplement, the public school, by teaching the language, history, and culture of the mother country. Parochial schools, where they exist, perform this function so far as the church group is concerned. Where church groups do not have parochial schools, a school of the second type is sometimes connected with the

---

[1] Frank V. Thompson, Superintendent of Schools, Boston, *The Schooling of the Immigrant.*

church. Usually such schools are on an entirely
secular basis. Sometimes, indeed, they are
sponsored by the freethinking element and used
for the inculcation of their ideas in the children.
Sometimes they are maintained jointly by a
number of immigrant societies. In a large Bohemian colony, for example, such a school is conducted through a joint committee, representing
practically all the societies among the freethinking element. From the fact that these
schools hold their longest sessions on Sunday,
though they also meet on Saturday and after
public-school hours on other days, they are
known popularly as "Sunday schools."

These schools, in purpose purely cultural, are
an important factor in the process of Americanization in that they help to prevent a break between the foreign-born parents and their American-born children. It is not generally realized
how often the children lose the language of their
parents unless they receive special instruction
in it. Not a few Italian children, for instance,
forget the native tongue of their parents as they
grow up. As many of the parents cannot speak
English, the result is that, however "American"
the children may be, they cannot carry their
parents along with them, as they could if they
were able to talk and read to them in their own
language and with due regard for their native
culture. Moreover, if Americans of various
racial descents can retain the language of their
fathers in addition to English, manifestly they
will enrich American life as well as their own.

# AMERICA VIA THE NEIGHBORHOOD

The libraries maintained by most immigrant groups, usually through certain societies, have substantially the same function as the racial schools. They consist mainly of books in the native language, especially its classics, and are intended to preserve a knowledge of the literature of the race.

The immediate neighborhood importance of such schools and libraries lies in the fact that they offer opportunity for sympathetic co-operation on the part of Americans. One social settlement, for example, invited a Carpatho-Russian group, which was conducting its school in cramped quarters, to transfer its sessions to the settlement. This hospitality was accepted, and has helped to relate the group more closely to the settlement. In some instances, sympathetic advances on the part of American agencies have resulted in merging racial libraries with public branch libraries and enlisting the active interest of the immigrant group.

## THE RACIAL CHURCH

A man's religion has to do with the depths of his nature. It is only to be expected that the immigrant finds his most satisfactory medium of religious communion in a church of his own race and language, the language in which his deepest feelings are most readily expressed.

The attitude of immigrant groups in this respect was expressed by a Syrian:

We are religious people and like to have our own church. We used to go to an American church, but we could not understand what was said and there was no Syrian priest, and we were not happy. So we decided to build our own church, and now we feel better.

In general, the racial church is a strongly conservative influence in the life of the immigrant, holding him fast to his traditional religious and moral anchorages. Unlike nationalistic organizations, racial churches are usually closely identified with local colony neighborhoods, and are a leading factor in the life of such neighborhoods. The church organizes itself closely around the religious motive and acts as a brake upon radical tendencies. Its attitude and influence differ in degree between races, creeds, and localities and individual churches. As a rule the Roman Catholic churches are the most conservative. Sometimes the brake is applied so hard and kept on so long that all forward motion seems to stop and some of the passengers prefer to get out and walk. Usually the church holds group progress down to a very moderate pace. Sometimes, however, it allows fairly rapid advance.

### FRENCH-CANADIAN INFLUENCES

What is probably the extreme of conservatism is represented by the Catholic churches of the French Canadians, and the Poles. While other churches contend, as these do, that the traditional faith of the immigrants must be preserved, these go farther than any other in holding that it is necessary to maintain intact all the traditional religious forms, especially the use

113

of the native language in religious services and instruction.

Although immigrants of these two races have been coming to the United States for fifty years or more, the instances in which any services or catechism classes in their churches are conducted in English still approximate zero. These churches hold that however important English is in secular intercourse, only the native language, the "tongue of the soul," is adequate for religious expression. When asked whether this holds true for the generations born in America, they reply that if only the American born were to be considered, English would probably suffice. But for the older foreign-born people and newly arrived immigrants the native language is necessary. It is vital, moreover, that young and old should hold religious communion together, in one tongue which both can understand. Otherwise children and parents drift apart, to the former's moral detriment.

Said one French-Canadian priest:

If Americanization means producing level-headed, law-abiding, industrious, and patriotic citizens, no better results could be shown than the young people we turn out.

In a recent great strike of textile workers, which was branded in many quarters as revolutionary, the fact stood out conspicuously that the French-Canadian workers did not take part, owing largely to the restraining influence of their churches.

While opposing radicalism, however, the French-Canadian churches are in some cases promoting progressive movements. Instances were found in New Bedford, Massachusetts, where parish credit unions had been organized by the priests on a co-operative basis. These were started by the deposits of twenty-five or more persons, on which interest is paid and from which loans are made, especially for home building. One priest in Woonsocket, Rhode Island, is planning a model village, in which tenements will be replaced by cottages, with ample space for fresh air and gardens.

In each of six parishes in New Bedford, again, there are societies to emphasize the importance of learning English and becoming naturalized. Besides co-operating with the public evening schools some of these societies have organized classes themselves. To make these measures more effective, a federation headed by a "league of presidents" has been formed to undertake a systematic campaign of naturalization. Stressing the importance of becoming voters and taking an active part in political affairs is characteristic, indeed, of most French-Canadian settlements, which, as a rule, figure actively in the political life of the community.

### CHURCH CITIZENS' CLUBS AMONG THE POLES

Among Polish churches, one was found where the priest had experimented with an English service, intended for the young people. "But the parents objected," said he, "so I gave it up." A rapidly increasing proportion of the priests, however, are of American birth, speak English fluently, and have an American point of view.

In Chicago, particularly, the Polish churches have fostered the development of "citizens' clubs." A typical example is that of "King Casimir the Great Polish Citizens' Club." This club was formed about six years ago. Its purposes are to naturalize the men of the church, to educate its members in political subjects, and to work for the general improvement of the district, which in this case is solidly Polish. The club has about three hundred members, and meets monthly, the active attendance being composed mainly of the men not yet naturalized. Meetings are usually conducted in Polish, but two-thirds of the members can now speak English and practically all of them can catch the drift of addresses in English.

To date, upward of two hundred and fifty men have been naturalized, and many more than that have been assisted in taking out first papers. For the past three years, a class in English and civics, meeting twice a week, with an attendance of twenty-five to thirty, has been conducted with a paid instructor. The club also concerns itself with such local matters as garbage collection and upkeep of streets, and sends frequent delegations to the city hall.

I always take some of the members along with me when I go on such errands [said the president], and tell them I want them to learn how to do such things for themselves.

It is claimed that a local alderman who failed to provide adequate lighting for the district was defeated for re-election through this club's opposition. As the officers of all the other Catholic church societies are members, the influence of the club extends to those societies. When the club took charge of the Liberty Loan campaigns in that parish, for example, it enlisted the officers of all the other church societies to canvass their own membership.

This club and others of its kind in near-by churches are now planning to organize a citizenship league among themselves, and it is likely that similar clubs will eventually form a city-wide federation with the purpose of relating the Polish people more closely to civic affairs. This type of organization has developed among Polish churches in other parts of the country.

The Polish church with which the citizens' club described above is connected has also, with the co-operation of two adjoining Polish parishes, established a combined home for working girls, medical dispensary, and day nursery. The three-story building in which these activities are carried on stands only a few doors away from an American social settlement. About fifty girls live at the home, paying their board. Some instruction in English, cooking, and sewing has been provided for them, and the young men of the parish, through their singing clubs, arrange entertainments and dances at the home.

Besides the three churches immediately responsible, the labor unions and some of the largest employers in the locality contribute to the support of the enterprise. The priest who is chiefly responsible says he hopes also to organize a hospital for working people, on a self-supporting basis. The health of many Polish women has been shattered, he says, as a result of childbirth without proper medical attention. Though it is hard to get the Polish women to go to American hospitals, a hospital conducted by their own race could, this priest thinks, do much to remedy the evil.

### OTHER CHURCH GROUPS

German churches, both Protestant and Catholic, are at present in a state of transition from the old order to the new. Though only a small minority as yet conduct all services in English, the majority use the two languages equally in the church, and mainly English in the Sunday school and the young people's societies. No instances were found, however, in which German churches were enlisting their members in such broader social and civic activities as those just mentioned.

Among the large Catholic groups, the Italian churches have gone farthest in modifying traditional forms. As a rule, they do not maintain parochial schools and in many cases the principal services are held in English. There is less hostility and more friendly co-operation on the part of Italian priests toward settlements and other social-service agencies. One Italian priest, whose attitude, though very exceptional, suggests the

118

direction in which others are moving, said he had rather opposed the building of the separate Italian church of which he is in charge.

Italians come over here to be Americans [he remarked], therefore they must be associated with Americans as much as possible. Amalgamation can take place only through natural association. The bishop of the diocese said he had orders to establish the church, however, so I gave in. But I got some Americans to teach in the Sunday school and thus far I have prevented the starting of any parochial school. The Italians here are determined that their children shall use the public school, and I know they would not send them to a parochial school.

This priest was born in Italy and came to America some fifteen years ago. He takes an active part in the general activities of his neighborhood, even attending the funerals of Protestant friends. In another neighborhood in Chicago an Italian Catholic church holds choir practice and presents plays in an American social settlement. An Italian Protestant church in Boston, the minister of which recently wrote a book in which he held that attempts at Americanization by coercion would drive many Italians back to Italy, is conducting a public forum and classes in English and civics.

Some significant examples of church outreachings were found among lesser known and newer groups of immigrants. In a Portuguese parish in Fall River, Massachusetts, for instance, the church has co-operated with the public schools to advertise classes in English, sewing, and cooking. One evening a week this church gives educational motion-picture shows, with talks by the priest in Portuguese and English. This priest has also helped to get his parishioners to join a local improvement association. Recently, he said, a deputation of Portuguese men went to the city hall to petition for a local sewer, but no one would listen to them. So he went himself and threatened to complain to the state sanitary inspector if the sewer was not put in. This brought results.

> Americanization is what I am striving for [he said], but it is slow work. All the Americanization plans that are being agitated so much are not reaching our people, because when it comes to any active part in these plans no attention is paid to us. Unless things are done differently, there is trouble ahead. Some day the people will rise up and take things into their own hands.

Similar instances were found in which Syrian churches, Catholic, Maronite, and Protestant, and so-called Uniat Catholic churches among the Ukrainians, were actively promoting English and citizenship and relating themselves with community movements.

### THE GREEK COMMUNITY

Especially interesting are the churches of the Greeks. There is a good deal of talk to-day about the desirability of the "community church." Well, the Greeks already have as a heritage community churches, which, though confined to their own race, provide a working model of a broadly democratic plan of organization.

120

## COLONY PIONEERING

In nearly every Greek colony of substantial size there exists what is called the "Orthodox Greek Community." Formed primarily for the purpose of establishing and maintaining a church, this community functions also as the representative organization of the colony. It is open to all Greeks of the Orthodox faith, which includes practically everyone. Leaders among the Greeks take the initiative in calling a general meeting. This meeting elects a president, a secretary, and a treasurer, several auditors, a school committee, and a board of directors. Everyone is expected to join the community and to pay a regular annual membership fee, usually about six dollars.

Larger contributions are made by the comparatively well-to-do. With the funds thus provided, a church is built and maintained. The elected officers manage the enterprise, including the engagement and, if desired, the discharge of the priest. The priest is thus accountable to the officers, and they in turn to the community, which meets for annual elections and at other times as needed. The president, not the priest, is the recognized head of the community, and is expected to represent it in all matters of general concern. There are now about seventy-five such Greek communities in the United States. Large cities have several, to meet the needs of different neighborhoods. New York, for instance, has four.

Here is a little story, as told by a leader, of how a Greek community took form in Atlanta:

Because we knew we could not live without religion all
the Greeks representing our different societies got together
to talk over having a church of our own. We united in
buying land and building the church, which is entirely paid
for. We have our own school, too, where our children are
taught. We bought all this property about fourteen years
ago; since then we have grown so that we have decided to
build a larger church, for which we have now raised enough
money.

This particular Greek community has related
itself with the general community round about
somewhat more than is usual.

Anybody is welcome at our church [said the president],
and some Syrians come. We are glad to have them, but
all our members are Greeks and we are proud that we built
the church ourselves. Graduation day in the school is
made a special occasion to which others in the neighborhood and people whom we know in work are invited. We
make many friends; we meet many Americans in our work;
we learn from them quickly how to do things and how to
speak English.

Recently a Syrian physician of the neighborhood was chosen to preside at the graduating
exercises. Officers of this community served on
Liberty Loan, Red Cross, and other war-time
committees, and assumed responsibility for these
campaigns in the Greek colony.

In the case of no other racial group are the
people and the church so intimately and democratically identified each with the other. Looking back in American history, however, a close
parallel may be found in the early Congregationalist communities of Puritan New England.
There church and community were one, and as

all the townspeople were Congregationalists, church affairs were considered and determined in town meeting. Gradually the secular or civic interests of these communities, as distinguished from church interests, expanded and assumed larger relative importance. The town meeting became the medium of local self-government.

The Orthodox community of America's Greek immigrants to-day contains within itself potentialities of similar expansion and civic usefulness. With adequate recognition and co-operation on the part of native Americans, it may readily be made the normal medium through which these Greek pioneers will become self-determining Americans and a contributing factor in American life. Similar possibilities hold true generally of the immigrant church.

# V

## COLONY PIONEERING
### (Continued)

THE local cultural organizations of immigrant colonies include a wide and interesting variety in addition to those described in the preceding chapter. The ways in which these organizations may relate the immigrant to the common life of America are equally varied.

### MUSIC AND DRAMATICS

Love of music and the drama is characteristic of nearly all immigrant groups, though differing among them in degree and in particular form of expression. Musical and dramatic societies abound. These societies are not a product of American conditions, and tend to die out as the foreign-born element diminishes and the colony gradually dissolves. They represent the continuation of old-country culture in America. For the most part, songs and plays are in the native language and have native themes.

Social settlements have to some extent utilized these cultural motives. Though more often attempting to work up musical or dramatic organizations of their own, instead of enlisting the interest of those already existing, settlements have in some instances followed the latter course.

Besides offering hospitality to such groups for meetings and performances confined to their own race, the settlements have helped to relate these group interests to the larger life of the neighborhood by general gatherings at which different races take turns in providing the entertainment and interpreting their own inherited culture.

By their own intrinsic worth and appeal, as well as through such friendly co-operation, these musical and dramatic societies have played no small part in bringing immigrant groups within the sympathetic consciousness of the community and thereby promoting closer relations. In New Bedford, Massachusetts, for instance, a chorus which was at first confined to a large French-Canadian colony has by its musical excellence made a community-wide appeal, and now gives concerts in the city's largest theater, seating six thousand people. In this same city several Portuguese bands figure prominently in various general celebrations.

The characteristic eisteddfods or singing contests of Welsh immigrants have in some instances been kept up, even where few of these immigrants still survive, as a feature in which the community as a whole takes a lively interest. The singing societies which have made the most general impression on America are those of the Germans. Originally neighborhood organizations among German immigrants, these societies, by their participation in public concerts and events, have done much to interrelate the German group with the American community. As a result of the feelings aroused by the war, these as well as other German-American organizations have become more or less disorganized, and it remains to be seen whether their cultural contribution to American life will be permanently cut off.

Music is a universal medium through which the immigrant and the native American, even though the former speaks not a word of English, may come into sympathy and accord. The drama is more limited in its racially uniting possibilities, in that its enjoyment ordinarily requires understanding of the language in which it is presented. Where such dramatic performances are in the form of pantomime or pageant, however, they also make universal appeal. Getting immigrant groups in their native costumes to participate in neighborhood and community pageants has become something of a fad, but while such occasional events are good as far as they go, they lack cultural roots. Much more significant are the saint's-day celebrations of many Italian colonies, which are sometimes so picturesque and beautiful that they draw spectators from the whole community and give them some real appreciation of the Italian immigrant's cultural background.

## AMERICANIZATION THROUGH ATHLETICS

There are a good many athletic societies of various kinds—wrestling, swimming, rowing, shooting, fencing, gymnastic—among immigrant groups. Reference here is not to the teams and clubs of American-born young people, which run to baseball, football, and other American sports, but to real immigrant organizations that carry over into America the forms of sport characteristic of old-country life. Greek colonies, for example, being composed mainly of young men, are particularly given to wrestling. Several settlements, notably Hull House in Chicago, have been able to establish contacts with such colonies by taking an interest in their wrestling bouts and providing better facilities for them. Branches of the Y. M. C. A. and the Young Men's Hebrew Association located near Greek colonies have found that without any special effort on their part Greek immigrants have joined their gymnastic groups.

The field of athletics, moreover, provides an excellent practical model of Americanization through participation on the part of immigrant groups. Many immigrant athletic societies are affiliated with the Amateur Athletic Union of America, take part in its contests, and are represented in its conventions and management. This affiliation has come about largely through the initiative of the societies themselves. The secretary of the A. A. U. writes:

It is natural, when athletes of foreign countries come to the United States, for them to wish to continue participating in the sports in which they are interested. In many cases they compete in our games before they know that there is an organization of their own countrymen with whom they can become affiliated. There are many advantages for clubs holding membership. . . . We have quite a number of foreign and foreign-American athletic organizations affiliated with the various district associations of the A. A. U.

# AMERICA VIA THE NEIGHBORHOOD

Participation in responsibility and management is regulated as follows:

The membership in these associations is limited to amateur organizations promoting some branch or branches of amateur athletic sports. These associations through their boards of managers are the sole judges of the qualifications of applicants for membership. In order to be accepted as members, clubs or organizations applying must agree to abide by the constitution, by-laws, and rules of the Amateur Athletic Union and of the individual association in which it is applying for membership, and to accept and enforce all decisions affecting or relating to such organization that may be made pursuant thereto by the board of governors of the Amateur Athletic Union, or by the board of managers of the association of which it is a member. Each association is allowed to be represented at the annual convention of the national body by six delegates and six alternates, which are elected by the clubs of the associations, and in this way the clubs have voice and vote in all of the affairs of the national body.

The Metropolitan Association of the A. A. U., with headquarters at New York, includes a dozen or more immigrant societies, representing Scandinavians, Germans, Hungarians, Finns, Bohemians, Jews, Scotch, Irish, and Greeks. These societies compete on even terms with those of native Americans and often win championships. A Bohemian rowing club, for instance, has taken championships in the metropolitan district, and a member of this club has been president of the New York Rowing Association, which includes all boat clubs within a radius of thirty miles of the city.

Each of the fifteen other associations of the A. A. U., which cover every state in the Union states the secretary, also has a number of such clubs as members.

AMERICANIZATION IN ATHLETICS
The A. A. U. unites all races.

BUILDING FOR THE FUTURE
Boys' gymnastic class of the *Sokol*, New York City.

## COLONY PIONEERING

Thus in the realm of athletics Americanization, as measured in terms of actual working partnership between immigrants and native Americans, may be said to approximate 100 per cent.

### THE TURN VEREIN TYPE

Of broadest scope among immigrant cultural organizations is the type of society represented by the German *turn verein*, the Scandinavian *turners*, the Bohemian *sokol*, and the Polish *falcons*. Starting with gymnastics, these societies develop musical, dramatic, educational, and social activities for men, women, and children, and have as their underlying purpose the promotion of all-around individual and social progress. In Europe they have been closely identified with popular struggles for a larger measure of democracy.

The *turn verein* was the rallying center of the German revolutionists of 1848, and was established in America by the revolutionists who came here as immigrants at that time—from among whom the late Carl Schurz, for example, rose to be a great American figure. In Bohemia the *sokols*, under cover of gymnastic drill, built up the national morale and determination which, when the World War brought the long-awaited day, snapped Bohemia free from the Austro-Hungarian yoke and aligned her with the forces of democracy. Similarly the Polish *falcons* prepared Poland to throw off the oppression of Russia.

# AMERICA VIA THE NEIGHBORHOOD

In America these societies have embodied the same spirit of freedom and democracy, but they have expressed this spirit in terms of loyalty to America. When the building of the *turn verein* of Chicago was burned down in the great fire of 1871 the only thing that the members saved, at risk of their lives, was the tablet bearing the names of those who fell with the Union armies in the war which put an end to slavery.

The activities of one *turn verein* in New York City may be cited as typical. This society has a membership of four hundred and fifty. Full membership is restricted to men, but women and children are taken in as auxiliary members. The society owns a building which contains a large hall for meetings and dramatics, a gymnasium, a restaurant, a library, and various smaller rooms. There are gymnastic classes of various kinds, and musical and singing groups, for both sexes and different ages, and a kindergarten for the little tots. Before the war a German-language school was conducted and a dramatic club presented plays in German. The older boys have a cadet company, which takes part in community celebrations and helped in the war drives. Educational lectures are held. A sprinkling of Italian, French, and Spanish members have come into the society quite naturally through living in the same neighborhood.

The *turn vereins* lay claim to having successfully infused into American life their cultural heritage of emphasis on systematic physical training. In many cities, it is said, the local

**GEDENKTAFEL**

der im Bürgerkriege von 1861–1865
gefallenen Mitglieder der
Chicago Turn-Gemeinde.

**GEFALLEN AUF DEM SCHLACHTFELDE:**

L. PFEIF, 2nd Lt., Co. F, 34th Rgt. Ill. Vol. In., Pittsb. Landg. M
B. v. HOLLEN, Ord. Sgt., Co. G, 24th Rgt., Ill. Vol. In., Perryville, Ky
C. KIRCHNER, Sgt., Co. G, 24th Rgt., Ill Vol In., Perryville, Ky
A. LAU, Sgt., Co. G, 24th Rgt., Ill. Vol In., Chickamauga, Ga.
L. STANGER, Sgt., Co. A, 24th Rgt., Ill. Vol In.
H. OHLL, Sgt., Co. A, 82nd Rgt. Ill., Chancellorsville, Va.
V. HEINZMANN, Sgt. Co. H, 1st Rgt Mich Vol Cav., Nine Run Creek
C. ENDERS, Private, Co C, 24th Rgt Ill Vol In., Perryville, Ky
G. RUNKWITZ, Co. G, 24th Rgt Ill., Perryville, Ky.
C. SCHENK, Co. G, 24th Rgt Ill.,
AI. WALTER, Co. G, 24th Rgt. Ill., Chickamauga, Ga
C. METZLER, Co. A, 24th Rgt. Ill., " "
E. LOEHR, Co. B, 82nd Rgt. Ill., Chancellorsville, Va.
L. FREIND, 9th Regiment Ill. Cav., Arkansas.

**IN GEFANGENSCHAFT ZU ANDERSONVILLE GESTORBEN:**

P. GEHRMAN, Corp., Co. G, 24th Rgt. Ill. Vol. In.
CH. DRESSEL, Co. G, 24th Rgt Ill. Vol. In.
C. SCHWARTZ, Co G, 24th Rgt " " "
F. SCHAEFER, Co H, 24th Rgt. " " "
R. MUELLER, 4th Rgt Ky Vol. Cav.

**ERTRUNKEN:**

C. KREY Co Union Cadets, bei St. Louis, Miss. River.
CH. KIRCHHOFF Co G, 24th Rgt Ill Vol In, Battle Creek, Tenn.
E. WEINRICH, Marine auf dem Kanonenboot Perry, Miss. River.
PH. LIEBRICH, Co D, 4th Rgt Ind Vol Cav, Ohio River.

**MEMORIAL OF THE CHICAGO TURN VEREIN**

This tablet, containing the names of members who gave their
lives to their adopted country as Union soldiers, was the only
thing saved when the society's hall was burned down in the great
fire of 1871.

10

societies, working out gradually to public notice from their German neighborhoods, were responsible for having physical training made a regular part of the public-school curriculum. A normal college to train teachers of physical education, which the national organization of the *turn vereins* established in 1866, is held by them to have been the first institution of its kind in America, and to have sent out graduates who greatly furthered the movement for physical training throughout the country.

### SIGNIFICANCE OF CULTURAL SOCIETIES

The deeper significance, not only of the type of society represented by the *turn verein*, but indeed of all immigrant cultural organizations, is forcibly brought out in a letter written by the president of the national *turn verein* body, the North American Gymnastic Union.[1]

The North American Gymnastic Union was founded in the year 1850. During the period of the Civil War its activities were practically suspended because of the voluntary enlistment of about 60 per cent of its membership in the Union army. It consists to-day of 194 societies, and its executive committee has bestowed upon 74 of these societies the diploma for fifty years' membership.

Candidates for admission must be of irreproachable character and must either be citizens of the United States or have taken the necessary steps for becoming citizens. It is the duty of the board of directors of each society to inquire at least once a year whether men admitted to membership on the declaration of their intention to become citizens

---

[1] Theo. E. Stempfel, Indianapolis, correspondence.

of the United States have actually become naturalized. Members who do not acquire the rights of citizenship within one year after they are requested to do so may be excluded from the society.

The Gymnastic Union was founded by political refugees of the German revolution of 1848 who attempted to abolish "kings by the grace of God" and to establish a German republic. The Union deemed it within its province to preserve and cultivate the German language, but not for the purpose of alleged "German propaganda," but as a means of education. It has always been the aim of the Gymnastic Union to assist in Americanizing the German immigrant, by infusing into his mind the spirit of democracy underlying American institutions. Could we have been more successful by speaking to him in the English language, unknown or only scantily known to him, or was it not better to address him in his native tongue? It is not alone the English language that makes the American; it is primarily the love of liberty, that glorious spirit of independence which animated the founders of this Republic. Is the father of an unbroken line of *Mayflower* ancestors, who satisfies the vanity of his daughter by opening his swollen purse for the purchase of the empty title of a European princeling, a better American than the obscure immigrant who speaks a broken English, but has a distinct feeling for the fundamental truth emanating from the Declaration of Independence?

In my opinion, the true Americanization of foreigners who come to our shores is more a matter of the spirit than a matter of language. In my opening address at the twenty-fifth biennial convention of the North American Gymnastic Union, held at Indianapolis on June 23, 1912, I said: "It seems to me that as Americans of German ancestry we should find particular satisfaction in the thought that voluntarily we preferred American to German citizenship, that our home and family have their roots in American soil, that our sons and daughters are growing up in an American atmosphere and American schools. The more the German in America fosters in himself the longing for the old fatherland, by fantastic pictures of his imagination, the less he will feel at home in his adopted country and the wider will be the gap between himself and his children. In Germany a gymnastic association like ours, with its outspoken democratic tendencies, would be under constant surveillance by the police. Let us rejoice, therefore, that we are living on American soil, and as Americans let us do our duty in contributing our share toward the development and perfection of the free institutions of our Republic."

I believe that night schools for the teaching of English and civics to the immigrants are an excellent medium of assimilation with their adopted country. . . . In my opinion it would be a mistake to suppress or hinder immigrants in the use of their native tongue when they are among themselves or with their families. I even consider it a crime against the principles of education if parents who next to English command another language neglect the opportunity of instructing their children in their native tongue. Every man of education ought to know a foreign language at least to the extent of being able to read it.

### ADAPTIVE ORGANIZATIONS

Besides organizations which are rooted in the culture of their native lands, but through which they relate themselves to American life, immigrant groups have developed other activities and organizations whose primary purpose is that of adapting the members to their new conditions of life.

To a large extent these activities have been developed by benefit societies, as an extension of their specific function of mutual insurance. Sometimes the new interests thus taken on become more important in the estimation of the members than the original benefit features.

Other societies, patterned after Old World models and including cultural interests, have a distinctly New World frontage, their foremost function being to adjust the immigrant to his American environment.

Activities of this sort—given in the order in which they usually develop in immigrant colonies —include charity, health, general education, English and naturalization, and participation in civic affairs.

## CHARITY AND HEALTH

In Atlanta the Greeks, through their societies and individually, have for some years co-operated actively with the Associated Charities.

An American friend of ours who is interested in the Associated Charities asked our help [said the president of the Greek community]. So I just put it up to our leaders, and we organized teams and canvassed among our people. They are charitable, and were glad to help. That was eight years ago. Every year since we have done the same thing.

Letters received from a number of American charity societies report substantial co-operation from organizations of immigrants, in the way of donations and advisory service. Many instances are found of immigrant societies contributing to hospitals. One society of Hungarians makes donations to fifteen or twenty. The care of the sick is a simple and urgent need which immigrants readily comprehend. A striking example of organization for the specific purpose of helping hospitals is provided by a large Bohemian colony in New York City. A Protestant Bohemian church, the pastor of which is so generally loved and respected that many of the freethinking and the nominally Catholic elements co-operate with him in matters of local welfare, had been accustomed to take a collection at Christmas for certain hospitals in the vicinity. One of the women of the church inquired whether this idea could not be extended. Encouraged by the pastor, she canvassed the Bohemian organizations of the colony, with the result that practically all of them, to the number of more than a hundred, elected delegates to form a representative society called Lidumil ("Love of the People") through which they contribute annually to half a dozen local hospitals.

Lidumil Society [states the secretary] has been in existence, for the benefit of humanity and good will of the people, for the past twelve years. Money is collected from the neighboring Bohemian clubs for this benefit and donated to near-by hospitals annually. The committee of three, who look after the poor and sick, donate these funds annually and see that the poor and sick are sent to hospitals until well, and without pay.

The amounts given to six hospitals last year included one donation of $800, one of $600, one of $500, three of $100, and one of $50, making a total of $2,250. The $500 contribution went toward an endowment of $7,500 for a hospital bed, of which $3,950 has already been paid.

This federation, initiated by the Bohemians themselves, suggests large possibilities for systematic co-operation between immigrant and native American forces.

In a broad sense, all immigrant societies are educational in that they bring the members together in a way which involves discussion, exchange of information, and practical experience in organized activity. A large proportion of societies have educational talks and lectures occasionally. Attention is confined here, however, to organizations which have developed educational activities in a more definite and regular way. Such societies are found among most immigrant groups, but present space will permit only a few typical examples.

In the midst of a large Hungarian colony in New York City there is an organization, formed ten years ago, called the Hungarian Free Lyceum. Like most Hungarian societies, its membership includes Hungarian Jews as well as Christian Magyars, and, unlike those of most immigrant groups, women as well as men. It is self-governing and self-supporting, necessary funds being provided through a membership fee of one dollar a year. Its objects are "to further the education and political knowledge" of its members and the Hungarian community, and to "acquaint them with American customs and institutions." Thus far, it has carried out these objects mainly through courses of lectures, some in Magyar and some in English. Until recently, when the society became affiliated with a social settlement in the neighborhood, its meetings have been held in a public school. They are open to the public, and the attendance at the English lectures includes others besides Hungarians.

A special point has been made of visual and imaginative appeal through stereopticon talks. Descriptions of natural scenery and centers of interest, such as "The National Parks of America," "Niagara and the Adirondacks," "Washington, the Metropolis of America," were used first to arouse interest. This led naturally into historical subjects, as, for instance, "The Discovery of America and Colonial History," and "The American Revolution and the Civil War." Then followed topics of civic and general appeal, such as "The Water-front and Transportation System of Our City," "Industrial Hazards," "The Influence of the Press," "The City's Educational Institutions," and "Problems of the Education of the Future." With a view to holding the interest of the foreign born and of interpreting Hungarian life to America, such subjects as "Modern Hungarian Poets," "The American Idea of Hungary," and the "Industrial and Social Transformation of Europe" were interspersed at intervals. The concluding lecture of the year in which those mentioned above were given had as its subject "The Americanization of Hungarians."

### A POLISH "UNIVERSITY"

A really remarkable enterprise is being conducted in a Polish colony in Chicago. This also had its beginning about ten years ago. It is known as "The Polish University" and is an undertaking in general self-education. It was initiated by a group of Socialists. At the outset some fifty men enrolled as members, paying one dollar a year. A program of weekly lectures, open to the public, was organized by educated men among the Poles, who contributed their services as lecturers. The aim, as expressed by one of the leaders, was "to stir the minds of the people about fundamental things and get them to do some fundamental thinking about the rudiments of things." As most of those to be reached were foreign born, their interest was enlisted by discussions relating to Poland's history, present problems, and future destiny. During the first few years most of the time was given to such subjects. Many of the lecturers, however, were American born and these questions were discussed largely from an American point of view and in the light of American experience.

Then the intellectual "drive" began.

Some Americans think [said one of the moving spirits] that we immigrants can comprehend only such thoughts as "I see a cat; the cat is black"—as the teachers in the evening schools make grown men repeat. But the minds of most immigrants are not quite so feeble as that. For the poor man, America is all work—work—work. We believe in work, all right, but we want thought and education to go along with it. So we took up questions about the beginning of things—the creation of the world, the theory of evolution, primitive man, the development of language. Sometimes we gave several weeks to one subject, explaining it as simply as possible. All the lectures were in Polish.

138

# COLONY PIONEERING

Most of our members could understand and speak ordinary English, but many others who attended the lectures could not. But obviously the use of Polish was necessary if such subjects, which are hard enough to grasp, anyway, and which involve many scientific terms and fine shades of meaning, were to be got across to our audiences.

Gradually, after getting some of these basic conceptions into people's minds, we came to subjects connected with America and with civic problems. But here we do more than have lectures. We go and see for ourselves how civic agencies work. At different times we have visited most of the public departments and institutions of this city. Every little while we take a week-end excursion to some city not far away and see how things are run there. We have good times, too; for example, this coming Saturday over two hundred and fifty of us are going out into the country for a big picnic together.

We hold our meetings at the public park center in the neighborhood. Our paying members have increased from fifty to more than two hundred, and the attendance at our lectures has grown proportionately; over a thousand people came to the last lecture. We Socialists have not tried particularly to spread our propaganda. Less than half of the paying members are Socialists, and most of the people who attend the lectures are not. We haven't preached "Americanization," either, or paid any special attention to naturalization, but practically all of our members are citizens who take an interest in civic affairs, and if what America wants is people who can think and act for themselves, then we're *doing* Americanization.

## JEWISH WORKMEN'S CIRCLE

Of all immigrants, the Jews run most to distinctly educational organizations, in which, although social and recreational features are present, first place is given to immediate instruction through classes, textbooks, lectures, and debates.

The longest established and most generally known educational agencies among the Jews, however, particularly the Jewish Educational Alliance, the Young Men's Hebrew Association, and various "institutes," hardly come within the limits of the present chapter, in that they are not directed and supported by the immigrant colony itself, but are maintained by Jewish philanthropists and controlled by nonresident boards.

In every Jewish neighborhood of any size educational societies which are really local in character spring up, usually in great profusion. Many of these consist of American-born young people. Of those which draw their membership mainly from the foreign born, one of the most important is the Workmen's Circle. This organization, of twenty-five years' standing, has some 70,000 members throughout the country, of whom nine-tenths are men. In Greater New York there are some 250 local branches, most of which are closely identified with the neighborhoods in which they are situated. The individual branches, self-governing and self-supporting, are free to run their local affairs as they choose; but they all pay dues to the national organization and comply with certain general regulations. Sick and death benefits are paid, and a sanitarium is maintained by the national organization; but educational interests are uppermost. Though the organization is not officially connected with any political party, a majority of its members are Socialists.

The educational aims are worked out through

lectures, classes, libraries, dramatics, and music.
The lectures and classes cover a wide range of
subjects, particular interest being taken in applied
science. Special textbooks are published by
the national headquarters and sold to the local
societies at cost. Special music, based on Jewish
folk songs, is likewise distributed, and much
attention is given to choral singing. The possibilities of education through the drama are
emphasized. Besides staging Yiddish translations of classic plays the Circle encourages its
members to write plays themselves and presents
publicly at Jewish theaters those which have
sufficient merit. Traveling assistants, maintained by the national organization, go about
constantly among the different locals, helping
them and stimulating their interest.

Cities which contain a number of locals have
a central representative committee, which in
turn has subcommittees on education, organization, benefit, health, and grievances. This last
subcommittee is the most important of all, as
it serves as a friendly court where differences
between members are reconciled. If members
who have grievances are not satisfied with this
subcommittee's recommendations, they may appeal to a local "supreme court," and as a last
resort to the national committee of the Circle.
This inner arrangement adjusts many misunder-
standings which otherwise would lead to litigation
and embitterment.

Though Yiddish is spoken in most locals because
the majority of members are foreign born, mem-

bers are urged to learn English and to attend public evening school, and a special committee assists them to become naturalized. Several of the locals in one city met in public schools for a time, and thus brought large numbers of foreign-born people into the school buildings. But the board of education barred the use of foreign languages, and they had to get out. The societies keenly resent this action by the board.

The only way we can reach many of our people [said an officer] is through their native tongue, and certainly it is better to teach them about American institutions in the only language they understand than not to teach them at all. It strikes us that the board of education is really defeating its own ends.

## CIVIC AFFAIRS

The line between the educational and civic interests of immigrant groups cannot be drawn at any fixed point. The educational activities which have been described involve, or lay the foundation of, civic interest and activity. But numerous organizations of immigrants concern themselves even more specifically and directly with civic affairs.

The most common civic concern is that which first presents itself to the immigrant—namely, naturalization and preparation for intelligent exercise of the rights and duties of citizenship. There are few racial groups who have not societies devoted to this initial stage of participation in American civic life.

In Brockton, Massachusetts, for example, a

Lithuanian "Citizens' Club" of three hundred members is promoting naturalization. In Philadelphia the same thing is being done by a club of Ukrainians; while in New Bedford, Massachusetts, a Portuguese society is conducting citizenship classes. An Italian club in Richmond has in four years helped over three hundred men to become naturalized, several of its members volunteering the necessary assistance. All but a minor percentage of the comparatively small Italian population of that city are now American citizens. A Greek club in Nashville is active likewise.

Not long ago [said one of its leaders] the commercial club of this city called a mass meeting of foreigners for the purpose of urging naturalization and citizenship. When my turn came to speak I told them that the Greeks had beaten them, because several years ago an organization of Greeks had started just such a movement, telling the people it was their duty to be naturalized. Probably 90 per cent of the Greeks in this community are citizens to-day.

A Syrian society, operating in a small colony of about seven hundred people in Birmingham, has assisted a hundred or more of the men to take out citizenship papers, while in a larger Syrian group in Boston a similar organization carried on during the war an aggressive naturalization campaign which resulted in some eight hundred applications for citizenship.

Still another instance is the more significant in that it pertains to a group usually regarded as un-American—namely, the French Canadians— and to a New England city where this group probably exhibits more solidarity than anywhere else. This is in Woonsocket, Rhode Island, where "the Independent Club" is working industriously on naturalization. Several French-Canadian lawyers prepare men for their examinations, and large numbers have become citizens. One of the leaders said that he alone had assisted over four hundred applicants. A campaign of political education has been organized among the women also, and the French-Canadian priests have enlisted to preach naturalization and active use of the vote.

An illustration of an immigrant group earnestly seeking guidance in the bewildering maze of "politics" which surrounds it is afforded by a little colony of Carpatho-Russians in New York City. This colony of some three hundred families is of comparatively recent growth. Several years ago, entirely on their own motion, they organized a "Russian-American Political Club," the membership of which, though confined to men, represents practically the whole colony. The club meets in a rented room of its own. On one of the walls is an American flag, and on the opposite wall a service flag with stars for the members who served in the war. The leader stated that this club had no reference whatever to the future of the Carpatho-Russian district in Europe, but was purely local in its purpose.

"You know we are very ignorant," he said, "and we want to learn about the American government."? The club was not affiliated with any party because "each party tells you it is the best, and we do not know which is the best."

More than half of the members are already naturalized, and they are instructing the others in English and civics. Some of the members attend a special English class, taught by a Russian woman, at a near-by settlement, and a few take part in a community council which meets there. Native Americans as well as leaders of their own race are invited to speak to the club on civic questions.

The immigrant's share in political parties and actual government will be considered in a later chapter. Substantial civic participation may take place through other than party and official channels, and immigrant groups are in fact participating in many ways in general community affairs.

### COMMUNITY BUILDINGS

One of their most substantial contributions to the community consists of the buildings which they have erected as meeting places. Such buildings are numerous and in many instances impressive in size and equipment. Moreover, reference here is not to the headquarters of regional and national associations of immigrants, but to local buildings which are primarily for neighborhood purposes.

In a Bohemian colony in New York City, for example, are three brick structures, each of several stories, which in appearance and equipment for social purposes compare favorably with any other private or public buildings in the district. A Ukrainian colony in the same city has its social center in a fine four-story brick building which it calls the "Ukrainian Settlement." In size this building stands comparison with the many American social settlements in that city, while as regards use by foreign-born adults it goes far beyond what any of the American settlements have been able to accomplish. The basement, equipped with a dozen or more pool and billiard tables, is thronged every night with men playing, smoking, and having a general good time. One floor is taken up by a theater, where at least one night a week plays are presented by the people themselves, and where frequent concerts and lectures are held with audiences that crowd the large room to its walls.

The story of this Ukrainian center is interesting. Asked why it was named a "settlement," the priest-leader replied:

Well, before we put up the building we visited different American institutions, and we found that those which were doing the kind of things we wanted to do were called settlements. We wanted to be like the Americans, so we called our center a settlement. But we have never been invited to join the federation of settlements in our city. Apparently only American settlements are admitted to that federation.

The several buildings mentioned are matched in many immigrant colonies. In erecting and maintaining such buildings, immigrant groups are first of all showing the community what can be accomplished through democratic initiative and collective action. In the second place they are relieving private philanthropy or public funds of the expense of supplying meeting places for them. In the third place, these centers often serve a larger use than that of one immigrant group. Racial courtesies are frequently exchanged in the use of such facilities. In one district where, let us say, a Polish colony has adequate meeting places and an adjacent Italian colony is not so well provided, the latter may avail itself of the former's hospitality; and *vice versa* where the conditions are reversed. The antipathies which are assumed to exist between certain races do not appear to figure in such exchanges, and a good deal of interracial neighborhood affiliation is taking place in this way.

Even native Americans use many of these immigrant centers. An example which stands out the more clearly because it occurs in a small city, Waukegan, Illinois, is supplied by a neat three-story building recently erected by a society of Slovenian immigrants. The cost was $50,000. Four hundred of these Slovenians contributed shares of $25 each, totaling $10,000, and the balance was lent by members of the group. The building contains a hall seating a thousand people, with well-equipped stage and a motion-picture machine. This hall has a kitchen connected with it, so that it may be used for banquets. There are pool tables, a gymnasium, and shower baths. A large and well-framed picture of Abraham Lincoln occupies a prominent place, and members said that pictures of Washington and Wilson would be bought as soon as the society could afford it. "We want good ones," said the caretaker, "and are saving the money for them now."

Because this is the best equipped building in the city and county and has the largest hall, it is already, though built only a year or so ago, being widely used outside the group. A number of labor unions meet there regularly. A near-by settlement has used it for gatherings for which it has not room itself. The leading women's club of the community has used it for motion-picture talks. The Rotary Club has used it for addresses by out-of-town speakers. The public schools, lacking such a large hall of their own, have used it for graduation exercises. Thus has a humble little colony of some fifteen hundred Slovenian immigrants not only met its own needs for a social center, but at the same time provided for a previously unfilled need of the local American community.

IMMIGRANT FEDERATIONS

Attention has thus far been confined to the strictly local activities of immigrant groups. There is a strong tendency on the part of each race, however, to interrelate these various local activities by means of city, regional, and national federations. Mention has already been made of the effective way in which over a hundred Bohemian societies are federated to assist hospitals. This case is exceptional in its distinctly

148

charitable purpose, but in Chicago there is a federation of Italian societies which is of even larger proportions, including upward of a hundred and twenty-five separate units. The general object of this latter federation is to stimulate the local societies and relate them more closely to community affairs. A large building in the center of the city, containing a number of large halls and smaller meeting rooms, has been leased for a period of five years. This building, states the secretary:

will be known as the Italian Halls, and will be used by the Italians of Chicago as their center, and will be rented for meeting purposes of all the Italian societies for dances and entertainments that the Italians of Chicago may give in the future. Americanization, social activities, and the betterment of economic conditions are the main projects. . . . A fund will be raised by the Italian societies of Chicago to redecorate and refinish the Halls within a very short time, to make them look as the finest halls in Chicago.

Until the war was won and most of the subject races which had been struggling for their freedom were launched as independent nations, many of the national federations of immigrant societies had devoted their energies to providing their brethren in the home lands with moral and material reinforcement. Now, however, that their old-country objectives have been attained, most of these federations are adopting programs chiefly concerned with conditions in America; in fact, if not in name, programs of Americanization.

AMERICA VIA THE NEIGHBORHOOD

The new policy of the Bohemian National
Alliance may be cited by way of illustration.
Recently the Alliance held a nation-wide con-
ference in Chicago. Here is what took place:

The committee on reorganization recast the constitution
completely. The Alliance was established in 1914 for the
purpose of supporting the movement for Czechoslovak
independence and the original constitution was framed
accordingly. For four years all activity was centered on
collecting money to finance the campaign of Professor
Masaryk; later, emphasis was placed on recruiting members
who were not naturalized in the United States for service
with the Czechoslovak army in France. During the last
year the Alliance was engaged in relief work for the needy
of the Czechoslovak Republic.

The new constitution, adopted unanimously by the
Chicago conference, omits all reference to the country from
which the members of the Alliance came, except for one
paragraph which provides that one of the aims of the
organization will be acquainting America with the life of
the Czechoslovak people and the development of the free
Czechoslovak Republic. The main object of the Alliance
has now become the good of its own members and of
Americans of Czechoslovak descent in general, and special
emphasis is laid on educational and cultural work in the
interest of sound Americanism; new arrivals from Bohemia
will be looked after and introduced to the spirit of American
institutions. As reconstructed, the organization will be the
representative body of American citizens, including Canadians of Czechoslovak blood, and will take the lead in
all matters affecting them. [1]

Other racial federations have announced similar
policies. The Sons of Italy, in particular, a
federation whose strength is mainly in the Eastern states, has announced that it will work

[1] *Czechoslovak Review*, December, 1919, p, 395.

systematically for Americanization among Italian immigrants. It is affiliating existing local societies and also organizing branches. To each branch it assigns a special representative called an "orator," whose duty it is to give educational lectures and to assist the members to learn English and become citizens and voters.

Not only through the nation-wide marshaling of their own initiative and resources, but also by entering into working relations with American organizations of kindred interests, are these immigrant groups effectively uniting with America.

Immigrant athletic societies become an integral part of the Amateur Athletic Union of America. Catholic and Protestant immigrant churches are included in the general denominational organizations of America. Societies of immigrant women are beginning to be received into membership upon their own application by the state and national federations of women's clubs. Finally, the mutual insurance interest, the basic feature of the great majority of immigrant societies, is drawing these organizations into a national body in which their representatives stand on an equal footing with native Americans. Thus far this body has concerned itself mostly with insurance statistics. But just as immigrant benefit societies have by a natural process enlarged their interests in different directions, so in time this national association of benefit societies may likewise enlarge its field of interest and activity. Meanwhile its name is a symbol of what it has already done to bring immigrant and native born together and of its unlimited possibilities in furthering such union. It is called the National Fraternal Congress of America.

\* \* \* \* \* \*

The facts presented in the preceding chapters show that the natural inclination of the immigrant is to relate himself to American life, and that forces inherent in the immigrant group and its American environment work toward that end. The facts show, further, that this natural process of Americanization affects the individual immigrant largely through his colony group, and proceeds by what seems to be a method of indirection. Instead of breaking away from racial heritages and lines of association, attempting to don immediately a complete new outfit of things "made in America," and live among and associate with native Americans, immigrants of each race generally settle in compact colony neighborhoods, cohere closely among themselves, and form their own associations and organizations. Thus they get their bearings, build up collective morale and resources, and eventually identify themselves with the surrounding American community.

This organic self-Americanization on the part of the immigrant himself is of primary importance. But it is not the whole solution of the problem.

Americanization, understood as actual participation in the going affairs of the community,
necessarily involves co-operation and partnership
between foreign and native born. Neither can
dispense with the other. The immigrant, on
his side, is manifestly willing and able to enter
into such a working partnership.

The question which now presents itself has to
do with the activities of native American agencies which work through the medium of the
neighborhood in order to establish such a relationship. How far, in the first place, are such
agencies worknig intelligently, with knowledge
and appreciation of the organized activities of
the immigrants themselves? How far, in the
second place, are they working organically, by
correlating their own activities with those of the
immigrants, taking full advantage of the initiative and momentum already existent, and thus
contributing to the Americanization not of
scattered individuals merely, but of immigrant
organizations and whole immigrant groups?

# VI

## THE SOCIAL SETTLEMENT APPROACH

THE American agency which is usually regarded as being most closely identified with the local neighborhood is the social settlement.

Though in a general way settlements have now become familiar to the public, the settlement approach and point of view may be better understood if we look back some thirty-five years to the beginning of the movement. The earliest definite presentation of the "settlement idea" was made by Canon Samuel A. Barnett, a clergyman of the Church of England. Mr. and Mrs. Barnett had taken up work in the parish of St. Jude's in the Whitechapel district of East London, and frequently visited the universities to describe the conditions and urge the needs of the people to whom they were ministering. In 1883, after ten years of such experience, Mr. Barnett, in an address delivered at Oxford University, crystallized his appeal in a concrete proposal.

"Something must be done" is the comment which follows the tale of how the poor live [he said]. "What can I do?" is a more healthy comment. And it is a sign of the time that this question is being widely asked, and by none more eagerly than the members of the universities. . . . The fact that the mass of the people live without knowledge, without hope, and often without health has come home to

154

open minds and consciences. . . . The thought of the
condition of the people has made a strange stirring in the
careless life of the universities, and many men feel themselves driven by a new spirit, possessed by a master idea.
They are eager in their talk and their inquiries, and they
ask, "What can we do to help the poor?"

I would suggest a settlement of university men, in the
midst of some great industrial center. . . . The settlers
will find themselves related to two distinct classes of "the
poor," and it will be well if they keep in mind the fact
that they must serve both those who, like the artisans,
need the necessaries of life, and also those who, like casual
laborers, need the necessaries for *livelihood.* . . . It will
be something if they are able to give to a few the higher
thoughts in which men's minds can move, to suggest other
forms of recreation, and to open a view over the course
of the river of life as it flows to the infinite sea. It will be
something if they create among a few a distaste for dirt
and disorder, if they make some discontented with their
degrading conditions. . . . It will be something if thus
they give to the one class the ideal of life, and stir up in
the other those feelings of self-respect without which increased means of livelihood will be useless. . . . Nothing
that is divine is alien to man, and nothing that can be learned
at the university is too good for East London.[1]

He advised a group of young men at Oxford,
who had consulted him as to how they might be
of service, to establish such a settlement, and
outlined some of the practical details. These
men should go to live in the Whitechapel district,
familiarize themselves with conditions there,
make friends with the people, and gradually enter
in a helpful way into all aspects of their life.
Some of the "settlers" should become local public
officials, as a means of acquiring recognized status

[1] Dr. Werner Picht, *Toynbee Hall and the English Settlements.*

and influence. In order to have a center of operation, quarters should be taken where a group of settlers should live and where various educational classes, clubs, and other opportunities should be offered to the people. Such of the settlers as could not afford to give their services gratuitously should receive payment from funds to be provided by philanthropy, preferably through universities, and one man should be placed in general charge of the enterprise.

This proposal resulted, the following year, in the founding of such a settlement as Mr. Barnett proposed. It was named Toynbee Hall, after Arnold Toynbee, an Oxford tutor who had served in Whitechapel a short time under Mr. Barnett's direction. Mr. Barnett himself was placed at its head as warden.

Thus the settlement as first conceived and carried out was an agency through which the educated, cultured, and better circumstanced classes might help "the poor."

### RISE OF AMERICAN SETTLEMENTS

In 1886, two years after Toynbee Hall was opened, the first American settlement was established on the lower East Side of New York by Stanton Coit. This was the Neighborhood Guild, which later became the University Settlement. Hull House in Chicago, the College Settlement in New York, and the South End House in Boston soon followed, and thenceforth the number of settlements rapidly increased. To-day some two hundred and twenty-five are

included in the National Federation of Settlements, and it is estimated that, counting all sizes
and varieties, there are probably five hundred
agencies in the country which come within the
meaning of the term "settlement."

Mr. Coit had lived for a time at Toynbee Hall
and was influenced by its example. His announced purpose was "to bring men and women
of education into close relations with the laboring
classes." Robert A. Woods, the head resident
of the South End House, had also lived at
Toynbee Hall. In an early paper Mr. Woods
expressed as follows his own conception of what
settlements could accomplish in this country.[1]

University settlements are capable of bringing to the
depressed sections of society its healing and saving influences, for the lack of which those sections are to so large
an extent as good as dead. The settlements are able to
take neighborhoods in cities, and by patience bring back
to them much of the healthy village life, so that the people
shall again know and care for one another. They will impart
a softer touch to what social powers now act there, and they
will bring streams from the higher sources of civilization to
refresh and arouse the people so that they shall no more go
back to the narrowness and gloom, and perhaps the brutality,
of their old existence.

The same motives appear in an early paper by
Miss Jane Addams of Hull House.[2]

I have divided the motives which constitute the subjective
pressure toward social settlements into three great lines:
the first contains the desire to make the entire social

---

[1] *Philanthropy and Social Progress, 1893,* "The University Settlement Idea."

[2] Miss Jane Addams, *ibid.,* "The Subjective Necessity for Social
Settlements."

organism democratic, to extend democracy beyond its political expression; the second is the impulse to share the race life and to bring as much as possible of social energy and the accumulation of civilization to those portions of the race which have little; the third springs from a certain renaissance of Christianity, a movement toward its early humanitarian aspects. . . . Nothing so deadens the sympathies and shrivels the power of enjoyment as the persistent keeping away from the great opportunities for helpfulness and a continual ignorance of the starvation struggles which make up the life of at least half the race. . . . We have in America a fast-growing number of cultivated young people who have no recognized outlet for their active faculties. . . . Our young people feel nervously the need of putting theory into action, and respond quickly to the settlement form of activity.

These quotations indicate that in America also the settlement was originally conceived as a medium through which the more favored elements of society might help "the poor." This is not to say that settlements were established as agencies for the giving of material relief. On the contrary, they were careful to differentiate themselves from charity societies, and have generally discountenanced the inclusion of material relief among their services. Furthermore, they have always maintained that they were dealing not with the poverty-stricken element especially, but chiefly with "the great hand-working class which is above the poverty line." [1] But in this contention they have not departed radically from Canon Barnett's view that "there are two distinct classes of 'the poor,'" . . . not only "those who, like casual laborers, need

[1] Albert J. Kennedy of South End House, Boston, correspondence.

the necessaries for *livelihood*," but also "those who, like the artisans, need the necessaries of life." Though American settlements have protested that they are working mainly with the latter class, as in fact they are, their attitude, as reflected in the authoritative quotations cited above, has been that this "great hand-working class" belongs to "the poor" in the sense expressed by Canon Barnett, and implied by such designations as "the depressed sections of society" and "those portions of the race which have little." In short, settlements appear to have conceived that their mission was for those elements of the population who, without their help, were assumed to be unable to do very much in the way of helping themselves.

## WHO ARE "THE POOR"?

But in the actual application of this conception there has been one important difference between England and the United States.

In England, where foreign immigrants are few compared with their numbers in America, settlements have usually been established among native English who are really "poor," if not in worldly goods always, at any rate in spirit and class status. The problem of the permanently "poor" in London and other English cities, the poor who inherit their poverty from their parents and pass it on to their children, has gnawed at the core of England's life for generations. Chronic poverty of livelihood has bred a certain chronic poverty of spirit, and this servility has been increased by the fact that in England "the poor" are regarded and treated as a "lower class."

Now in America, although some settlements work with elements of the population corresponding to these English poor, the majority are located among groups of foreign immigrants. It appears to have been assumed that in America the immigrants are "the poor." Is this assumption borne out by the facts?

True it is that the average immigrant, when he lands in America, is encumbered by little money or material goods. But he does not remain in this condition very long; he quickly gets an industrial foothold, saves, and in many cases becomes erelong the owner of a little home. What immigrant groups are capable of doing in such ways as erecting large buildings of their own and contributing funds to American agencies has already been noted. But more essential than his material condition is the immigrant's whole spirit and outlook. The immigrant left his native land because he was not content to become one of "the poor" over there. His is the spirit of the pioneer, and the pioneer's vigor and initiative. In view of the manifold activities of immigrant groups, does it not appear that, far from being "poor" in the deeper implication of the term, the immigrant is rich in the essentials that make for progress?

## THE SLUM

There are two types of neighborhood in this country, however, in which settlements are working, which more nearly correspond to the neighborhoods of the poor in English cities.

One of these types is the "slum." Properly speaking, a "slum" is not a normal neighborhood at all, least of all an immigrant neighborhood. It has no organic unity; rather is it a human conglomeration of which the outward shell may have a neighborhood look, but in which real neighborhood substance and organization are lacking. "Red light districts" are slums in the true sense. So are the "Chinatowns" that figure in sightseeing tours; not their wholesome kernel of real Chinese life, but the zone of murky resorts supported by a nondescript and more or less degenerate element of "Americans." Cheap rooming districts, with their nomadic life, often become outright slums.

Immigrants figure in districts of these kinds in two ways. While getting their bearings and having to make shift with the cheapest quarters available, they may find themselves in a slum. But they are there through necessity, and are not long in getting out. In the onward progress of the immigrant group shiftless or vicious individuals may be left behind in a district which eventually runs down and becomes a slum, or they may be thrown into such a district by a backwash. In that case they become part of the slum. But instances of this sort are not frequent among the foreign born. They occur oftener in the first generation of American born.

Under slum conditions, a settlement provides a sort of quasi-neighborhood life for those who will accept its hospitality. Furthermore, by the educational advantages it offers, it helps those who still have some ambition to rise above their environment and get out of the district. Thus particularly it saves some of the children from demoralization.

"We measure our success by the families who move away," said the head resident of one settlement. This remark is typical of the slum situation.

### "POOR WHITE" AMERICANS

Another class in this country which corresponds with "the poor" in England is the native American stock that has "petered out." Passing reference was made in the second chapter to some run-down Americans who lingered in the midst of a vigorous community of Jewish immigrants. The "pine barrens" of New Jersey, the back districts of New England, and various other parts of the country contain specimens of this sort, not only as scattered individuals, but sometimes forming the majority of whole communities. Doubtless the best known example is that of a certain portion of the "poor whites" of the South—not the rugged though illiterate mountaineers, but a contingent employed chiefly as mill hands in the cities. These people, of American descent for generations, are truly "the poor." It is an interesting fact that most of the settlements in the South are working not primarily among immigrants, whose numbers are still few in that region, but among this particular element of "poor whites."

# THE SOCIAL SETTLEMENT APPROACH

A majority of the Southerners interviewed in the course of this study remarked that they had "no foreign problem in their communities," and pointed out that the immigrants were ambitious and progressive. The situation as regards the poor whites was described as considerably different. They usually live in the most run-down and ramshackle part of the city. Some of the houses are without water supply, and the occupants have either to catch rain or buy water from people who have wells. Very few own their shacks. A large proportion of the women and nearly all the children work in the mills. Coming from the backwoods villages, they have next to no education. Few read even the newspapers. Few belong to societies or attend church. Life is for them a dull round of drudgery and monotony. They have little recreation. When not working, sleeping, or eating, they just sit around and talk, listlessly.

Here is a typical story told by a man of this sort who eventually woke up:

My experience is that of the average. I lived in a small country town, son of poor people, uneducated. I went to school three years. As soon as I was old enough I went to work in the cotton mill, where I worked nineteen years. I went to work in the early morning and came home in the evening, never read a newspaper, never went to the library, never went outside the village. The social settlement here meant nothing to us men. We went there for an occasional shower, that was all. We were illiterate, ignorant people, with no initiative, no interest. We never did anything, and yet I never knew a mill employee to be satisfied. He is always grumbling, but he doesn't know what to do about it. We never heard of a union. Just before the strike, five years ago, I picked up a mill news in the mill and read an account of a meeting of owners; one sentence I read over and over again—"In union there is strength." This hit me hard, so when the strike came I was in it until it broke. There are injunctions against me in three mills for trying to unionize the men, which is against the law. As a result of the union my whole life has been changed. You can see I ain't an educated man, but what education I have is from the union. It is my whole life.

Usually only the children and a few of the women of this element come to the settlements. The men do not respond to the constant efforts to attract them.

These people lack initiative and wait to have everything done for them [said one settlement worker].

There is little ambition among them [said another], and they do not care particularly about coming to the settlement. We almost have to beg them to come.

Another referred to them as "down and outs."

What we aim to do [said another] is to give them the standards of American life that we think they should have. We try to put them on their feet and help them eventually to move into a better neighborhood.

Significant comparisons were made between the "poor whites" and the immigrants.

We find fewer problems in the homes of our immigrant women than in those of the Americans [said one].

Among a hundred American families that I know [said another] there are more than a hundred children of school age who are staying away from school. The compulsory-attendance law is not enforced. But the teachers don't worry about this because, they say, the "mill children are slow and stupid and hold the others back."

These immigrants [another commented, referring to a Slovak group] are citizens and go and do their voting; Americans are the ones who are slack.

It was generally reported that the immigrants are gradually buying homes of their own, whereas most of these "poor whites" are content to scrape along as tenants.

These comparisons are cited to bring out the essential difference between the truly poor and the typical foreign immigrant, who, leaving his native land, takes his destiny in his own hands and comes to America in quest of freedom and a larger life. In considering the settlement approach, this difference suggests at the outset that in so far as settlements are, or conduct themselves as, agencies for helping "the poor," their application to the case of the immigrant is limited.

### RESULTS AND MODIFICATIONS

Two questions present themselves. First, what actual results have settlements obtained in dealing with immigrant groups? Second, what modifications of the original "settlement idea" have been brought about or may be necessary in consequence of the settlement's experience with the immigrant? These two questions indicate the limits within which the present chapter will be kept. The purpose of our brief study is to concentrate upon the activities of settlements that affect the Americanization of the immigrant through the medium of the neighborhood.[1] Americanization is understood as self-dependent, democratic participation in the affairs of the local community and the larger life of America. By the immigrant is meant the foreign-born adult. How far has the settlement furthered such responsible, self-directing neighborhood activity on the part of men and women of foreign birth?

In the large, settlements have performed two distinct though practically inseparable functions. One is interpretation; the other is direct local activity.

### INTERPRETATION

There can be no doubt that the settlement has been of immense service in interpreting the immigrant to native Americans. Before the advent of settlements, immigrant groups were commonly viewed only from the outside, as solid masses of "foreigners," or as so many "Dagoes" or "Hunkies." Slight notice was taken of differences in the characteristics, historical backgrounds, and old-country heritages of different groups, and individual immigrants were looked upon more as ditch-diggers and pick-swingers than as human beings. There was little real sympathy for the immigrant and still less understanding of him. While there were exceptions,

---

[1] Readers who are especially interested in settlements are referred to *The Settlement Horizon*, by Robert A. Woods and Albert J. Kennedy of South End House, Boston; soon to be published by the Russell Sage Foundation of New York City. This is an exhaustive presentment of the activities of American settlements, considered from every angle.

the attitude of most Americans toward the immigrant was one of indifference, if not of outright antipathy.

Many Americans, perhaps the majority, feel the same way to-day. But the settlements have modified the attitude of a large number. Living in the midst of immigrant groups, the settlement workers saw their life from the inside, and they interpreted it sympathetically and intelligently to native Americans. Books by settlement workers of national reputation, which have been accepted as classics in this field, come at once to mind. In every community where settlements are situated similar interpretation has been carried on, if not through press and platform, at least through everyday intercourse between settlement workers and others.

Settlements first caught the popular imagination for the immigrant. The interest, sympathy, and degree of understanding thus aroused in his behalf have naturally and inevitably led to closer and better relations between native and immigrant Americans. As a result, previously existing American agencies, such as charity organization societies, have concerned themselves more actively with the problems and needs of immigrant neighborhoods, and have dealt with them more intelligently and co-operatively, as, for instance, by employing immigrant or foreign-speaking workers and by consulting with immigrant leaders. Public schools have been similarly influenced by the settlement's example, especially in the development of school social centers. Settlements have also largely inspired newer forms of neighborhood work such as neighborhood associations and community councils.

The question of how far these other neighborhood activities have enlisted the responsible participation of the immigrant will be deferred until a later chapter. Meanwhile it is reasonable to assume that some degree of participation has resulted, and that the total product for the country must be large. As the mediator, the settlement must be credited with a good part in this result. Thus the settlement's interpretation of the immigrant to the American public eventually yields a concrete return to the immigrant neighborhood.

The settlement also interprets America to the immigrant. But here the case and the method are different. For just as the native American, with the American point of view inborn, is best fitted to interpret the immigrant to Americans, in terms which the latter will understand, so by the same reasoning it is the immigrant himself, with the inborn point of view of his race and understanding of its language, who can best interpret America to his own group. Of course, to perform this task adequately the immigrant interpreter must have had at least as much experience with American life as the average settlement worker has had with the life of the immigrant. It is at this point that the foreign-language press serves its own purpose and the purpose of America. It interprets America to the immigrant in the same way that settlement workers interpret the immigrant to America.

The analogy may be continued. Settlement workers do not and cannot interpret the immigrant to America completely. The immigrant does a good deal himself, in part by word, but mostly by act. Just so the immigrant leader does not and cannot interpret America to his own people completely. Something is to be done by settlement workers and other Americans, partly by word, but here again mostly by living example. In other words, it is through what the settlement does, more than through what its workers say, that its most effective interpretation of America must be accomplished. Thus the settlement's first function, that of interpretation, identifies itself with its second function—local action.

### INHERENT LIMITATIONS

An agency which is not an integral and accepted part of an immigrant group may nevertheless convey to others the essential facts about that group. Indeed, being an "outsider" involves a freedom from bias, and a breadth and impartiality of viewpoint, which are essential for adequate interpretation. But when it comes to direct action, to winning the participation of an immigrant group in definite activities, the question of how far the agency is an integral part of the group bears vitally upon the results. For this reason it is desirable to understand the exact status of the settlement in the immigrant neighborhood. The following characteristics, common to practically all settlements, are pertinent from this point of view.

The funds with which the settlement is established and supported are in the main donated by persons living outside of the neighborhood and belonging to a different economic and social stratum. In other words, the financial support of the settlement is philanthropic. This was inherent in the "settlement idea" as originally expressed.

The governing board of the settlement, by whatever name it may be called, is as a rule composed of people who live outside the neighborhood, contributors and others who are of the same social status. The control of funds, and therefore in last analysis the control of policies, is ordinarily in the hands of this board. In some cases its control is purely nominal and actual control is left with the head worker. But though the head worker is presumably in closer touch with the neighborhood than the board is, and may disburse the funds more intelligently and sympathetically, when all is said he, and not the people of the neighborhood, decides how these funds shall be used. The people of the neighborhood, therefore, have no more control of funds in this case than they do when the board itself exercises control. Such control of funds from above was also implied in the original conception of settlements.

Settlements are seldom established through the motion or upon the initiative of the neighborhood itself. They are there not because the people express a desire for them, but because some philanthropic individual or group thinks that they will do the neighborhood good.

Lastly, settlements are tied to a given locality by their physical plant—their land and buildings. The degree to which they are tied varies in different cases. A settlement with a small plant, in which comparatively little capital is invested, would be able to dispose of it if desired at a lesser sacrifice than another with a large and elaborate plant. From the point of view of most settlement workers, this identity with locality is not disadvantageous, but is, rather, in accord with the settlement's purpose of relating itself as fully as possible to local conditions.

However, immigrant groups do not ordinarily remain in one locality, but move on to better districts as they progress. A locality which was settled solidly by Italians ten years ago may to-day have no Italian residents at all. The Italian colony may have moved out, and an equally solid Polish colony may have taken its place. Under such circumstances, the inner organizations of the Italian group move with the group, and the headquarters and meeting places of its societies are transferred to the new location of the colony, or, if some scattering has taken place, to that of its major contingent. The settlement, however, remains where it is, its relations with the Italian group come to an end and it begins to cultivate similar relations with the Poles. Though there are significant instances of settlements which have pulled up stakes and followed their groups to new localities, these are exceptional.

Whether or not settlements can accomplish most by staying where they are, and however difficult may be the practical obstacles in the way of moving, the fact remains that settlements are not as a rule identified continuously with a given immigrant group. Such being the case, it is not to be expected that the settlement can play the same intimate part in the life of the group that its own organizations play.

The settlement workers themselves are for the most part people who have not lived in the neighborhood before. They are assumed to be persons of superior education and culture, who are used to a different environment, but who, when they enter settlement work, go to live in the neighborhood which they are to serve. This likewise was provided at the outset. It was assumed, however, that these persons would cast their lot, without reservations, in the neighborhood to which they went. Not only by living there, but by having as far as possible recognized self-supporting functions such as those of local officials, they were to become an integral and accepted part of the neighborhood. While it was proposed that some of them should live together in a working center and receive such modest payment as might be necessary, it was contemplated that others would live either as individuals or families here and there throughout the neighborhood. The "settlement" was first thought of not as an institution, but as the act of residence on the part of a group, not of "settlement workers," as they are called to-day, but of "settlers." Men as well as women were to be enlisted. In fact, Canon Barnett's appeal was addressed primarily to men.

## DEPARTURES FROM ORIGINAL IDEAL

American settlements have developed certain modifications of the original ideal. If a rapid increase of settlements was desirable, then some of these modifications were necessary. People who are willing to give up permanently their accustomed surroundings for the kind of neighborhood which settlements serve, and who are also the sort of people to do so acceptably and successfully, are not to be had on order. Happily there are a good many such rare persons in American settlements to-day, not only among the well-known leaders, but among the inconspicuous rank and file. There are still many who, supporting themselves independently, live permanently at the settlement and devote all or part of their time to its activities.

In general, however, settlement work has come to be regarded as a profession, or as training for more remunerative forms of social work. As such it has appealed to cultivated young people, and more particularly to young women, whose experience is limited and whose characters are still in the formative stage. Such workers pass on from one settlement to another or enter other fields as more attractive opportunities present themselves. To some extent settlements have had the misfortune to become a fad, and to attract not a few dilettantes whose interest in the neighborhood is superficial and ephemeral. In so far as the influence of settlements is dependent upon the permanency of residence, the richness of experience and the ripeness of personality of their members, it will probably be granted that present conditions leave something to be desired.

It is also true that the development of settlements on the institutional side has outstripped their development in other respects. Settlement buildings, and the more or less formal activities carried on within those buildings, have taken first place over activities distributed throughout the neighborhood. Instances in which settlement workers live outside the settlement house are exceedingly rare. Rare, also, are instances of family life among settlement workers. In general, settlements are made up of single men and women, mostly women, who live in congregate houses; men and women sometimes in the same building and sometimes separate.

Congregated thus, settlement workers lead a group life of their own, which is not a little different in its comforts, its natural interests, and its general outlook from the life of the surrounding neighborhood. In fact, to the neighborhood the settlement is usually something of a riddle.

These characteristics of the settlement have been mentioned because they bear upon the effectiveness of its direct activities in the neighborhood and the extent to which the participation of the neighborhood can be enlisted. With reference particularly to immigrant neighborhoods and foreign-born adults, they indicate limitations inherent in the settlement. These elements in the situation should be kept in mind in considering the settlement's local activities.

### NATIVE-BORN YOUNG PEOPLE

The most familiar of such activities are those closely connected with the settlement as an institution—the regular clubs and classes and the occasional parties and other gatherings which are organized by the settlement and meet there. These are numerous and varied.

The proportion of foreign-born adults comprised in such settlement groups, however, is small. In the case of men it is almost negligible; in that of women somewhat larger. Native-born children and young people, from kindergarten age up to the time of marriage, make up the great majority.

Such club and class groups play an important part in the lives of these young people. Their immediate contribution is wholesome sociability combined with some specific instruction. The ideal in view, however, is to make these groups little nuclei of democracy. The degree to which this ideal is fulfilled varies greatly from one settlement to another, depending upon the breadth of vision and the skill of the workers in charge, but in the large a good deal is accomplished. Each group, in proportion to the age of its members, is developed along lines of self-government. Frequently the different groups are co-ordinated, through delegates to one central council, or to senior and junior councils. Because of the lack of definite functions these councils are often only forms. They become real in proportion to their actual powers and responsibilities. Clubs of different settlements in the same city frequently enter inter-settlement competitions or federations. Athletic and debating contests figure most prominently among the boys, while the girls specialize in leagues for social good times. An important aspect of these group and inter-group activities is that they bring together individuals of different racial stocks.

One of the most fully developed inter-settlement organizations has been built up in connection with summer caddy service at a golfing resort. A settlement in Boston worked out this plan. Boys from the neighborhood who needed an outing, but whose parents could not afford to pay their expenses, were taken to the White Mountains. There, under the supervision of workers from the settlement, they camped near the golf course, and served as caddies during the summer. Their earnings on the links not only paid all their expenses, but left them a surplus to take home. The caddy service was incidental, a practical setting for the real object, which was the promotion of healthy group spirit and co-operation. More and more responsibility was gradually demanded from the boys and eventually a corps of "sergeants" was developed.

Brought closely together in this way, the boys came to know and work with one another far better than would have been possible in their crowded city neighborhood. When they returned in the fall they remained a unified group in spirit, even though they were scattered through various clubs and classes. They stimulated the other boys all along the line, while the sergeants became the real backbone of the boys' work. These results did not come all at once, but accumulated through several years, the same sergeants and some of the same boys being taken to the camp each year. When the undertaking had successfully passed the experimental stage settlement groups from other neighborhoods joined in. Local identity was preserved by having separate camps. But the different groups were organized into a league, and to some extent during the summer, but mainly after their return to the city, they have held joint meetings and athletic contests. Thus each local group, conscious first of itself, has been brought into a consciousness of the larger community through alliance and friendly rivalry.

## INFLUENCING PARENTS THROUGH CHILDREN

Such activities constitute participation in the community life of America on the part of the children and young people of native birth who are mainly enlisted. Settlements are undoubtedly doing much to assimilate the generation born in America of foreign parentage. But inasmuch as this volume is concerned specifically with the foreign-born immigrant, it follows that the activities just described are pertinent only in so far as they influence the immigrant himself. In what ways and how far does this result follow?

Obviously the young people carry back from the settlement into their homes American influences and standards. To distinguish the influences due to settlements, however, from those due to the public school, the library, and other institutions is practically impossible. All that can be said is that the settlement's contribution is more distinctly that of informal neighborliness.

Sometimes the process of reaching the parents through the children overreaches itself. The children get or think they get so far beyond their parents as "Americans" that children and parents lose touch, and the latter, instead of being led on by their children, withdraw into their shells. This often occurs tragically in orthodox Jewish homes. The young people gradually break away from the orthodox regulations of their parents, and the home is disorganized. The same thing sometimes occurs in Italian homes, when the girls, adopting the American conception of "women's rights," find the traditionally strict protection with which their parents surround them very irksome, and consequently revolt. This problem exists to some degree in every racial group. Another closely related problem is the adjustment of marital squabbles in immigrant families. Immigrant leaders often criticize settlements for persuading women to hale their husbands into court. They say that families are sometimes broken up by these "American" methods, when the trouble could have been settled peaceably from the inside and the family kept intact by more conciliatory methods and more consideration for the old-country point of view.

It is during this critical period of adjustment to American conditions that the organizations and influences which originate among the immigrants themselves are of vital importance in holding parents and children together. It is essential to successful Americanization that these forces, instead of being disregarded or opposed, should be capitalized by American agencies within common-sense limits.

The ways in which settlements influence immigrants through their children are so intangible, so interwoven with the many other influences, that it is impossible to trace them to their conclusions, except through certain definite tests. One such test is the extent to which the foreign-born parents are actively related to the settlement. The proportion of adult immigrants who are enrolled in the settlement's organized clubs and classes is not very great, but it is larger in the case of women than in that of men.

### REACHING THE MOTHERS

The approach to the adults via the children succeeds best with the mothers. It begins in the

179

health clinics and milk stations to which the mothers are invited to bring their infants. Usually these clinics are operated by separate health agencies, but they are held at the settlement house and regarded by the neighborhood as being part of its work; so the settlement gets the benefit of the interest thus aroused. In racially mixed neighborhoods it is often in the clinic, while waiting their babies' turns for examination, that mothers of different races first rub elbows and begin to compare notes about such absorbing questions as teething and colic. Next the settlement kindergarten steps in, appealing to the mother as the personality of her little ones begins to unfold. Usually the mothers of the class are organized into a club which meets regularly with the kindergartner as leader, and often becomes the nucleus of a larger group.

During the school years the settlement not only supplements the school through its classes and clubs for children, but serves as intermediary and interpreter between the foreign-born parents and the school authorities. The former, though ambitious for their children's education, are often perplexed, if not estranged, by certain school regulations and rigidities. The latter, hampered by administrative red tape and a great mass of inner detail, often lack the time or the patience to explain things sympathetically to the halting immigrant parents. The settlements render a helpful service to both, and their influence has also done much to socialize the attitude of the public schools more fully. During vacations, and after the children have completed their schooling, the settlement still commends itself to the parents by providing wholesome recreation and interests during the morally critical period of adolescence, when the street, the "movies," and the dance halls contain so many alluring temptations.

Thus the interest of the mothers is enlisted in what the settlement stands for, and, building upon this interest, the settlement draws the mothers themselves into its organized activities. The obvious approach might appear to be a class in English, and this route is often tried.   But in general a "class" is too formal and formidable a beginning.  Informal social clubs, with English picked up incidentally, or a class organized later, are much more effective, especially with middle-aged women.

Most settlements of any size have one or more women's clubs, which they regard as the most substantial part of their organized work.  Even in immigrant neighborhoods, however, many, if not a majority, of these clubs are composed of native-born women or women who have been in America since girlhood and speak English fluently.  This is partly because most settlements have no workers who understand and speak the foreign languages of the neighborhood, and so have been unable to reach or hold the immigrant woman whose knowledge of English is scant.  But to an increasing extent settlements have become alive to the constructive possibilities of the foreign-language approach, and have taken on foreign-speaking workers—that is, workers equipped with both English and the foreign tongues of the neighborhood. As a result, the number of clubs composed mainly of foreign-born women has constantly increased.

### WOMEN'S CLUBS

The largest and most successful of these are, as a rule, made up of women of one race. One settlement which is situated in an almost solidly Polish neighborhood in Chicago has a Polish mothers' club of over two hundred. One of the settlement workers serves as leader, but the members elect officers, partly from among themselves and partly from the settlement staff. Some of the meetings are purely social, and some educational, with talks by outside speakers on child care, school problems, and civic questions. Both as a club and as individuals these women assist the settlement in numerous ways. For instance, they serve as matrons and tactfully enforce proper standards at "community dances" for the young people, which are run by the settlement to compete with the commercial dance halls. The club has an active interest in local political reforms, and it took a vigorous part in the various war drives.

The story of the origin and gradual development of this club, as told by the present leader, is interesting:

After repeated efforts to bring together a group of our Polish neighbors had failed we appealed to the United Charities worker in our district for help.

# THE SOCIAL SETTLEMENT APPROACH

We knew our women needed help other than financial, that an occasional social gathering would break in upon the dull routine of their days and inspire and strengthen them to take up their task with new courage, and that we would grow to know them better if we could meet them outside their homes. The Charity Workers readily co-operated, and made the pension issued to certain families in our neighborhood conditional upon their attendance at the Settlement Mothers' Club. Four women attended regularly that winter, the number occasionally augmented by a new member or a visitor. Games were played, friendly talk and always a coffeeklach wound up the meeting. Gradually the club grew as our people gained confidence in us and began to regard the meeting as an event to anticipate rather than dread as a necessary adjunct to their pension.

. . . Recently the character of the club has changed in a general way. Regular employment, better wages, and the interest of many neighbors who no longer need us, but who realize our need of them, have tended to make the club almost self-governing.

. . . All meetings are conducted in English, but the president, being a young Polish woman, repeats in Polish the proceedings that everyone may understand and participate. We have occasionally had some one to address the meeting in Polish, though the speaker usually uses English and depends upon a club member to interpret. Stereopticon talks are the style most frequently used. About 60 per cent speak English.

The club now numbers 216 members, about 75 per cent of whom are foreign born.

Another settlement, situated not far from the one just mentioned, in a neighborhood which was till recently almost as solidly Italian as the other is Polish, has a substantial club of Italian women. Organized some ten years ago, this club now numbers over a hundred members, and is so popular that its membership has been restricted to prevent its becoming unwieldy. In age its members range from seventeen to eighty years, but the majority are in middle life. Italian women are hard to free from the traditional restriction to the home, and it took an entire year to get this club under way. One of the settlement workers who spoke Italian canvassed the neighborhood, first arousing the interest of the women and then winning the consent of the Italian men. The settlement worker who is the club leader at present also speaks Italian, and though many of the members can now speak passable English, most of the meetings are conducted in Italian because that makes them feel more "at home." After each meeting an English class is held for such of the members as care to attend.

This club, at its own wish, does not elect officers or bother much about self-government, preferring to get along, as the members say, without quarreling over who shall fill the offices, and content to intrust their destinies to the settlement leader who has proved herself the friend of them all. The meetings follow about the same lines as those of the club of Polish mothers previously described, combining sociability and self-education in proportions to suit. During the war these Italian women were enthusiastic in their response to all the local demands.

Clubs of Jewish women are frequently large and vigorous. One club connected with a Jewish settlement in Pittsburgh, has a membership of about eight hundred, and devotes itself chiefly to assisting needy Jewish families. This particular type of society appeals strongly to foreign-born Jewish women. Another strong club of Jewish women has been built up by a settlement in New York City, which has developed the approach through health campaigns and visiting nursing more specifically than any other in the country. It has been in existence nearly twenty years, and has now about one hundred and fifty members, mostly middle-aged women. It elects its own officers, but is largely guided by a volunteer leader. Meetings are held weekly, the first one each month being given to business, the second to a "literary" topic, the third to civic questions, and the fourth to a musical and social program. This club has not taken a definite part in neighborhood movements, and nearly half of its members now live outside the locality. It has, however, created a mutual loan fund through deposits by the members, which is frequently drawn upon, especially just before holidays. Meetings are conducted in Yiddish, but a good many of the women join English classes at the settlement.

Here is an account of another Jewish women's club, connected with a Jewish settlement in Buffalo:

This has now been in existence some twelve years. It came together first in a small way. About a dozen women, who were met by our domestic educator in the course of her home visits, had meetings monthly and sometimes oftener at the Jewish Community Building, where they had lectures and talks in their own language by physicians and occasionally some lay people. They began to consider health and welfare of children, then, as our people liked activity, participation in tangible action, they began to hold parties of various kinds.

Under the guidance of the domestic educator the number of mothers steadily increased, some of the mothers bringing in friends of their own and others being added through the natural extension of the work. In discussing the welfare of their own children, the idea was presented to them that it would be a fine thing to have a place where children could be taken care of while their mothers did the necessary shopping or attended club meetings or went to the movies, and so they began to plan for the establishment of such a place, which they called a nursery. They have worked with much enthusiasm to raise funds to establish the home. Fairs to which members contributed their own handiwork, dances, card parties, package parties, have taught them organization methods and management.

As their funds grew larger their ideas underwent some process of change. There has been an outcry against sending poor Jewish children who are left orphans to non-Jewish orphan asylums. It is not always possible to send children needing temporary care to the Jewish Orphan Asylum at Rochester, which takes children for long periods of time, nor has it always been possible to find private Jewish boarding homes for such children at the time that such homes were needed, so they decided that this home of theirs, when it came into being, could take children needing temporary care until the proper disposition could be made.

The membership has now grown to over four hundred. There are three classes of membership, adjusted to the varying incomes of their members. They have bought a house which they have remodeled, redecorated, and equipped with up-to-date plumbing. They plan to have a trained nurse in charge of the children, a matron, a laundress, and a maid. It looks as if the children would be properly supervised. The club has become incorporated, and I think it is bound to be successful in the accomplishment of its purpose. In this practical way one mothers' club has found its own work in its own community.

## COMBINING DIFFERENT RACES

Racially mixed women's clubs are not so frequent or so successful. The differences of language and race are such obstacles that these clubs are usually composed of women who have been in the country for some time; in fact, the largest single element is almost always native born. In many clubs that are reported to be made up of immigrant women, practically all the members prove to be native born, though of different racial stocks. Attention is confined here, however, to those in which foreign-born women form a substantial proportion.

One such club includes Italian, Spanish, and native-born women. It is young but promising, numbering about forty members. During the war it served as a Red Cross auxiliary. Though the Italian and Spanish members cannot speak much English, they are making progress in learning it at their meetings. Another club, in Boston, contains about fifty Jewish, Italian, and Irish-American women, and is likely soon to take in some Syrians. It emphasizes sociability, and is largely responsible for a spirit of mutual respect and neighborliness in a racially mixed district. Its big event is an annual New Year's Eve party, to which the whole neighborhood is invited. At the grand finale, as the clock strikes twelve, all those present join hands in a circle and wish one another a Happy New Year.

Another club of mothers in New York City, known as the "Neighborhood Civic Club," is a real force in the neighborhood. It has about seventy-five members, including Bohemians, Hungarians, and Irish-Americans. It began as a purely social club, but gradually, under the guidance of the settlement, became interested in civic matters. Frequent parties, dances, and plays are given under its auspices. Since the advent of woman suffrage, some of the members have been very active in arousing political interest among the women of their district, and a good many of the club meetings are devoted to political and civic questions. At one meeting, for instance, the women's police reserve, a volunteer body of the district which includes some of the club members, were present as guests, and their work was informally discussed.

The writer was present at an annual election of officers. The head resident of the settlement, who had been serving as president, stated that it was not necessary to elect her again, and suggested that at least other nominations be made. The members, however, insisted on having her, but at the same time chided her a little for not attending all the meetings of late, as she used to. Recently this club has been used as the nucleus of a community council which centers in the settlement.

### IMMIGRANT WOMEN AS A CIVIC FORCE

Another settlement, in the racially mixed stock-yards section of Chicago, has three women's clubs which form a closely interrelated group. One is composed entirely of Bohemian women, many of whom could not speak English when they joined. As the native-born daughters of these women grew up, they wanted a club, too, so they organized as the "Daughters of Bohemia." A few years ago they thought it more appropriate, especially as they had taken in some friends who were not of Bohemian descent, to change their name to "Daughters of America." They meet alternately by themselves and with the mothers. The third group is a larger club, with members representing half a dozen different races, of both foreign and native birth. The first two clubs figure as sections of this last one, into which their members graduate, so to speak, as they outgrow the smaller units. In the case of all three sociability is combined with educational and civic interests, and the main club carries out an ambitious program of addresses by well-known people of the city. All are partly self-governing and partly directed by leaders from the settlement.

Through the influence of the head resident of the settlement, especially since women have had the vote, these clubs have been the medium for arousing the foreign-born women of the district to agitate for local improvements and cleaner politics. The head resident tells how this awakening of the women was gradually brought about:

I had noticed the great number of wagons filled with garbage that passed my door, and seldom a wagon closed or covered, going through this part of the city summer and winter, day after day, a great, ugly procession of them. At last I followed them and found they went a few blocks west from our settlement house. There the city was pouring in its refuse, bringing it from the other parts of the city. I, of course, was shocked. It seemed to me an outrage. I did not know quite what to do, but one day an awakened Bohemian woman came and asked me to go to the city hall with her to protest.

We went and we protested. We were treated with great politeness, but nothing happened. Then we went on protesting. After nineteen years of working and protesting with this locality against this injustice, there came an awakening in the state and the women were given the municipal vote. They at once began to use it. The very week after we got it we went to the city hall. We had asked and asked for a commission to study the question of garbage collection and disposal and said we wanted a report and a city plan for a system of garbage disposal. Before, as I said, we had always been treated with futile politeness. The strange thing was that when we came to the city hall after receiving this tool to work with, and we had made the same appeal, to our surprise at once the health committee voted that the finance committee be requested to appoint a commission with a ten-thousand-dollar appropriation to make the report. To our delight it went right through the finance committee, and two women were put on the commission. It went to the City Council, where again without delay it went through—two women members, ten-thousand-dollar appropriation, and all. The women of that locality had been awakened.

We organized a Women's Civic League for the ward. I was made chairman. The experience revealed the ward to itself, and a civic consciousness arose. The southeast end of the ward, which is English-speaking, came over to help us. They wrote some very clever songs, such as "Wanted, a Man," and sang them all over the ward. The Polish women organized. The Bohemian women already had so many organizations that they did not organize separately, but worked with us. We asked all

190

the nominees to come out and declare themselves. We held meetings which were very educational. With them we had music and songs. We brought all sides of the ward together as nothing else had done. As a result there was a registration of over 5,000 women, of all the nationalities in the ward. It brought into ward politics new women, fine, intelligent women, who never before knew about an alderman, and it brought out as nominee the finest man that ever came out in the ward; and though this man was not elected, he came within so few votes of getting in that the sway of the corrupt boss who had formerly held the ward in his hand was given a deathblow.

## FEDERATIONS

There is an increasing tendency for local settlement clubs of women to affiliate in district or city-wide groups. In Boston a federation of this kind included the clubs from five settlements. At each of these in turn sociable meetings were held under the direction of a committee made up of two representatives from each club. This arrangement was given up during the war, but it is likely to be revived. Sometimes the clubs enter broader leagues, extending beyond the settlement sphere. In Chicago, for example, a racially mixed club takes part with clubs of both foreign-born and native women in a program of group singing at a municipal pier. Such clubs are beginning to join the state federations of women's clubs and to take part in the activities of their district subdivisions. Thus the local clubs of immigrant women are being interrelated with the general American community.

The foregoing examples are sufficient to indicate

the types of organization into which settlements, by appealing primarily to the interests of motherhood and the home, have succeeded in drawing foreign - born women. Though these women's clubs are guided and directed by the settlement, and do not stand wholly on their own feet like self-originating organizations of immigrant women, still they involve responsible participation on the part of the club members in settlement, neighborhood, and community affairs, and they are a medium of large potential value in infusing immigrant neighborhoods with vital American motives.

In view of the traditional position of women in most immigrant groups, which restricts them closely to the home and thereby limits their direct contact with American influences, it is particularly important that they should be reached and enlisted in such ways. Thus the foreign-born mother is brought into somewhat the same sphere of interests as her native-born children, and the whole atmosphere of the immigrant home is affected at its source. Reviewing what settlements have accomplished, one of the outstanding leaders in this field gives it as his judgment that this neighborhood type of women's club is on the whole the settlement's most distinctive single contribution.[1]

---

[1] Robert A. Woods of South End House, Boston, correspondence.

A REFRESHING STREAM

This fountain, bubbling up in front of the University of Chicago Settlement, for all who will to partake, and always thronged with children, seems to stand for the settlement spirit of helpfulness.

# VII

## THE SETTLEMENT'S LARGER OPPORTUNITIES

THE man, not the woman, is the determining factor in immigrant groups. This is due not alone to his position in the old country. There from time immemorial he has been the lord and master of the home. But the great adventure of establishing a new home in America gives him even more responsibility and authority. He is the explorer. In many cases he comes to America first, to get the lay of the land before bringing his wife and children. He is the pioneer. He must hew out a way for himself and his family in this New World. He is the breadwinner and the guardian, on whom the mother and her brood depend for livelihood and protection. Consequently his is the deciding voice.

In order to enlist the vital strength of the immigrant group, settlements must reach and interest the men. The number and variety of societies organized by immigrant men on their own initiative and through their own resources prove that they are willing and able to organize for purposes which appeal to them. How far have settlements succeeded in organizing them?

### MEN'S CLUBS—MINUS THE MEN

Here is a different story.

Quotation may be made from a report on this

very subject, which was presented to the National Federation of Settlements in 1917, by one of the veteran settlement workers of the country.[1] This report not only gives the facts, but analyzes the causes:

The subject of settlement men's clubs and that of Arctic orange groves have this in common, that not only are their data somewhat meager and indefinite, but the evidence at hand appears to show that neither is at present in a conspicuously flourishing condition.

All discussion on this point would be in a fair way of being ended if one were able to point to a flourishing settlement men's club either existent or, if defunct, with unimpeachable evidence of its once flourishing condition. Frequently I have had referred to me flourishing settlement men's clubs, and I have thought that, had I possessed a plentiful supply of salt, I might have succeeded in catching one or more. But as I have approached, the bird has either taken wing and flown away or has proved to be plucked or already in cold storage. I have not canvassed the entire country, and so live in hope, but wherever I have turned the testimony has been of a uniformly depressing character. One director that I approached the other day with high anticipation, following the lead of our secretary, replied, "I am afraid I can't tell you anything very encouraging about men's clubs." He didn't. The head worker of a leading New York settlement made this response: "I feel that settlements at large have not made good in any way along this line. My own so-called success has been pitiful." From a house in the Middle West comes this statement, "Our work has not been successful with men." A well-known Eastern settlement leader, who is also well informed about other settlements, writes, "As yet we have never done any very successful thing and we do not know of anybody who has."

---

[1] William E. McLennan, head worker, Welcome Hall, Buffalo, New York, pamphlet.

# LARGER OPPORTUNITIES

Dr. Graham Taylor, who knows well the ups and downs of settlement work, says, "You have a tough subject in dealing with settlement work with men, because very little of it is successful enough to furnish either encouragement or suggestions."

Taking up the "causes for the failure—the difficulties in the way—of organizing settlement men's clubs," this report finds certain fundamental obstacles connected with settlement residents, equipment, and methods:

Under the head of residents, Doctor Taylor names two weaknesses: Residents are not acquainted with the men of the neighborhood, and some residents are not personally prepared to work with the men. I quote Doctor Taylor's words: "One reason for the failure to rally and hold men is that too few residents are personally enough acquainted with the men in the neighborhood. This is due in part to the fact that residents are too much off the field or transient in residence to be in touch with the habits, resorts, and fellowships of the local men. This lack of acquaintance is also due, possibly principally due, to the lack of time on the part of residents to cultivate an acquaintance with local men." Doctor Taylor cites his own experience: "The comradeship of political meetings and in campaigns, which has always been so wide open to me, has all along inspired my wish that I could follow it up between campaigns. But it takes time especially in the evenings and on the occasions upon which men resort to the street corners, barber shops, saloons, and their front doorsteps in summer, which I have never had at command."
Another chief reason for failure has to do with the personality of the residents. "Too few men residents," says Doctor Taylor, "are a man's kind of a man." I think we know pretty well what Doctor Taylor means, though it would be difficult to define just what is included by the phrase, a "man's kind of a man." It is not enough

to say he is a manly man. That leaves too much for granted. Possibly we will not miss it much if we say that such a man must be democratic, generous, modest, fearless, and possessing, as a matter of course, a sense of humor. I wonder if we may not apply the same test to our women residents. Certainly, if successful men's clubs are ever established in certain settlements, women residents must have something to do with them, a good deal to do with them, if there are no men in residence, or, worse, if the men who are there are not the right sort.

The second cause of failure, so far as the settlement itself is concerned, has to do with equipment, or, rather, the lack of proper equipment. Miss Trenholm of East Side House, New York, touches the heart of this weakness when she says, "I feel that men of our neighborhood will not come freely into the settlement house until separate quarters, and even separate entrances, are provided for them." Men will come to our houses without these separate quarters, but they will not come freely or in goodly numbers. It is perfectly natural that men of means build private clubs for themselves. It is not that they want to get away from society or that they love darkness rather than light, but rather that they want to be by themselves at times and enjoy their own society. "Most men's clubs," says Doctor Taylor, "in and out of settlements, to be successful, must have the exclusive use of the room they occupy. They do not always make good use of the space. and often do not need to use it all the while, but they are seldom satisfied to share it with other organizations. If Chicago Commons had lodge halls to offer the many orders which require privacy and lockers for regalia, we could get practically all of them to meet under our roof." Yes, and by meeting under the settlement roof they would soon come to regard the settlement in a new light and be inclined to identify themselves with the settlement's work.

The third cause of failure, with respect to the settlement's own efforts for men, pertains to method, or, rather, what is fundamental to method, the understanding of men and the purpose of organizing them. George A. Bellamy, of

# LARGER OPPORTUNITIES

Hiram House, Cleveland, seems to me to put his finger on a decidedly weak spot when he says, "I believe we have tried too many milk-and-water methods." What those methods are is suggested by Mr. Bellamy's next statement: "We must give the men of our community ideals worthy of them. We should interest them in politics, in the drama, in music, in group organizations, with definite hard struggles ahead of them which call to the colors the strongest and brainiest leadership in the neighborhood." It is a mistake to assume that all men, or even a majority of them, are children or feeble-minded. They cannot be held by the motives and methods that appeal only to small children.

The author of the report states that, as the net result of his inquiries, he knows of only one substantial settlement club of adult men, this being one which he found in existence at his own settlement when he went there as head worker. He describes it as follows:

### A SUCCESSFUL ITALIAN CLUB

The Welcome Hall Italian Men's Club was organized March 11, 1914, with less than ten members. It has steadily grown until it now numbers seventy-five in good standing, which means with all dues paid. According to its constitution, which is published in both Italian and English, its object is "to promote the best interests of its members physically, educationally, and socially, to develop the spirit of good citizenship, and to insure its members, their wives and children." According to the same authority, its members "shall consist of men of good moral character who shall be from eighteen to forty-five years of age." The business meeting is held on the first Wednesday evening of each month, the social evening on the third Wednesday evening, and special meetings at the call of the president. The dues are twenty-five cents a month.

The initiation fee is according to age, from two dollars to six dollars. The money secured from these dues and fees, after running and special expenses are paid, is set aside chiefly as funeral benefits for the members and their families, an amount being named which will meet, or go a long way toward meeting, the expense of a humble funeral. At the present time there is a surplus on hand amounting to above $300. Another consideration is noted in Articles IX and XIII of the constitution. To each member after his death are to be sent flowers worth five dollars, and to his memory is to be erected a monument to cost fifty dollars, on which shall be inscribed the deceased member's name and the fact that he was in good and regular standing in the Welcome Hall Men's Club.

During the more than three years' existence of the club I do not recall the omission of a single monthly meeting except in the middle of summer. The meetings appear never to drag on account of not having interesting themes for discussion. I was once present through a long session, when the subject was whether at a coming dance children would be admitted "wit or witout parents." For a long time it seemed that the "wits" and "witouts" were about evenly divided, but the former finally won. The members have visited our summer camp several times, paying their own expenses. Every year they have a banquet of a somewhat formal and formidable character. Last March the food was prepared wholly in the Italian manner, cooked and served by the men themselves. We all not only survived, but enjoyed the feast.

### BASIC PRINCIPLES

The club serves to illustrate—and this is, as I have said, the chief reason for citing it—some of the principles and methods which I believe to be fundamental in a successful settlement men's club—principles and methods which were referred to in the earlier part of this paper in naming the things to avoid. It also shows how certain obstacles were overcome.

# LARGER OPPORTUNITIES

*The club has ideals.* These were not published and I am not sure that the members were or are conscious of them. But they were there just the same. One of the ideals was to provide for death in the family through the mutual efforts and sacrifices of the members. With the exception of five or six persons, all these men are employed at almost starvation wages. It has meant real sacrifice for them to pay their initiation fees and dues. They have had a growing civic spirit. Within the past fortnight they gave out of their treasury, without the slightest suggestion from the outside, fifty dollars for the benefit of the Allied bazaar.

*The club is self-governing and democratic in the truest sense. Its relation to the settlement has been permitted to develop freely.* The members had some assistance in the beginning, but their ideas were allowed to control everything. We have kept our hands off, even when the club has appeared to be wasting its time on some insignificant matter. We have felt that nothing is really insignificant that helps men to find themselves and to understand their own business. A democracy must inevitably waste time and make mistakes. The greatest mistake, however, would be to try to prevent it from making mistakes. Babies learn to walk by falling down. This club has never had an outsider for a leader. If one had appeared he might have killed it.

*The language and race and, I might say, the religious, difficulties have been met by keeping the club Italian.* The admission of Germans, Poles, Syrians, and Americans, not to mention Irish, would inevitably have made trouble. The way to cosmopolitanism is through nationality, just as love of all mankind is usually through family love. We come to love all children by loving our own.

The foregoing report applies to all settlement men's clubs, and not alone to those of immigrants. It is significant, therefore, and conclusive as evidence against the notion that immigrants are harder to organize than native Americans, that the one successful club to which the author points is composed of men of foreign birth. Two other facts also are significant. The first is that the reasons assigned for failure to reach the adult men of the neighborhood are very closely related to the limitations which, as previously noted, are inherent in the settlement idea. The second is that the one club described is patterned after the mutual insurance societies which are so numerous among the immigrants. In other words, instead of trying to coax Italian men to come into something that to them looked strange and vague, this settlement adopted the form to which they naturally responded, and then allowed this form of organization to adapt itself gradually to the larger purposes in view.

## OTHER EXAMPLES

Besides the settlement men's club just described, there are at present a few others composed largely of adult foreign-born men. One is a club of Polish fathers in Chicago. It grew out of the Polish mothers' club previously mentioned. The women challenged the men, who had been coming to the parties, to form as good a club as theirs, and the men accepted the challenge. Their club has about a hundred members, but the average attendance is something under half that number. Though it elects its own officers, it has a leader from the settlement. Its meetings are mostly for informal sociability, but in various ways it helps out in settlement affairs in conjunction with the mothers' group. There is also an Italian club in a Cleveland settlement which has about a hundred and twenty-five members, including foreign and native born. It is composed mainly of shopkeepers and business men, and acts as a sort of local improvement association in its solidly Italian neighborhood. Though originally organized by the head resident of the settlement, it functions now on its own initiative. It is regarded as the backbone of the neighborhood.

As respects racially mixed men's clubs, while there are some groups of native-born young men of various racial stocks such as that which grew out of the caddy-camp enterprise, only one has been discovered which brings together foreign-born men of different races. This one is remarkable. The settlement with which it is connected is in Milwaukee, situated in a neighborhood predominantly Polish, with a minority of Germans.

Eight Polish Catholic churches, averaging a thousand children each in parochial schools, tell the story [writes the head worker]. In our men's club of two hundred members we have many races, but chiefly Germans and Poles. About a third of the members are foreign born and practically all the others are of foreign parentage. This club is fifteen years old. Members are hand picked, program strong met each year, an *absolutely free open forum*, good-fellowship a cementing power—a club that has done things and is not afraid of the cars, has always stood up and fought. The members of our young men's clubs all look forward to becoming twenty-one years old, when they can graduate into the men's club. I believe this club is really the most influential club in civic affairs in the city, except the City Club. I'm sure we count for more in civic matters than the University Club, of which I am a member.

The head worker of this particular settlement, be it said, is a real "man's man," and to his rugged personality is due much of the vital interest which the men of the neighborhood take in this organization. By bringing foreign-born and native-born fathers and sons together in one effective working body this club is making a signal contribution to Americanization.

### ADULT CLUBS

It appears, then, that while settlements have had substantial success in organizing clubs of immigrant women, especially women of one race, there has been almost complete failure to organize the men. Indeed, the very success which settlements have had with young people and women appears to have worked against their success with men. When immigrant men, of the average laboring type, are asked what they think of the settlement, the usual answer is a shrug of the shoulders and the remark, "Oh, well, it's all right for the women and children." The incentives supplied by the settlement have not proved sufficient to attract men except in a few instances, and in only one instance, so far as present information goes, have they been strong enough to unite men of different races in the same organization. Whether the approach to the adults has been through the children, as in the main it has been, or whether it has been made directly, such are the actual results.

### LEADERSHIP OF NATIVE BORN

One way in which the settlement might reach the foreign-born adults is by training its American-reared young people to be leaders of immigrant groups. Such leadership on the part of individuals or of organizations would serve to interrelate the foreign born with American life.

Instances of this kind of leadership, however, are comparatively scarce. There are several reasons for this. One is the pronounced tendency on the part of native-born young people to move out of immigrant neighborhoods into American districts, especially when they marry and start life for themselves. Settlements, by instilling young people with the American point of view, contribute to this natural tendency, and to some extent deliberately encourage it, particularly in the case of more energetic and ambitious individuals. Although moving out may be a progressive step for the young folks themselves, it takes away potential leaders from the immigrant group. In this respect the settlement is subtracting from the assets of its own neighborhood.

It may be asked whether the young people who move out become leaders in the localities to which they go. Though doubtless there are a substantial number of instances where such is the case, it has been possible to trace only a few. Moreover, the young people move largely into districts of the native born, so that whatever leadership they may develop has no direct bearing upon the Americanization of the foreign-born immigrant.

Another reason why the settlement does not produce more local leaders is that these young people who remain in the neighborhood are often so imbued with the settlement atmosphere that they lose their appreciation of the vital interests of the foreign-born adults and become unacceptable as leaders. Here, again, a natural tendency in the American-reared to feel and think differently from the foreign born is furthered by the settlement. The young people move in a settlement circle that few of the foreign-born adults enter. The leadership of such of them as become leaders is usually confined to this circle and does not extend throughout the neighborhood.

### SELF-ASSERTION OF "ALUMNI"

Though it is difficult to find instances for which the settlement is responsible of native-born leaders of foreign-born groups, there are some interesting cases in which organizations composed of the first generation of native born have concerned themselves with the foreign-born element. Sometimes these organizations are composed of persons who still live in the neighborhood, but usually they are made up of those who have moved away but still retain their interest. In either case, the members represent a point of view between that of the immigrant neighborhood and that of the settlement. They have come under settlement influence, and, consciously or unconsciously, are actuated by the settlement idea.

One case, which is significant in several ways, centers in a predominantly Jewish neighborhood in New York City. Though Italians have of late been coming into the district, they have not been drawn into the settlement activities. This settlement, which is one of the oldest in the country, has always emphasized educational self-governing clubs, with the aim of developing self-reliance, public spirit, and leadership. The attitude of the settlement workers has been unusually democratic, and in earlier years the managing board consisted of the workers. But later this settlement, like others, came to have a board of trustees whose members had never lived in the neighborhood. Several years ago a disagreement arose between the head worker and the board, and the former resigned. A majority of the board were inclined to discontinue the settlement on the ground that the results accomplished did not warrant the large expense involved, which was met entirely by outside philanthropy.

At this stage, aroused by one of the residents, the "alumni" of the settlement—that is, the former members of its clubs, entered a protest, which they backed up by raising four thousand dollars among themselves. Most of these alumni had not lived in the settlement neighborhood for some years. They were scattered throughout the city and included many successful business and professional men, as indicated by the fact that three thousand dollars of their fund was contributed by six persons. This gift was accompanied by a request for representation on the board.

In the face of this demonstration, the conservative members of the board withdrew, and half a dozen of the alumni, all former residents of the neighborhood, were elected to serve with a dozen or so of the more liberal trustees on a new board. A young man who had been born in the neighborhood and had lived there until shortly before this happened, and who had been closely identified with the settlement, was elected head worker. This reorganization has increased the exceptionally active interest of the alumni in the settlement and the neighborhood. But the situation strikingly illustrates negative as well as positive aspects of the settlement's relation to the foreign-born people immediately about it.

There are a hundred and twenty-five different settlement clubs, with an almost solidly Jewish membership of about twenty-five hundred. Indeed, this settlement seethes with club activity. But practically all the members of these clubs are either native born or came over as little children and now count as native born. Only to a small extent does the settlement include immigrant adults. Its gymnasium attracts some of the younger men. It has one Yiddish-speaking mothers' club of fifty members. Foreign-born adults come to lectures, especially when they are given in Yiddish. Some benefit societies of foreign-born men meet at the settlement, but have no part in its inner affairs.

# LARGER OPPORTUNITIES

We feel that our settlement is for the young people [said the head worker]. We've tried in the past to get the foreign born, but we've found that the old people and the young people can't be mixed, at least not by the settlement. Our job is with the young people. Anyway, they use up all our space. Just the other day we had to refuse a request for meeting room from a society of foreign born, the Workmen's Circle, simply because we didn't have any room to spare.

At the same time the head worker stated that many of the labor unions of the neighborhood included both foreign and native born, and that some of the young men who graduated from settlement clubs were leaders in these unions.

The second outstanding fact about the club enrollment is that nearly all the members of the thirty-five "senior" clubs have married and scattered to various parts of the city. Yet they take the most active interest in settlement affairs and are still more or less of the neighborhood in spirit, though not in residence. The qualifying terms "more or less" are used advisedly. At any rate, many of the senior club members belong to this neighborhood more than they do to any other. Asked whether they did not identify themselves with the neighborhoods in which they lived, the head worker replied, "They seem to prefer to come back to the settlement."

Thus the controlling element within the settlement comes from outside the locality in which it is situated. For these clubs are the most important and have the largest voice in the settlement's activities. Most of the club leaders are drawn from these alumni. The latter have also concerned themselves more specifically with the welfare of the neighborhood through several clubs of their own. One organization which was more active in former years than at present is called the Guild Civic Union, and is thus described in a leaflet which it issued:

The Union's work is done by a group of young men and women living now or formerly in this neighborhood, having an understanding of its people and their needs. It has been for a long time a largely unconscious response to the civic needs of our neighborhood. It is now taking a more completely organized form. The Union's workers are all people who through long residence or association with the neighborhood have been enabled to gauge the needs here in the most accurate of ways—by measuring their neighbors' civic problems by their own experiences. The Union is local civic pride vitalized. It is a conscious striving for reform of conditions which affect and reach directly the lives of the workers in our enterprise.

This organization has taken a leading part in heading off a political deal to sell a local playground for private use, bringing about the abolition of the last horse cars, providing comfort stations and additional footpaths over bridges, repairing pavements, operating an experimental school center, and arousing interest in political contests. To-day the same sort of activity is being carried on by another club.

But how far have these things been done [one of the workers was asked] in a way which involves the active participation of the foreign-born residents of the neighborhood?

Well, not so very much [was the reply]. The quickest way is for some of the members, who know the ropes and have some influence, to get in touch with the necessary public officials and get things done in short order. Sometimes we have taken the foreign born in by circulating petitions, speaking before their societies, and getting up big mass meetings.

One instance was related, however, in which a big result was accomplished by working through the foreign born. Jewish peddlers' stands had overrun the streets, the peddlers "squatting" wherever they wanted to display their wares. The city authorities could have arrested and penalized them all, but, realizing that many of them were ignorant of the laws and not wishing to alienate the local Jewish element by undue harshness, they appealed to one of the settlement workers to try persuasion. For several months this man, with the aid of an interpreter, held conferences with the peddlers.

I sweat blood [he said], laboring to make those fellows understand the situation, but finally I succeeded. The result was that they agreed voluntarily to limit and regulate the business themselves, and since then there has been no further trouble. It was well worth the effort.

### AN OFFSHOOT ASSOCIATION

In another case in New York City an organization of native-born young people still living in the neighborhood has independently undertaken activities which enlist the foreign born. Some fifteen years ago a settlement organized a group of boys of Italian parentage as a social and dramatic club. After they had stuck together for nearly ten years, and had grown up to be young men, they decided to stand on their own feet and be self-supporting as a separate organization. They rented quarters in the neighborhood, and for a while had a hard time financially. Finally they won out and now occupy a rented three-story house. From twenty members they have increased to a hundred and fifty.

They call themselves a "Community Association" because their aim from the beginning has been to do something for the local community. They lend their rooms for meetings of other local organizations, and they are trying to preserve the bonds between children and parents. The members bring their mothers and fathers to special meetings, at which Italian speakers explain differences between American life and life in Italy, and ways in which immigrants can best adjust themselves. The club conducted a vigorous naturalization campaign. Its members went into the saloons and cafés, where men congregated, and in many cases took men to the naturalization courts themselves. During the war, in which many of its own members served, it assisted in all war drives, raised about $75,000 for the Liberty Loans, and contributed from its own treasury to the Knights of Columbus, the Salvation Army, and the Red Cross. During political campaigns the club, which is nonpartisan, holds neighborhood meetings at which the different candidates are invited to speak.

The attitude of this club toward settlements is interesting. It will not acknowledge that its own existence is mainly due to a settlement, and it is not conscious that the furnishings of its clubhouse plainly testify to settlement influence. It does not affiliate much with the local settlements, its members stating that they do not wish to be connected with institutions which are not self-supporting. They say that their aim is to develop a general neighborhood center which will be supported by the neighborhood itself.

## NEIGHBORHOOD VISITING

So far we have been chiefly concerned with settlement club work, and the extent to which it influences foreign-born adults, either directly or through their children. The settlement also makes direct contacts with individual adults through various forms of service administered from the settlement house and through systematic visiting in the neighborhood.

These services include supplying miscellaneous information, individual assistance in naturalization, and sometimes, though this is not generally approved by settlements, giving material relief in cases of distress. Visiting takes various forms, from that of general neighborliness, either to get acquainted or to maintain friendly relations, to such more specific forms as nursing, instruction in housekeeping, collecting savings, and canvassing for campaigns of one sort or another. Such visiting represents, in large measure, the extension of the settlement's service out into the neighborhood.

The chief purpose of both these lines of activity

is to reach the adults, and, as far as personal contacts go, it is mainly the adults who are reached. Though the items of assistance given from day to day often seem slight, the total service rendered over any considerable period is great. In the case of a settlement which has been working in its neighborhood for years, it amounts to an immense contribution in terms of human helpfulness. While the neighborhood people figure chiefly as the beneficiaries, it is obvious that a good deal of actual participation on their own part is enlisted.

The least tangible, but perhaps the most important, element in this participation is the development of a community of feeling. The adults with whom such human contacts are established, and who share such friendly services, come to have somewhat different attitudes in consequence. Through the multiplication of individual reactions, the neighborhood is infused with new sympathies, new ideals, and new motives for action. Settlements are becoming increasingly conscious of what may thus be accomplished. "Constructive gossip," they call it, the idea being to make topics of neighborhood betterment so interesting to the neighborhood people in a newsy, gossipy way that they will be discussed by housewives on the doorsteps and by the men in their lodges, in competition with the story of Mrs. Kulinski's last row with her husband.

The local gossip is capable of being made a means of disseminating new ideas and standards and of enlarging and refining vision. . . . Here is a germ . . . a principle which began to be developed through the whole scheme of settlements as a means of introducing the ripe results of civilization into the circulatory system of working-class life.[1]

As illustrating how the contact between settlement workers and neighborhood people may produce results more directly than through the medium of "gossip," an incident was told of an Italian woman who had recently moved into an Irish neighborhood. She came to the settlement to say that the little children in the block were liable to fall into some ditches which had been left open in the course of construction work on an adjoining street, and to ask if these ditches could not be covered. The settlement worker suggested that she find out how many little children there were in the block. So the Italian woman visited every family in the block. There proved to be over twenty little tots. Complaint was made to the street department, and the ditches were covered. The best of it was that the Italian woman herself had a part in this detail of neighborhood improvement, and that her neighborly service at once installed her in the good graces of her Irish neighbors. Similar illustrations could be multiplied.

Direct contact between the settlement and the neighborhood reached its maximum during the war. The government turned to the settlements as the readiest agencies for reaching the neighborhoods in which they were situated. Workers

[1] Robert A. Woods and Albert J. Kennedy, Manuscript of *The Settlement Horizon.*

from the settlements canvassed their neighborhoods fully and came to know them far better than ever before, and the foreign born responded to visits, came to the settlements for information and help, and assisted in numerous ways as they never had before.

The war made the neighborhood conscious of itself, and brought the neighborhood at large and the settlement into closer relationship. The people felt then that they and the government and the settlement were partners in a common cause—the winning of the war.

Such is the almost universal testimony of settlement workers. The war supplied the occasion and the motive; the results obtained demonstrate that, given motives sufficiently vital, the settlements are in a position to get neighborhood co-operation.

### MOBILIZING THE NEIGHBORHOOD

The final goal which settlements have had in view beyond their club and class groups and their service to individuals, has been to help organize the neighborhood as a whole—to marshal the forces and equipment necessary for progress, and then to provide such inspiration and guidance as may be needed to bring the neighborhood up to a plane of entire self-direction. In this role the settlement appears as the representative and accredited leader of the neighborhood, in interpreting it to itself and enabling it to make the most of its resources.

## LARGER OPPORTUNITIES

There are two ways, closely related and yet distinct, in which a neighborhood may be thus assisted. One is to bring in reinforcement from without. The other is to develop the forces inherent in the neighborhood itself, and such organization as has grown out of its own initiative. Settlements have obtained their more tangible results mainly in the first of these two ways.

### REINFORCEMENT FROM WITHOUT

The settlement's interpretation of the immigrant has stimulated activity in his behalf on the part of agencies already established, and also the rise of new agencies of neighborhood character. Not satisfied with general interpretation, the settlements have directly urged the specific needs of their neighborhoods upon such public or private agencies as could properly meet them. Frequently they have gone farther and played the part of pioneers. They have initiated certain activities, carried them through the stage of experiment until both the need and the concrete means of meeting it were clearly demonstrated, and then got them established on a permanent basis under other auspices. In many instances the first playgrounds, school buildings, parks, public baths, branch libraries, and kindred improvements in given neighborhoods have been secured mainly through the settlement initiative. Neighborhood environments have been greatly enriched by these reinforcements from without. That this is regarded by settlements as one of their greatest contributions is indicated in the following statement:

As to the municipal playgrounds, baths, etc., which have resulted from settlement initiative, the development of such experiments under settlement auspices and their transfer to the municipality are one of the settlements' most important, and in a sense most ingenious, contributions to Americanism. The settlements more than any other agency disintegrated and displaced the method of local politics by jobs, contracts, and other favors to the few, with a policy of tangible benefits for all, in which all participate on a democratic basis, getting the most telling kind of kindergarten education in the downright significance of democracy. Personally, I doubt whether there has been any other single phase of the movement for Americanization that has been more important than this, and it is absolutely and, in a sense, exclusively a settlement method.[1]

This study, however, is concerned with these results primarily as they involve responsible participation on the part of the immigrant. In other words, how far do immigrant neighborhoods share in obtaining these improvements and in their subsequent control? Unless the neighborhood has such an active share, its relation to the improvement is simply that of a beneficiary or consumer, and not that of a copartner or joint producer.

The extent to which the neighborhood enters into the directing of these improvements, after they are obtained, will be taken up in a later chapter when the most important of such agencies are considered. Attention will be confined at

---

[1] Robert A. Woods, correspondence.

this point to neighborhood participation in securing them.

## LITTLE NEIGHBORHOOD PARTICIPATION

As a rule, neighborhood participation is small compared with the part played by the settlement workers. The latter undertake to speak for the neighborhood in presenting to the public authorities, or to some private organization, what they regard as a neighborhood need. They initiate and maintain a demand that this need be met in a certain way. If they are persistent enough, and can bring to bear sufficient pressure, their request is granted and the particular improvement is carried out. In this process the neighborhood itself figures actively hardly at all.

Sometimes, when a settlement thinks it necessary to arouse a wider demand, it calls together the officers of other private and public agencies operating in the neighborhood, as, for example, the secretary of the charity society, the visiting nurse, the school principal, and the playground director, and gets them to unite with it for the object in view. Although these officers are seldom residents of the neighborhood, their united opinion is assumed to constitute a real expression on the neighborhood's part.

The reasons for proceeding in this way, instead of in a way which actually enlists the neighborhood, are quite understandable. The settlement's general motive, to promote the local welfare, is good. The specific object in view, as for instance a playground, is good. The need is believed to be urgent. Therefore the quickest and surest way to obtain the desired object appears to be the best way. To attempt to secure an organized demand on the part of the people of the neighborhood would take a lot of time. Besides, some element in the neighborhood might not agree with the settlement as to the urgency of the need and the best way of meeting it. So, the settlement workers argue, as long as they have the situation in hand and really represent the neighborhood, their best plan is to do the thing themselves, *for* the neighborhood, rather than to take the longer and slower route of having it done *by* the neighborhood.

The settlement's policy in this respect is admitted and defended in the following statement:

There is of course no manner of doubt that faced with the necessity of getting something done either by direct appeal to the city at large or through a long, tedious educational process of the local citizenship, they have waived the values entailed by the latter method and chosen the former. This has been very largely true in the matter of securing playgrounds, baths, and certain recreational provisions. This kind of thing, however, has been done with the eyes open. Settlements have known that it was the less desirable way, but they have chosen it because in the light of larger human needs it seemed the only thing to do.[1]

### CO-OPERATION WITH IMMIGRANT FORCES

How far, in their efforts to secure local improvements, do settlements go beyond short-cut and not altogether democratic methods, and help

---

[1] Albert J. Kennedy, assistant secretary of the National Federation of Settlements, correspondence.

the neighborhood to obtain similar results in its own way and through its own powers? In the case of immigrant neighborhoods, this question resolves itself into one of still larger scope and significance.

Immigrant neighborhoods usually abound in organizations formed and maintained without assistance of any kind from native Americans. Many of these organizations carry on Americanizing activities of the most fundamental sort, and are reaching out in an effort to unite more fully with the American community. They constitute reservoirs of power which may be turned to greater constructive use if the proper connections are established by American agencies. It has been assumed that the American agency which is closest to these immigrant groups, inasmuch as it is situated right in their midst, is the settlement. To what extent has the settlement taken advantage of its opportunities? How far has it related itself to immigrant organizations, and undertaken to guide them into fuller participation in American life? In what degree does the settlement figure as the immigrant neighborhood's accredited representative?

The answer to these questions must be largely unfavorable. Many settlements are totally ignorant of the inherent immigrant forces which surround them, or know them only in a vague way which is of little avail for practical purposes. For example, a certain well-known settlement has been working for years in a district composed of a number of racial groups, yet the head worker was unable to give any definite information about

the organizations or leaders of these different
groups, and frankly admitted that no connections
whatever had been made with them. He explained that the racial character of the district
had changed in recent years. But of course it
is part of a settlement's job to know a changing
neighborhood as it is to-day, not as it used to be.

In another district where there are half a dozen
principal groups and two hundred or more immigrant organizations, some of them remarkably
progressive, the several settlements which call
this their neighborhood have only a fractional
and indefinite knowledge of these societies. In
many cases, when settlement workers were asked,
"What immigrant organizations are there in your
locality?" the answer has been, "We don't
know; we have never really tried to find out."

Where settlements are somewhat acquainted
with such organizations, they are often indifferent, if not positively opposed to them, and regard
them as "nationalistic" or "clannish" affairs,
to be broken down rather than built upon. Even
settlements which have some sympathetic understanding of such organizations have done but
little to draw them into any concerted neighborhood movement. Sometimes a few individuals,
mostly native born, who are assumed to represent
the immigrant groups, are called into conference
by the settlement, along with the social workers
of the district; but the common organic life of
immigrant groups, and the foreign-born leaders
who really represent these groups, have been
taken very little into account. Instead of trying

to infuse existing immigrant organizations with the spirit and practice of Americanism, most settlements have attempted to start entirely new organizations after their own ideas.

The intrinsic unwisdom of such a policy has been pointed out by one of the foremost exponents of settlement philosophy.

The presumption is always against having a settlement introduce any new institutional scheme. It is always in favor of falling in with the current of what is already advancing in the neighborhood. In an enterprise of the people's own, you find them under a kind of momentum which can never be so well artificially aroused. . . . The settlement ought to be represented, so far as possible, in every organization that has any visible influence in the local community . . . the development of independent social forms is so important.[1]

Largely as a result of their failure to carry into practice the fundamental principle of social economy which has been thus clearly stated in theory, settlements are not accepted by immigrant neighborhoods in a representative capacity. There are a good many instances of specific activities which are somewhat representative, but so far as present information goes, instances of settlements which have come to have a generally representative status in their neighborhood are very few indeed.

### ATTITUDE OF IMMIGRANT GROUPS

Immigrant leaders of many different races, degrees of education, and points of view have

[1] Robert A. Woods, *Philanthropy and Social Progress, 1893.* "The University Settlement Idea."

been questioned as to their attitude toward settlements. Their replies have a striking unanimity. Nearly all expressed a good-natured friendliness for settlements, and a willingness to co-operate with them, coupled with the remark previously quoted that "they are all right for women and children." Some told of their own children going to settlements for a "good time." Some spoke of the many personal services which settlements render to individuals in need of advice or help. But as to the settlement's really representing them and their groups in any substantial sense, their comment was all to the contrary.

They're like all the rest [said one]. A bunch of people planning for us and deciding what is good for us without consulting us or taking us into their confidence. No one but a member of our own race can really understand us.

Another highly educated man, of broad experience, after referring to the "kind and generous spirit" of a certain settlement working among his race, and the good it was doing among the young people, pointed out that it was not reaching the deeper life of the foreign born.

The ladies at the settlement do not understand the problem of Americanization [he said]. It is slow, and cannot be brought about by forcing people to give up their language or to be present at meetings where they cannot understand what is said.

Another, a woman, felt that settlements were

just scratching the surface and do not have any real understanding of the people they are trying to work with. It is always a question of putting something over and not of trying to get at the bottom of things.

An editor of racial cast was more sweeping:

No outside agency can undertake to tell my people what to do. We believe in freedom and equal opportunity for the attainment of the highest growth and development. This must come from the people themselves, through their societies and education after their own ideas. The influence of the settlements in our life is negligible. If they were to disappear overnight, the life, growth, and development of my people and their assimilation into American life would go on just the same.

Such general criticisms, from the viewpoints of racial groups, were supplemented by others from non-racial angles. Labor leaders, while granting that settlements often try to cultivate friendly relations with unions, and that the latter sometimes accept their hospitality for meetings, say that such relations can never be substantial, for the simple reason that settlements are supported and controlled by the very interests against which the unions are contending. Political leaders hold that their parties "have been doing for years the sort of thing the settlement is doing, only we have done it more democratically." In some cases leaders of radical groups complain that the settlement virtually excludes them. "But we are an element in the neighborhood, and so how can the settlement represent the neighborhood when it shuts us out?"

It can hardly be said, therefore, that settlements have established such close and organic connections with the inherent forces of immigrant neighborhoods as really to represent them. However, there are a good many partial exceptions to this rule. These are significant, first, as evidencing the methods by which more successful results are obtained, and, second, as affording a demonstration of the settlement's larger possibilities.

In citing a few examples of this sort, there is no intention of comparing these particular settlements with others in any general way. Many settlements are larger and are obtaining larger results in other respects than the institutions mentioned here. Nor are these the only ones which are succeeding in these particular ways. The examples cited below are intended to illustrate certain typical problems of immigrant neighborhoods, on the one hand, and on the other the measurably successful application of certain general principles in meeting these problems.

### THE MEXICAN PROBLEM

The latest and as yet least organized immigrants in the United States are the Mexicans. Their numbers are rapidly increasing in California and the Southwest, and they are gradually working northward. In Mexico their condition has been abject. They come nearer to being truly "poor" than any other immigrant group in the country. They are a problem, therefore, from that angle. But they present another and more difficult problem. The memory of our forcible "Americanization" of Mexican territory in the war of 1848 has naturally colored the attitude of Mexicans toward the United States, and even these untutored immigrants come here in a state of suspended judgment as to how far American professions are borne out by facts. If these immigrants are to be Americanized in a better way than that of 1848, not only must they be helped materially, they must be relieved of their inherited misgivings. In that case they will accept the United States as their adopted country. Otherwise they may make ideal tinder for the flames of bitter and destructive revolutionism.

Such is the problem, but the way in which generally it is being dealt with is suggested by the following statement.

In this city [writes the head worker of a settlement in Los Angeles] Mexicans receive the worst treatment accorded any group. This is true in wages, in living conditions, in industry generally, and also in our courts of justice. The Mexican undeniably sees the very worst side of American life. Most of our Mexican laborers were imported by the railroad companies, the agricultural and mining interests, as cheap labor. The Mexicans were misled by promises of wages that seemed high to them in Mexico. They arrived in the United States to find conditions wholly different. No matter how poorly they lived at home, they expected it to be different here. Notably in the case of one railroad company, they have been treated like cattle. The disappointment and injustice embitter them.

Now this particular settlement is trying to solve the Mexican problem in its own neighborhood. The Mexican immigrants are Catholics. This is a Catholic settlement. Here is the way it is going about its task.

# AMERICA VIA THE NEIGHBORHOOD

We are working in a neighborhood of the foreign born, 90 per cent of whom are Mexicans. Our plan of work is co-operative, but the development of full co-operation is slow. The Mexican laborer's status in his own country has been virtually that of a serf. He is used to the paternalism of the *hacendado*. We hope to foster a self-governing organization just as soon as we find a competent Spanish-speaking leader. We employ a Spanish-speaking field worker. We talk things over with our neighbors. We consult them, and they consult us in every kind of perplexity.

During the war we found the foreign born, including the Mexicans, willing to take an active part in all campaigns when they understood the real situation. In food conservation, home gardens, Liberty Loans, Red Cross, War Savings campaigns, they gave co-operation and service.

The settlement in its general work is open on equal terms to all of any race or creed, without the slightest compromise or conviction. In its religious work it is Catholic. The house was built by the bishop of the diocese. The Settlement Association, which equips and maintains the work and determines the policy, is composed of Catholics, though the Association is not a religious society. The settlement neighbors are fully 90 per cent Catholic. We believe that because the settlement is harmonious with the religious background of the Mexican people it has an unusual opportunity to cultivate a love for American ideals and to build up a responsible American citizenship with their co-operation. Thus far we have established a confidence among many of our neighbors that, after all, the United States stands for an ideal of liberty, equality, justice which all men desire to approach. As Father T—— said to me last Sunday, "Share with them [the Mexican people] all that is best in your splendid civilization, illumine it with kindness, and they will be Americans through love of what America means."

Thus has this settlement identified itself with these Mexican immigrants and made itself their

representative. Through the fortunate medium
of common religious faith, it is bringing to bear
upon them an influence which is at once conservative and adaptive. In the face of adverse
conditions, it is helping them, on the one hand,
to preserve and assert their self-respect as a
group, while on the other it is by its own example
winning their respect for America. Recognizing
that this immigrant group is as yet in its earliest
formative stage, the settlement is laying a sound
foundation for the future.

### ORGANIC CORRELATION

Another settlement, situated in the midst of
several colonies, in New York City, has undertaken on an unusual scale to relate these different
groups to the settlement and also to correlate
them with one another through common interests and activities. Its approach has been to
offer the hospitality of the settlement to immigrant organizations which lack adequate
meeting places of their own, and then, if this
invitation is accepted, to enlist the organization
as far as practicable in the settlement's local work.

A number of Russian, Bohemian, Hungarian,
and Italian societies are now holding their regular
meetings at this settlement. One of the Russian
societies is a benefit and educational society, and
another is a group of young women. Particularly
interesting is the fact that the choir of a Russian
church and a school for teaching the Russian
language to the children also meet there. By
relating itself to the cultural interests of these

immigrants, the settlement has aroused their interest in its own adaptive activities, and has enrolled some of them in a special class in English and civics, taught by a Russian-speaking teacher.

The Czechoslovak Arts Club, which previously met at the branch library, but needed more room, now meets at the settlement, and a group of artists is more closely identified with it as the Czechoslovak Arts Department. An Italian benefit society meets there, and a Hungarian-American athletic club uses the settlement gymnasium.

Besides forming these connections with societies organized by the immigrants themselves, the settlement has organized two new societies, one composed of Hungarians and the other of Italians. A special feature has been made of using abandoned saloons, somewhat remodeled, as the meeting places for these clubs. The settlement bears the expense of equipment and rental and provides a paid leader for each club. The club is expected to defray any other current expenses. It is also supposed to be self-governing within the limits of the supervision exercised by the settlement, particularly through the paid leader, but some very practical problems have already arisen in consequence of this division of authority. Both the clubs have shown considerable vigor. A Hungarian Free Lyceum, which originated independently of the settlement, now meets in the quarters of the Hungarian club.

The corresponding organization of Italians is known as the United Community Club. Its name conveys the suggestion that it is intended as the nucleus for uniting at least the Italian organizations in the neighborhood through one central body, and to that end it has co-operated actively with the settlement in a movement for a "Community House." Most of the funds for this project were obtained by the settlement from outside philanthropists, but local Italian organizations and neighborhood people have made substantial donations. A former residence has been bought and remodeled. The satisfactory control of this clubhouse presents a problem. The head worker of the settlement says that there will probably be three committees. One will be the "West Side Committee," representing the philanthropic element. Another will be the "House Council," representing the Italian organizations, and any others which use the clubhouse. Each of these will meet separately. Then there will be a joint "Executive Committee" representing the other two bodies. "This seems to everybody very democratic and businesslike," says the head worker, "but the details we have not worked out yet." How practicable this plan will prove, and what degree of local initiative can be developed under it, remains to be seen, but the experiment is interesting.[1]

---

[1] Since the foregoing account was written this Community House has been opened, substantially under the plan of organization above indicated. About a dozen Italian societies meet there, as do also two women's clubs of racially mixed membership. The tendency, in line with the basic principle of association along lines of race, appears to be toward a predominantly Italian constituency. Club and class work for children is carried on there by the settlement.

The settlement has co-operated with the local and state educational authorities and the naturalization officials in organizing two schools of citizenship, one for Bohemians and the other for Italians. Both meet in public-school buildings and both have a large enrollment. In working them up, the settlement enlisted the co-operation of individual leaders, organizations, and foreign-language newspapers in each group.

These connections have been made with each group separately, but the settlement hopes gradually to correlate its group activities. Informally, it is working toward this end through gatherings, such as plays and entertainments, to which all elements in the neighborhood are invited. English-speaking individuals of different races are brought together in common organizations, particularly in an active body called the Women's Civic League. An attempt to form more organic connections between the societies of the different racial groups, and between the immigrant and native elements, is being made through a community council which centers in the settlement. This, the head worker states, "is made up of representatives of organizations and delegates at large." Though it is as yet in an embryonic and uncertain state, it "has great possibilities."

RECIPROCITY ESSENTIAL

In the situation just described, however, there is a marked tendency toward centralization of local activities in the settlement, so far as concerns their ultimate control. This settlement has related immigrant organizations to itself and brought them under its own influence more than it has related itself to them and put itself under their influence as well. It has not become their recognized representative or given them a substantial part in the shaping of the settlement's general policy. This is not to say that such representativeness is not present in some degree, but simply that it is very minor as compared with the extension of the settlement's own "sphere of influence."

Such a one-sided relationship between the settlement and the neighborhood is inadequate as an expression of local democracy. There needs to be a copartnership, in which the voice of the neighborhood counts for at least as much as that of the settlement. Indeed, as the measure of neighborhood self-direction becomes greater the role of the settlement *per se* should become proportionately less. In any event, if democratic progress is to be made, the current of influence must flow from the neighborhood in as well as from the settlement out. The relationship must be one of reciprocity. There are other settlements which show more of a tendency to develop in this way.

### UNITY OUT OF VARIETY

Here is the story, briefly told by the head worker, of how one settlement in Cleveland is working to develop a unified neighborhood out of racial variety, and at the same time to identify itself with the natural interests of the different elements and give them an opportunity to shape its activities.

We tried at first the obvious "English class for foreign women," making a house-to-house canvass of the neighborhood. This was a failure, as we were entirely unknown to the neighbors at that time, and the sudden invitation to learn English was regarded with suspicion as part of a plan of the American government to "make soldiers of their husbands." Our actual English classes have not been very successful except for a few weeks when we were fortunate enough to have a remarkably gifted teacher. The secret of successful teaching of English obviously lies in the personality of the teacher. The men are too tired to make much effort themselves and require unusual stimulus.

A worker speaking Polish and Lithuanian succeeded in organizing a Lithuanian Women's Club, and the American Women's Club did what we felt to be the best kind of Americanization work, an exchange of hospitality. The Lithuanians were invited to the American Christmas celebration and gave in return a quaint Lithuanian Christmas party to the American Club. Other mixed parties followed, resulting in very pleasant relations between individuals, and the two groups combined in weekly meetings during the summer to knit for the Red Cross. The Americans were unwilling to admit the Lithuanian group as a whole, however, and it is only recently that I have been able to get them to admit a few as individual members. I hope ultimately to get the Lithuanian women all into the so-called American group, which is composed of Irish, German, Norwegian, Scotch, and English. This sort of thing, the actual mingling of the American of limited opportunities with the foreign born is, I believe, peculiarly the settlement's opportunity.

Our largest piece of Americanization work was the American Pageant we organized in the neighborhood in the spring of 1918. As there are in this district Poles, Lithuanians, Slovaks, and Rumanians besides the original Irish and German-American inhabitants, all more or less isolated from one another, we felt that the best way of amalgamating them was to make known to one another and to the general public the contribution of color and grace each had brought to America.

A neighborhood committee was organized to manage the affair and was composed of representatives of all the different nationalities. It met monthly or oftener from January to May, so the members had an opportunity of knowing one another and working together. I had suggested a "Pageant of Nations," or "Cosmopolitan," but the committee insisted that "American Pageant" was the proper name for it, for, as a Croatian said in halting English, "We are all Americans, whatever our homeland." I felt that the committee meetings in themselves were educational in working toward the overcoming of national prejudice, and the Pageant itself, with three hundred people taking part in the costumes and dances of six nationalities, was educational both to those taking part and to the native Americans who saw it.

Since last spring we have been the headquarters for the meetings of many national societies, both of men and of women, which is gradually bringing us into friendly relations with the members. It might be interesting to know that fourteen Lithuanian societies, one Polish-Lithuanian, two Polish, one Slovak, and one Jugo-Slav are meeting here either weekly or monthly, besides numerous Lithuanian mass meetings, lectures, and plays.

The neighborhood does not as yet participate in the general control of the house, but this spring we organized a house council for the management, in co-operation with the resident workers, of social and athletic affairs. It is composed of two delegates from each senior club and includes, therefore, besides young people of the second generation of German and Irish Americans, representatives from the Jugo-Slav Gymnastic League and the Polish Club, who, though foreign born and speaking very broken English, nevertheless take an active part and are on one or two committees.

It is getting people to work together that will finally solve the problem, I believe. I have been pleased recently to be asked by the Lithuanians to serve on the executive committee of their Red Cross, and wish there could be more reciprocal service of this kind.

### CO-OPERATIVE PARTNERSHIP

Two settlements have gone farther than any others, on the whole, in establishing co-operation and partnership between themselves and their neighborhoods.

In the case of one of these settlements situated in New York City, the fact which first impresses a visitor is that the workers, instead of living in a house by themselves, occupy individual apartments in a local tenement, along with families of the neighborhood. This means that they are brought into close contact with the daily life of their neighbors, and that they themselves are looked upon more as real neighbors, who share the common life.

Another co-operative feature is that although final decision as to policies rests with a board of trustees and funds are mainly supplied through philanthropy, the general regulation of club activities is left to a house council, composed of delegates from the organized groups within the settlement. This council assigns rooms for the different clubs, arranges general gatherings, decides upon standards of orderliness, administers any necessary discipline, and has the entire responsibility for collecting all club rentals.

"SHARE AND SHARE ALIKE"

Hudson Guild. New York, is unique among American settlements in that its workers live in a tenement with some of their Irish and Italian neighbors.

Though the head worker retains the power of veto, he has seldom used it, although on occasion the council has voted in opposition to his known views on certain subjects. Consequently the people who use the settlement feel that it is really theirs. They feel that they, and not the settlement workers, are running things.

A farm and summer camp are conducted in a similar co-operative way. A farm committee, composed of neighborhood people, advises with the general manager employed by the settlement, and regulates the summer camp, for which a portion of the ground is used. Every one who goes to the camp contributes a stipulated quota of farm labor, and several buildings have been erected largely by such voluntary work. Full co-operative ownership and management of the farm are the ultimate aim.

A still more definitely co-operative activity is a little grocery store, in which the settlement itself, some of its workers, and about a hundred and twenty neighborhood people figure as shareholders on an equal footing, with the practical object of knocking something off the high cost of living. Underlying and growing out of all this teamwork between the settlement and its neighbors is a manifest spirit of co-operation in a common purpose.

The settlement is cited as exemplifying both a general attitude and a definite working plan which are truly democratic. Yet there are limits to what this particular settlement has thus far accomplished. Though Italian immigrants are

235

a large and increasing element in the district, the settlement has not yet drawn them into its own activities or related itself to theirs in any substantial measure. Its membership consists largely of American-born people of Irish and German parentage. The Irish element, especially, has shown a disposition to keep things in its own hands, and is none too cordial toward the Italians. One gets the impression that the settlement constituency regards itself as a superior clique, and that consequently the settlement has developed intensively within its own membership rather than extensively by identifying itself with the interests of the neighborhood as a whole.

The second settlement is much like the one just described in its general attitude, but it is situated in Milwaukee in a neighborhood composed largely of foreign born, and has in some respects gone farther than the first in its application of democratic principles to the local situation.

The "Club and Camp Council" of this settlement, which has as its purpose "to control the various clubs in their relations to one another, to the house and to the community," and "to foster and manage Camp X——, and to administer its finances," is composed of two delegates from each of the settlement's clubs, with only one representative of the board of directors, and one of the settlement workers. This council, says the head worker, "actually runs" the clubs and the camp. For eleven years it has financed the latter entirely, raising funds sufficient to provide working capital and to cover a deficit of a thousand dollars or more each year. The council, the head worker further states, "has a number of foreign born on it," who have responsible and equal participation with the native born in the activities under its control.

This settlement has also gone beyond any other in neighborhood representation on its board of trustees. A number of other settlements, though only a small percentage of the entire number, include present or former residents of the neighborhood on their boards, but these individuals are usually picked by the board itself and form only a small contingent of its full membership. On the board of this settlement five of the fifteen members are neighborhood people. Furthermore, they are not selected by the other members, but are elected by the most important organizations connected with the settlement. Thus they are the actual representatives of these bodies.

The whole point of view of this settlement is distinctly outlooking. This is evidenced especially by the Men's Community Club, which was referred to before as probably the most remarkable settlement men's club now in existence, in that it has united in vigorous action some one hundred and fifty men of different races, of whom a third are of foreign birth and the rest of foreign parentage. The settlement has not attempted to keep this club a satellite moving within a prescribed settlement orbit. On the contrary, the club has concerned itself so widely and effectively with the civic affairs of its neighborhood and of the community that its influence is felt throughout the city.

## THE LESSONS OF EXPERIENCE

Certain general conclusions which point the way to larger success in the future may now be drawn from the settlement's experience with immigrant groups.

The most fundamental conclusion—to answer now a question which was raised in the preceding chapter—is that settlements have regarded and treated the immigrant as belonging to "the poor." This is not to say, be it repeated, that they have dispensed material alms, nor is there any quarrel with their contention that they are not, like charity societies, working among those elements of the population which are below the poverty line. But the facts which have now been presented show that in general, in their relation with the immigrant, settlements have conducted themselves *as though they were* ministering to "the poor" in the sense of "the depressed sections of society," and "those portions of the race which have little." They have dispensed immaterial alms, so to speak, and, notwithstanding the immigrant's demonstrated capacity for self-direction, have adopted toward him, in general, a policy of philanthropic paternalism. Consequently, the results which settlements have actually accomplished, when measured in terms of such democratic participation on the part of the immigrant adult as Americanization is here understood to mean, are not greatly impressive.

238

The facts also show that the settlement's inherent limitations, as pointed out in the preceding chapter—namely, outside boards, outside control of funds, shortage of permanent "settlers" of the right kind, institutionalism and physical immobility—are closely related, both as cause and effect, to the settlement's policy toward the immigrant, and constitute kindred obstacles which stand in the way of fully democratic achievement.

Notwithstanding these limitations, settlements have been able to enlist many children and young people of foreign parentage. The largely recreational motives held out have been sufficient to attract those who have not yet reached the responsibilities of adult self - dependence. But though, as may well be reiterated, such young people of foreign parentage constitute a distinct and serious Americanization problem in themselves, they are not the immigrant. In the case of immigrant adults, settlements have enrolled a considerable number of women in their activities. Dependence rather than self-assertion, and the monotony and drudgery of the household, have been the accepted lot of most women of foreign birth. They are willing to accept the settlement's kindly help, especially as it appeals to their instincts of motherhood, and offers them a little relief from their dull round of care. In its larger implications and possibilities, the settlement's work with immigrant women is of great importance.

It is in reaching the immigrant man and the larger group interests which are shaped by him that the settlement falls most decidedly short. The man is a self-reliant pioneer fighting his own way and that of his family. So intense is the struggle of life for him that only the most vital and practical motives are sufficient to move him. He is able to manage his own affairs. Therefore he resents what he considers a patronizing attitude on the settlement's part. He declines to come in merely as a beneficiary. He objects to what he believes is an attempt by the settlement to control the affairs and the destiny of his group. He instinctively feels and recoils from a certain implication of his own dependency in the usual settlement attitude—as expressed, for instance, in the statement that

The settlement has tried to make the adjustment between the *organizing classes* and the *hand workers*.[1]

There can be no question that the general principle of having neighborhood houses located in the midst of immigrant colonies is sound. But it is only as the settlement broadens its conception of its mission and as it breaks away from its usual limitations that it achieves substantial and durable results with the men. It is only as it gives the immigrant a voice in determining its activities and policies, only as it is represented before him by workers who impress him as strong and practical, only as it relates itself to the whole range of his interests, that the settlement enlists the co-operation of

[1] Albert J. Kennedy, assistant secretary, National Federation of Settlements, correspondence. Italics are supplied by the author to bring out the essential point of view.

the whole immigrant group. Even then it is impossible for the settlement, remaining fixed in one spot, fully to identify itself with mobile groups which as they get ahead move on to better localities. Under such conditions, the settlement is confronted with the alternatives of moving on with the group or of doing the best it can with each passing group while it abides. In either case, the degree to which it helps to Americanize the immigrant group will depend upon the degree to which it treats the immigrant not as an inferior or a beneficiary, but as a copartner.

Settlements are coming to realize that their whole conception and plan of operation need to be more fully democratized. This was apparent in much of the discussion at the meeting of the National Federation of Settlements, held in Philadelphia in 1919. Such realization was voiced especially in an address made by John L. Elliott, who was elected president of the Federation. Mr. Elliott is the head resident of Hudson Guild, New York, and one of the foremost settlement workers in the country.

Settlements have worked more *for* than *with* their neighbors [said Mr. Elliott]. They try to boss their neighbors too much. They talk too much about democracy and practice it too little. Real co-operation is what is most needed. In future the settlement must make more important appeals to people, not little petty appeals, but big ones. We have not had half enough faith in our neighbors and in their ability to do things for themselves. The organization of the community on the basis of its own powers is the fundamental task to which we must henceforth address ourselves.

# VIII

## CHURCH, SCHOOL, AND LIBRARY

SOME other American agencies, though they are not assumed to be as closely connected as the social settlement with the particular neighborhoods in which they are situated, are carrying on local activities and have a distinctly neighborhood character. Three of the most important of these are the church, the school, and the library. These three agencies will be discussed from the same point of view as that from which settlements have been considered. In what ways and to what extent do they interrelate themselves organically with immigrant neighborhoods? How far have they enlisted immigrant organizations in effective teamwork? In what measure do immigrant neighborhoods have a responsible share in the local activities of these agencies?

### THE CATHOLIC PLAN

The place of the immigrant's racial church in his neighborhood life has already been discussed. At this point reference is made to churches which are not identified with any one race and whose principal services are conducted in English.

As the proportion of Catholic immigrants is far greater than that of Protestants, the Catholic Church in America enrolls the foreign born in much greater numbers than do the various Protestant churches. There are more Catholic than Protestant churches in immigrant neighborhoods, and they are more closely related to their neighborhoods through their parish organization. However, English-speaking Catholic churches, even those located in the midst of Catholic immigrants, include comparatively few of them in their congregations. This is because the great mass of immigrants belong to racial churches of their own. Frequently the latter are not restricted to parish lines, because immigrants of their respective races are expected to concentrate in them.

The English-speaking Catholic churches are composed mainly of native-born Americans and English-speaking immigrants from the British Isles, chiefly the Irish. Some immigrants of other races become connected with them as they become accustomed to English as their common medium of speech. Of non-English-speaking immigrants it is usually only scattered individuals or little clusters who have no racial church of their own who attend an English-speaking church. The Catholic Church recognizes and encourages church affiliation on racial lines. These national or foreign-speaking Catholic churches, as they are called, are included within the general organization of the Catholic Church in America. It is apparent, therefore, that while the general organization brings all Catholic churches within one fold, the local English-speaking Catholic churches include comparatively few immigrants.

The connection with the church of such as are so included is usually confined to attending mass and to some personal contact with the priests through confession and otherwise. As a rule, they do not become an active part of the various religious, beneficial, charitable, or educational societies within the church. This is not to say that a considerable number of immigrants are not gradually absorbed into the general church body, and thus actively enlisted in its parish affairs. Such has been the result, especially in the case of immigrants who do not live within reach of a racial church.

If a substantial number of immigrants of the same race come to attend an English-speaking Catholic church, they are often organized separately with a priest speaking their own language. If the group continues to grow, it may develop into an entirely separate congregation with a church of its own. Here again the general policy is followed of recognizing differences of race and language and providing each racial group with the opportunity and responsibility of a church of its own.

The great help which this can be to a group of immigrants which has not yet reached full self-dependence is admirably exemplified by a Catholic church in Los Angeles which ministers especially to a large colony of Mexican immigrants. This church and the Catholic settlement previously mentioned work in close co-operation. The following quotation is taken from a letter written by the priest in charge of the services for Mexicans:

You ask which are the chief results in the direction of Americanizing the Mexicans. If I put aside the Christian activities of the settlement, whose final result is to make up a good American citizen, I don't see but the work of anti-Americanization here and there and everywhere. Because:

1. Mexicans are considered as of an inferior race.
2. They are undervalued in their work.
3. They are underpaid.
4. They are nicknamed.
5. The papers tell of the bad things they do, never the good things.
6. City Council seems not to care for their neighborhood, their dirty housing, their unsanitary environment, their house of prostitution, their immoral gatherings, their immoral literature, and their subversive papers and socialistic or anarchistic madcap leaders.
7. They resent the brutal treatment of their bosses, and the contempt wherewith they are looked upon almost everywhere. So they do not care a bit for this thing called "Americanization."

In particular, you want to know why we find it necessary to deal with Mexicans as a separate group. The Mexicans we deal with are of the lowest class, perfectly ignorant of English and unable to learn it. Furthermore, they are very poor, have very poor clothes, cannot pay pew rent in the church. So they feel ashamed to be mingled with better-off people, and yet their souls are as valuable as the others. So we have to give them all facilities to prompt them to come to church on Sundays. And they come. Six, seven, eight, and nine o'clock Masses are crowded with these poor Mexicans. Eleven-o'clock Mass is for English-speaking people. The attitude of the other members is one of sympathy toward them all. Sometimes they are a little too sensitive and run away from these our beloved Mexicans, because their appearance and their manners lack the amenities of an attractive countenance. But they come to us with filial confidence and call us padres. Thanks to God, there are many Americans who recognize the wrongs of the past and are to start the good work of Americanizing people in the most sympathetic and efficient manner.

### PROTESTANT ACTIVITIES

Protestant churches are at an obvious disadvantage in relation to immigrant neighborhoods, because most of these neighborhoods are of Catholic complexion. Nevertheless, there are a good many Protestant immigrants, and the plan followed by Protestant denominations in their case is somewhat like that of the Catholic Church, but does not place so much responsibility on each racial group. Many foreign-language Protestant churches, organized and supported by immigrant groups, are included in the general denominational organizations. At the same time, the different American denominations establish a great many mission churches for immigrants. Frequently their aim is, not to develop these as self-dependent and self-governing churches, but to continue them as dependent missions, meanwhile graduating some of the immigrants, but more especially their children, into the church by which the mission is supported.

Sometimes Protestant missions are opened in neighborhoods which are predominantly Catholic. Sometimes Catholic immigrants come to form the majority of the population in neighborhoods which were formerly composed of American Protestants. When such changes occur the Protestant churches in these neighborhoods usually sell the church building and re-establish themselves elsewhere. Sometimes, for sentimental reasons, they cling to their old church edifice, the members returning to it for the services. In this case, the church bears little relation to the neighborhood other than simply being there. Not infrequently, however, as its older members die or fall away, it tries to build up a local congregation, thus becoming virtually a mission.

Such Protestant missions usually appeal to the immigrant first through so-called institutional activities, patterned after those of the settlements. Through these activities and the Sunday school, they reach a good many children, some women and a few men, who are attracted by the "good time" and the educational opportunities. However, only a small proportion of adults who have been Catholics even nominally become permanently attached to the Protestant church. Recruits come mainly from the children as they grow up. As a rule, Protestant missions and churches are not organic factors in neighborhoods of Catholic immigrants.

When working among Protestant immigrants they can, of course, accomplish more. A striking example is that of a Presbyterian church situated in one of the most fashionable sections of New York City, and drawing its congregation chiefly from well-to-do and wealthy Americans. Not many years ago this element composed the whole surrounding district, but to-day, owing to a great shift of population, a large colony of Bohemian immigrants lies only a few blocks away. The Bohemians in America have in general broken away from the Catholicism which was forced upon them at home. Most of them have become freethinkers, but some are Protestants.

This particular church used to maintain a mission in the Bohemian colony, but it got such a good response and was so well impressed with the people that it gave up the mission and took its members into the main church. Some foreign-born Bohemians and a substantial number of the first native-born generation are now full members of this church, cordially welcomed by the others and sharing in church offices and responsibilities. A third of the children in the Sunday school are of Bohemian parentage. There is a special Bible class for non-English-speaking Bohemian women, with a Bohemian-speaking teacher, from which they graduate into the general women's groups. Very few of the fashionable and wealthy members have left because of this "immigrant invasion." The spirit which prevails is that of democratic religious fellowship.

### THE COMMUNITY CHURCH

Though the number of undenominational "community churches" is increasing, none was discovered which was succeeding in building up membership in immigrant neighborhoods. But the development of community service and of willingness to co-operate with one another and with other agencies and interests is marked in churches of all denominations. The national sweep of this new spirit through the majority of Protestant denominations is expressed in the broad social program of the Federal Council of the Churches of Christ in America and that of the Interchurch World Movement. As respects the Catholic Church, it has found similar expression in the National Catholic Welfare Council. While in strictly churchly functions each particular church is still restricted to its own congregation, in relation to neighborhood affairs the different churches show more and more willingness to co-operate with one another and with secular organizations. From the point of view of such broader interests, churches can no longer be set apart as purely "religious" bodies. They are interrelated with community activities.

### SCHOOL AND NEIGHBORHOOD

If you ask ten immigrants who have been in America long enough to rear families what American institution is most effective in making the immigrant part and parcel of American life, nine will reply "the public school."

This reply is significant in two respects. It means, first, that the immigrant is thinking not of himself, but of his children. He sees them go into the kindergarten as little Poles or Italians or Finns, babbling in the tongues of their parents, and at the end of half a dozen years or more he sees them emerge, looking, talking, thinking, and behaving generally like full-fledged "Americans." Vicariously, he sees himself at one with the life of America in this wonderful metamorphosis. No wonder that the public school looms so large in his mind. But his answer has a still deeper significance. It voices the adult immigrant's own hunger for education, his intuitive grasp of the fact that education is the foundation of progress. He craves education; but with his way to win and his family to rear, he cannot go to school as the children do. He must get what he can outside the classroom, in grown-up ways. He must find it in his daily life.

The initial volume in this series deals specifically with the "schooling" of the immigrant. But there are aspects of the school which lie outside its institutional routine, which pertain, so to speak, not to its "department of the interior," but to its relations with the surrounding immigrant neighborhood.

How far does the public school relate itself to the daily life of the adult immigrant? In what broader and more practical ways than those of the classroom does it become a real force in his life, uniting him, as well as his children, with America? How far does it make itself a constructive factor in the life of the whole group? To what extent does it enlist mothers and fathers, and the immigrant neighborhood as a whole, in mutual co-operation?

There are several definite channels through which these relationships may be established.

## KINDERGARTEN MOTHERS' CLUBS

The first one is that of the kindergarten mothers' club. Many schools have no kindergartens, and of those which have them, only a minority have mothers' clubs of this kind. Some schools, however, have successfully utilized the kindergarten as the stepping-stone to organized activities among immigrant women.

The mothers' contact with the kindergartner is usually more frequent and more informal than with the grade teacher. Often the mothers bring the little ones to the kindergarten and call for them. The kindergartner visits the mothers in their homes. She is able to help them individually in many ways, and every little while she arranges parties and meetings. Through such approaches she may organize a regular club, officered and increasingly directed by the mothers themselves, and having many possible lines of development.

A successful club of this sort in Boston, where such clubs have received special attention, is thus described by the kindergartner:

In this district a mothers' club of fifty to sixty members meets regularly once a month, with an attendance of about thirty-five usually, sometimes more. Care of children's eyes, teeth, and general health are some of the topics discussed, also each year there is a cooking demonstration of practical help to the mothers. The mothers hold all the offices of the club, as president, treasurer, etc., arrange the program each year with a little help, and elect their own officers at the annual meeting in May. They have contributed to a shoe fund in the school, Red Cross work, baby hygiene, and have done various kinds of sewing and knitting during the war. They have had several entertainments in the evening since the club was started in 1914. The money has always been given to something for the school. The mothers take part in the entertainments sometimes, some also act as ushers, and others sell home-made candy during the evening, contributed by the mothers.

In another instance the kindergarten reports a similar club of forty mothers:

Our mothers' club is well attended at our monthly meetings. We have had a great variety of subjects for discussion. A committee of mothers secures the speakers. Physicians, dietitians, nurses, educators have been among our speakers. Next year at the request of the mothers we plan to turn our attention to "our own community" and see what we can do for its betterment.

Once a year, in Boston, there is held a general meeting of all clubs as well as of kindergarten mothers who are not organized in clubs, and thus the different local groups are brought together in a broader community of interest. A systematic effort is made gradually to enroll these kindergarten mothers in English and citizenship classes. These are often taught by the kindergartner so that the informal spirit and relationship may be preserved in them, but sometimes it is more practicable to refer the mothers to the evening-school classes.

In the organization and continuance of mothers' classes in Americanization [states a school official] it is worthy of note that those women whose children have attended kindergarten are the most active. They are closely in touch with the school, understand its purposes, and, because of the mothers' meetings and home visiting, have confidence in the teacher.

## PARENTS' ASSOCIATIONS

Parents' and teachers' associations are the second channel through which the school may reach immigrant neighborhoods. Such associations sometimes grow naturally out of the kindergarten mothers' clubs.

If the school followed up the connections started by the kindergarten, and enlisted the co-operation of the children of all ages in reaching their parents [said a kindergartner], the position of the school in the neighborhood would be greatly strengthened and it could become in a true sense a neighborhood center.

Parents' associations are an attempt to organize neighborhood interest and participation in the school. Theoretically, they include fathers as well as mothers. Their immediate function is to maintain an alternating current between the school and the body of parents, and to promote mutual understanding and co-operation. It would be difficult to set limits to what such an association might ultimately accomplish by working along these comprehensive lines.

But such large possibilities are a long way from being realized, at least so far as immigrant neighborhoods are concerned. One of the chief reasons why there are not more parents' associations is to be found in the discouraging and managerial attitude of many school principals.

253

If a parents' association is really to amount to anything [many principals have said in substance], we must surrender something of our own prerogatives. Naturally, if we make this surrender we want something in return. The tendency of such associations is to "butt in" to our school affairs and to cause more bother than they're worth. So we're not very strong for them. Then, too, with the multitude of routine details of administration and the official red tape with which we are burdened, we simply haven't got the time.

To such general objections, principals of schools in immigrant neighborhoods often add the further one that "the parents are ignorant and don't speak much English, so of course we could not have an association here." Even when such associations are organized the principal usually keeps such a tight hold on them that they do not get very far on their own feet.

### SUCCESSFUL EXAMPLES

Nevertheless, instances of measurably successful parents' associations composed wholly or partly of immigrant women are sufficiently numerous to prove their practicability. One such association in Atlanta includes Jewish and Syrian women. The president for the past six years has been a kindly American woman, who says modestly that she "doesn't know much about parliamentary procedure, but enjoys people." She has taken special pains to draw in Jewish and Syrian women, and whenever possible to put them on committees. One practical difficulty which keeps immigrant women from joining the association in larger numbers is that they have to stay at home to take care of their children. Those who do join take a real interest. The association has helped the school in such ways as supplying medicine chests and buying books for special classes. During the war it co-operated with the local Red Cross auxiliary. It obtains funds by holding rummage sales and getting up entertainments. The president makes a special point of taking immigrant women to the meetings of a city-wide federation of the local associations.

Associations made up of immigrant women of different races are less frequently successful than those in which the members are of the same race. A school in a predominantly Italian neighborhood of Boston, for example, has an association with a membership of some three hundred Italian mothers, which has greatly strengthened the school in its local influence. The successful organization and growth of this association have been due largely to the fact that the school principal is of Italian parentage and able to talk to these women in their native tongue. The association is especially helpful in connection with entertainments and other special occasions.

It is a fact in accord with the educational zeal of the Jews that Jewish mothers are found in parents' associations in proportions exceeding other races. In many cases they are thus intermingled with native Americans. It is also true that the largest and most active associations composed mainly of immigrant women are those whose membership is Jewish. A school situated in the center of a solidly Jewish district in New York City has such an association of eight hundred members. It has co-operated in providing school luncheons, equipment for a dental clinic, and the like. Its most important contribution, however, has been helping to promote an evening community center at the school.

In many cities all the local associations are united in a central federation where each is represented by delegates. These central bodies, besides co-operating with the different associations in their local affairs, represent them in such general movements as those for increasing the pay of teachers and for providing better school equipment. During the war they were active in all the patriotic drives. At the meetings foreign-born delegates are brought into direct working relations with those of native birth. Each delegate carries back a report to her local, and the locals are represented on various special committees. What such a broadening of experience may mean to a foreign-born mother was simply expressed by one who said that it had been a "great thing" in her life, and was "like an education."

### PROBLEMS AND POSSIBILITIES

The future progress of these associations in immigrant neighborhoods appears to depend on several practical factors. Some representative of the school should be able to speak the native tongue or tongues of the immigrant people, and the meetings should be conducted largely, and at first almost wholly, in the native tongue. Otherwise only the English-speaking minority can be reached. In racially mixed neighborhoods a school might in the beginning organize the association in racial sections, on the plan of one of the settlement women's clubs mentioned in a previous chapter; or, following the lead of many labor unions, it might have one general organization, but arrange to have discussion and motions translated at the meetings into the different languages. This could be done by some of the women themselves. Of course, it would be a good deal of a "bother," but the results might justify the pains. Gradually, especially through the formation of English classes, the association could be put on an English-speaking basis.

Another essential to success is that the principal and teachers, while co-operating in every way, should keep hands off the actual direction, as far as possible leaving this to the parents themselves. The last and most vital requirement is that the association should have real powers and responsibilities and definite activities. One of its chief functions might well be that of promoting two other neighborhood extensions of the school which are now to be considered— namely, the evening school and the social center.

### SOCIALIZED EVENING SCHOOLS

The great majority of public evening-school classes in English and civics for adult immigrants, though they may start with a large enrollment, dwindle to small proportions or die out altogether. It is not the purpose of this volume to consider the strictly pedagogical reasons for this lack of success, but rather to indicate the fundamental failure to interrelate such classes with the neighborhood life of the immigrant group, and to cite some examples which point the way to success.

As a rule, evening-school classes in English and civics are nothing more than classes. They are purely instructional, and therefore handicapped in competing with recreation for the tired workman's leisure. The teachers do not—indeed, the latest pedagogical theory is that they should not —speak the native tongue of the pupils, nor is very much done to make the latter feel "at home." In short, the classes are not humanized and socialized.

How can this deficiency be met, and how can the evening school for immigrants be organized as a constructive neighborhood force?

First of all, classes for immigrants cannot be regarded as a strictly pedagogical problem of giving technically correct instruction in a technically correct way. The larger problem involved is that of interesting the immigrant in the life of America, and as far as possible interrelating him with that life through the class itself. This is a unique, practical, and essentially human problem, which must receive the most careful consideration. In place of merely a "class," there must be a group of coworkers. If pedagogics necessitate the instructor's confining himself to English, there should be added to the evening-school staff one or more "general assistants in humanity," speaking the language of the immigrant and preferably living in the neighborhood. Their function would be first to work up classes through neighborhood visiting, and then to serve as mutual friend and interpreter, outside the work of the classroom, between the immigrant pupils and the teacher. This in itself would do a good deal to make the evening school a neighborly affair.

## COMMUNITY NIGHT

There are two other ways in which evening schools may be linked with the neighborhood. One, which is rapidly coming into use, is the "community night." The school meets, for example, four evenings a week. The first three evenings are devoted to work in the classroom. The fourth, however, is given to a social get-together, and is usually open not only to the members of the classes, but to their friends, and, in fact, the whole neighborhood. Games, dancing, concerts, and entertainments, interspersed occasionally with addresses on subjects of interest —during the war, patriotic rallies—make up the program on these occasions. Sometimes paid "community workers" are employed to develop such programs, and volunteer assistants are enlisted.

The class members are supposed to be the hosts, and the others come as their guests. Though the degree to which this nominal relationship becomes real depends mainly on the attitude of the principal and teachers, it is certain that such community nights make the evening schools much more attractive and give them a more important place in the neighborhood. In racially mixed neighborhoods they also serve to bring immigrants of different races into personal contact and thus to encourage the formation of interracial neighborhood ties.

### EVENING SCHOOL COUNCILS

In New York City a more advanced step in socializing the evening schools has been taken. School councils, made up of delegates selected by each class, have been organized to run the community nights, in co-operation with the teachers and the community worker. In this particular city fifteen or more schools are supposed to be operating on this plan. But again, the genuineness of the thing depends on the attitude of the principal. Several principals said it was not practical to grant more than a limited amount of self-direction to such councils, because otherwise the pupils "would get the upper hand."

The most successful example which was found was a school the principal of which had helped to extend the initiative of the pupils without being afraid that they would do too much. In this case the first step which the principal took was to make a brief survey of the neighborhood, in order to get a line on its natural interests and

260

its actual needs. He then called a general meeting, with speakers in foreign languages, and made every effort to get suggestions from the people themselves. An Armenian group asked, for instance, for help in forming a chorus, and this was given. The school was then widely advertised in the neighborhood, especially through the foreign-language papers.

Immigrants of seventeen different races enrolled, and were formed into as many classes in English and civics. There were also six classes of native Americans on general subjects. When these classes had somewhat got their bearings they were all asked to elect one delegate each to the executive committee of a central "students' council." The classes also met together and elected general officers. The council holds a short meeting one evening a week, particularly to work out the community-night program, but also to discuss anything else in which the members may be interested. An orchestra, public-speaking classes, debating clubs, and dramatics have developed in this way. A Chinese young man, for instance, wrote a clever little sketch which was given on one of the community nights. A school newspaper was started, partly to help with the English, and became the "organ" of the whole group to which the different elements were eager to contribute.

The general testimony is that the community nights, and, still more, the students' councils, have greatly contributed to the attendance and success of the classes. They have humanized the school.

What is still more important, they have integrated the evening school with the neighborhood, and brought adult immigrants to share more actively in school and neighborhood affairs. Several of the principals expressed the conviction that such socialized evening schools were the best foundations for full-fledged school centers.

## SCHOOL CENTERS

School centers (often called community or social centers, which does not distinguish them from similar centers under other auspices) were widely hailed when they first appeared, as the means through which the school would relate itself in larger democratic ways with the surrounding community. and become truly the "people's house" and the "town meeting brought to life." But gradually these claims have abated as the facts of actual experience have emerged.

School centers situated in immigrant neighborhoods have been very successful in attracting the native-born young people, and in developing active and responsible participation on their part. They draw largely from those who have attended the grade school, and so form a sort of social continuation department for the school's alumni. But comparatively few have interested immigrant adults sufficiently to make the centers a direct, organic force among the foreign born. From this point of view, indeed, the evening schools with their community nights and students' councils are turning out better. The centers must be given the credit for suggesting some of the innovations which the socialized evening schools have adopted, but now the child seems in a fair way to outstrip its parent. In the evening school the adult immigrant is already there, and the classes in English and citizenship provide a very practical interest through which he may be held. The center has first to catch the immigrant, and then to hold him, and this it has not accomplished to any striking degree.

### SUCCESS WITH YOUNG PEOPLE

As regards young people, the results are good, and indirectly these results affect the foreign-born parents. So far as the directors of the centers have been willing to leave initiative and control to the young people, centers which are largely self-governing have grown up. Following lines of natural interest, the activities of these centers are chiefly recreational, consisting of athletics, dancing, social clubs, entertainments, and dramatics, with debating and forums as the more serious features.

Besides being self-governing, many centers, particularly those run during the summer months when schools are not in session, partially support themselves upon the proceeds of entertainments. This demonstration of the practicability of a considerable measure of local self-support is in itself a signal contribution. It means that the expansion of any one center's usefulness is not necessarily limited by the municipal funds available in the central treasury of the school department. It puts the center on a more self-dependent basis, as the people who use it also share in its support. Thus, in their work with young people, the centers are accumulating practical experience and working out practical methods which, with modifications and more vital appeals, may eventually help them to succeed with immigrant adults.

## OBSTACLES TO REACHING ADULTS

For their lack of success thus far in reaching foreign-born men and women there are many reasons. One is that the school buildings themselves are not attractive. They are regarded as places for children. Their interior equipment is inadequate. Most of the rooms are fitted with desks of children's size, which are uncomfortable for an adult and which cannot be moved out of the way. The paraphernalia of the classroom, visible everywhere, hardly suggest sociability. Otherwise the rooms are bare and dismal, and the only one suitable for good-sized meetings is the auditorium.

The red tape and restrictions imposed by the school authorities are discouraging. They usually require closing by half past ten, which is about the hour that an average meeting of immigrant men gets well under way. The comfort of smoking is not usually allowed. As a rule labor unions and political organizations, particularly if they are radical, are not as such permitted to use the buildings, and thus two of the basic interests of an immigrant neighborhood are barred out.

Worst of all, though here again the authorities sometimes take a broader view, all meetings must be conducted in English and the use of any foreign language is prohibited. This regulation automatically keeps out the very element that it is most important for the center to reach; namely—the adult non-English-speaking immigrant. Even in the case of those who have acquired enough English to squeeze in under the rules, it necessarily, as one man observed, "limits freedom of expression," just as the expression of Americans in a foreign country would be limited if they could conduct meetings only in the language of that country.

The attitude of the directors of the centers who are employed by the school department is often more managerial than co-operative, and as officials they lack close touch with the neighborhood. Many of the centers have "neighborhood committees," whose nominal function is to advise with the director concerning neighborhood affairs, while the center's council runs the routine activities within the school building. Actually these committees amount to very little. In few cases do they include immigrants who really represent their groups. Usually they are composed of the social workers of the district, who do not live there. In many instances, where centers have been started under private auspices and have had tolerably active committees of this kind, transfer to the school has resulted in conflict between the director and the committee, and either disrupted the latter altogether or reduced it to a nonentity which simply "follows the leader"—that is, the director. When the directors change, as they often do, one personal machine stops going and another has to be set up.

SOME BETTER RESULTS

Some centers have met with substantial success among adult immigrants because they have used co-operative methods.

In New York City, among a dozen centers which are typical of the best, several have developed active women's clubs which include a considerable proportion of foreign-born women, though mostly those who have been in America some years and represent the less "foreign" element in their neighborhoods. At several schools the International Ladies' Garment Workers' unions conduct so-called "unity centers" of their own, with classes in English and many other subjects. These consist chiefly of Jewish girls of foreign and native birth, and have a tremendous attendance, which is drawn only in part, however, from the immediate neighborhood.

Though in no case among this group of a dozen centers has a club of immigrant men been organized by the center itself, in several cases pre-

266

viously existing organizations formed by the men meet at the center and are more or less identified with it. In one instance a group of some fifty Ukrainian men and women asked the privilege of organizing classes of their own at the center in such subjects as arithmetic and history. Though they could not speak English, they were allowed to meet there and to carry on their classes with a teacher paid by themselves. In another case a group of Russian workmen asked the privilege of conducting classes in similar subjects in their native language. At first this request was refused, but later granted on condition that they include an English class, which they did. "What we want," said their leader, "is kindness, and to learn English in simple, everyday terms." They also had classes in arithmetic, applied geometry, physics, and chemistry, electrical and machine work, and automobile repairing. The men paid for the instruction themselves.

In another center a co-operative high-school course was conducted by a hundred and fifty young men and women, mostly Jewish. All were English-speaking, but all except twenty-odd were foreign born. These students wished to pass the State Regents' examination. They had found private commercial schools unsatisfactory, and objected to the public high schools because they took too long and did not give sufficient opportunity for self-expression. This school they organized, conducted, and financed entirely by themselves. They employed their own teachers and followed their own methods. Besides classes, they had general meetings for discussion.

Our school is really a force for Americanization in this neighborhood [said the chairman], because it is giving us the opportunity for self-expression and co-operation. We are gradually becoming Americans without losing our individuality or feeling we have anything to be ashamed of.

Another center, situated in the midst of an all-Jewish population, has a Jewish director who lives in the neighborhood and understands it. Here a branch of the Workmen's Circle, largely composed of Socialists, has organized a chorus and an orchestra and conducted an open forum. A group of Jewish labor unions for a time carried on some classes at this center, until official red tape, and especially the prohibition of foreign languages, alienated them. If it were not for such troublesome restrictions, the director states, the neighborhood would use the center much more. Settlements, he says, are regarded as philanthropic institutions, whereas the school "is supported by the people and belongs to the people." Another director, who frankly admitted that thus far he had not been able to reach adults, said he knew that he could do so if he could give the Socialists a responsible part in running the center. They were the most active element in the neighborhood, but the authorities would not permit this affiliation. He told of two forums which were carried on in the same center, one by a Socialist group and the other by Republican politicians. The latter ran motion pictures and general entertainments, attracted mostly women and children, and gradually died out. The other held vigorous and intelligent discussions, was largely attended by men, and grew stronger as it went along.

## EFFECTIVE METHODS

One of the most striking examples of a school that has become the generally accepted center of an immigrant neighborhood is a high school situated in a district of Chicago composed largely of Bohemians and Poles. Through the influence of Bohemian-American members of the school board, a fine new high school was built there. Besides classrooms with a pupil capacity of three thousand, the new building contained an auditorium seating several thousand, a dining room accommodating twelve hundred, a kitchen, and various other facilities. Up to the time of this building's completion the number of high-school pupils in the district was comparatively small. Skeptics said it would take fifty years to fill the school to capacity.

But a local committee was organized, the neighborhood was thoroughly canvassed, speakers addressed all the Bohemian and Polish organizations, the high-school chorus and orchestra gave concerts for them, and the foreign-language newspapers were enlisted to carry on a sustained campaign of publicity. As a result, in one year after the building was erected the regular high-school attendance increased from eight hundred to three thousand, while at times, including day and evening classes, clubs and various community groups, the school has been used by over six thousand people. Most of the big meetings of the Bohemian and Polish groups are held there. The people of the community regard it as their natural gathering place.

## UNIFYING THE SCHOOL

At present, responsibility for the public-school's administration is, as a rule, divided among several officials. The day school is under one principal; the evening school, if one is carried on in the same building, is under another principal; the social center, if there is one, is under a third official, usually called a director. Not only are there three separate officials, with three separate organizations, but co-operation between the three is often less evident than competition and friction.

In consequence, constructive co-ordination of these several neighborhood extensions of the school is exceptional. The parents' associations are not utilized, as they might be, to promote both the evening school and the center. The evening school in turn, with its ready-at-hand group of adult immigrants, is not used as a solid foundation for the center. The center goes its own way, without either the parents' association or the evening school, and reaches mainly native-born young people. Everyone concerned is tangled up in three different kinds of official red tape.

Manifestly such a situation involves lost

A COMMUNITY BANQUET IN CHICAGO

At the Harrison Technical High School Center. The banqueters included Americans of Bohemian, Polish, Scandinavian, Russian, and native birth; Protestants, Catholics, Jews, and free-thinkers; laborers, business men, teachers, and city officials.

motion, confusion, and a division of forces within the school which can hardly be expected to make for teamwork outside. If the school is to do its best constructive work in the neighborhood, it should be so organized that it will respond readily and without internal friction to neighborhood demands as they arise. This means that the whole school should be headed by one official, not three, with such specialized assisttants as are needed. This official would then be in a position to enlist maximum neighborhood co-operation at every point.

## PARK CENTERS

Park centers with activities similar to school centers have developed especially in Chicago. "Small parks" are widely distributed throughout the more congested districts of that city. These are equipped with athletic fields, swimming pools, playgrounds, and field houses. The field houses contain baths, gymnasiums, reading rooms, game rooms, rooms for club meetings, auditoriums, and branches of the public library. The extent to which these parks, and especially those which are situated in immigrant neighborhoods, are used by the children and young people is nothing less than wonderful. They swarm with youngsters.

In the adult immigrant life of their neighborhoods these parks in general play a larger part than do the public schools. Individual immigrants resort to them in great numbers. The mothers sit with their babies in the shade and visit with one another in little groups. The men smoke and chat on the benches. Both sexes make plenty of use of the shower baths. A great many societies of immigrant men and women hold their regular meetings in the field houses. Though the connection between these societies and the center does not as a rule extend beyond the former's meeting there, that is a good foundation upon which closer relations may gradually be built.

Musical and athletic societies, however, usually participate in the general contests and concerts, and sometimes, as in one case where nearly a dozen singing societies meet at the same park, joint committees are formed to arrange joint programs. Frequently adult groups take part in general patriotic celebrations and pageants, which are worked up by the center and in which co-operation on the part of the neighborhood is usually enlisted. In most instances the parks are situated in districts composed predominantly of one race, and so are used almost entirely by that race alone; or, if they are in mixed districts, the tendency is for the race which is in the majority to identify itself with the park, while the others use it comparatively little.

Like the schools, the park centers are hampered by official restrictions. For the most part, political organizations and labor unions are excluded from meeting there. One official, however, who has the general supervision of a group of parks, stands squarely for letting such groups in, so that the center may more fully represent the real interests of the neighborhood.

Participation of the neighborhood in the actual direction of these park centers, through councils like those of the school centers, is not favored by the majority of the park officials. They think, with many school principals, that such councils interfere with their own control and are more bother than they are worth. In most of the parks no such councils have developed. The official referred to above, however, is strongly in favor of councils of this kind, and has in the past developed several fairly successful ones, which have for one reason or another ceased to exist. One great obstacle to maintaining such councils has been the frequent change of park directors, due to civil-service transfers and promotions.

There is a regulation that, inasmuch as the parks are public agencies, no admission fees shall be charged for entertainments or events held there. This prevents the development of such partially self-supporting and self-governing centers as those previously mentioned in connection with the public schools. Otherwise, in Chicago and elsewhere, park centers have thus far worked out with results not so very different from those of school centers.

## THE BRANCH LIBRARY'S SUCCESS

Some librarians seem to be more concerned with the way their books look on the shelves, and with other matters of interior routine, than they are with the practical use to which the books are put. Others, while striving to augment the circulation of their books, have in mind only to increase the number of individual readers. Many, however, conceive the library as an organic part of the community, which may be not only a place of books, but a general center with a broadly educational motive. To a remarkable extent this conception of the library has been carried into practice. This statement applies especially to branch libraries, whose function it is to serve the people living immediately about them. In many instances branch libraries have related themselves very effectively with the life of immigrant neighborhoods. Though, like settlements, schools, and parks, they reach young people in largest numbers, considering their resources they have been more successful in enlisting foreign-born adults, not only individually, but in neighborhood groups.

This result appears to be due mainly to the libraries' recognition of two fundamental facts and their use of methods based on these facts. The first of these facts is that most of the immigrants who come to America want to read. They want to read about the life of their native land for the same reason that an American living abroad would want to read about the life of America, simply because it is the life they have known since childhood, and reading about it brings the comfort and sense of identity given by old familiar things. They want to read about America for just the opposite reason—because it is their new world of infinite promise, to which they want to adjust themselves as soon as they can.

The second and companion fact is that these immigrants cannot at first read any English, and if they come here as adults they scarcely ever master it sufficiently to read with real satisfaction. How many educated Americans, who are supposed to have learned some foreign language, do their customary reading in that language? What, then, could be expected of the average untutored immigrant? He not only prefers, he is practically compelled, to do most of his reading in his native tongue. This, indeed, is the main reason for the existence of the foreign-language press in America.

## INTELLIGENT APPROACH

The libraries which are most successful in reaching the immigrant shape their methods according to these fundamental facts. Their first step is to install a supply of books printed in the leading foreign languages of the neighborhood, some about the old country and some about America. The latter are not confined to lesson books in English and civics, for "lessons" are always forbidding, but include simple biographies of Washington and Lincoln and other great Americans whose names the immigrants know, and translations of rugged American fiction of a sort that grips the immigrant's imagination, such as *Uncle Tom's Cabin,* Cooper's Indian tales, and the like.

The immigrant groups themselves are consulted in selecting books, and as far as practicable their suggestions are followed. This is the first opportunity of enlisting the immigrant's interest and makes him consider himself a partner in the undertaking from the start. One instance is particularly significant. A library in New York situated near a Chinese colony called upon the more educated leaders of this colony to suggest Chinese books. There was a ready and grateful response. When the books came the librarians were unable to index them, so the co-operation of some Chinese students was enlisted. The result was that the Chinese used these books, came into friendly relations with the library, and later began to read books in English. In some instances immigrant organizations which formerly maintained libraries of their own have turned their books over to the public library.

The next step is to bring the special foreign-language collection, as well as books in simple English, to the attention of the immigrants. This is done in various and often ingenious ways. Library assistants who speak the languages of the neighborhood are practically indispensable. Lists of books and explanatory circulars are printed in the different languages, and are sent to the parents via the children, since the latter usually come to the library first. Through the co-operation of the principals, the children in the public schools are asked to take the same message home.

As far as time permits, the library workers visit parents themselves. In some cases they get lists of all newly arrived immigrants and call upon them, and also visit the English classes in evening schools to make the library facilities known. They arrange "old home" exhibits, to which the different races are invited to bring cherished mementos and handiwork of the old country, and they display the work of local artists. They offer the use of the library for meetings. They organize clubs among the young people who frequent the library, and get up plays and entertainments to which the parents are invited. They speak at the meetings of immigrant societies. They enlist the assistance of the foreign-language newspapers. They often secure substantial co-operation from the priests and ministers of immigrant churches, who usually do not suspect the public library of proselytizing. Through the foreign-language assistants especially every effort is made to make every immigrant who visits the library want to come again. Librarians emphasize this as the most vital touch of all.

### A CONVINCING DEMONSTRATION

A convincing demonstration of such co-operative methods was made by a librarian of Passaic, New Jersey, where the laboring element consisted mainly of Hungarian, Bohemian, Ger-

man, Italian, and Russian immigrants. A fund
of $5,000, with which to buy books, was contrib-
uted to the library by an interested citizen, with
the stipulation that the books should be those
which the working people wanted. In the
librarian's own words, here is what transpired:

When it became known that the library would buy books
in foreign languages the different nationalities which
formed that town's cosmopolitan population got together
and made a concerted appeal to the trustees for their own
books. I have with me one of these petitions. They all
breathed the same spirit, and were expressed in the same
halting English. But what pleased me most was the way
people of different interests had combined in an appeal for
their own nationality; singing societies, working with
church societies, gymnastic societies and benevolent insurance societies. Our societies did not end their usefulness with the petition, for, in reply to their request, we
told the people we would have to ask their assistance in
selecting the books. These different societies each selected
two members to represent them on a library committee,
and this was the case with every nationality, a committee
composed of two members from each society, and the
librarian as chairman. We soon found we could rely on
their advice, for they took great pride in showing us what
good things there were in their literatures. When we
actually purchased the books advised by the committee
the news spread like wildfire among their own people, so
we usually had a waiting list long before the books were
ready for circulation.

We are also indebted to them for their co-operation in
connection with public lectures carried on in the library.
The library was meeting all the expense of the free lectures
in English, but the foreigners thought it would not be right
to ask the trustees to spend money for lectures which only
appeal to foreign-speaking people, so if the library would
grant the use of the hall they would secure and pay the

lecturer, and see that the man and his subject were acceptable to the library. They also secured the audience, which in every case overflowed the hall. When the state tuberculosis committee had a campaign in the library the different nationalities had their evenings at which foreign doctors made their addresses, using the slides and material provided by the state. We had these addresses in eight foreign languages in addition to English, and all agreed that an Italian doctor held the audience better and got more discussion than anyone else during the campaign.[1]

## THE WHOLE STORY

The whole spirit and process of such organic Americanization as is possible through the medium of the library is expressed in the following description of the work of one of the branch libraries of New York City. This account is positively refreshing in its grasp of the necessity of sympathetic dealing with the immigrant. Its significance, moreover, is not confined to the library alone. With the library as its text, it represents the whole story of the immigrant's organic union with the life of America.

Take the developing work as it goes on at our Seward Park branch. We are in the very heart of the Jewish ghetto. Our foreign department is a large and important one, yet in no library is it less possible to limit the foreign work within a special division. The population in the ten blocks immediately surrounding the library is between 16,000 and 17,000. You could walk from one end of it to the other within five minutes. The people are nearly all of the one race, but the population shifts constantly as the newer immigrants come in and the older ones, having made a

---

[1] Miss J. Maud Campbell, *Library Journal*, November, 1913.

little money, move out and up. Most of these Jews
from Russia are orthodox believers, conservative, devout,
law-abiding. In their midst, however, is a radical group of
eager, tumultuous young thinkers, speakers, and writers.
They are, in great part, Socialists, atheists, anarchists—
the intellectuals of the East Side. They are striving, by
every means in their power, to undermine the conservatism
of their race. Radical and conservative newspapers exist
side by side. Orthodox and radical schools compete with
one another. Settlements there are, but their work is
largely physical and hardly touches the life of the adult
first generation. The inner life of the older folks, mostly
newcomers, is often intensely foreign. To talk of foreign
work as a phase or department in such a neighborhood is
surely folly. All the work of the library must be foreign,
if it is to be effective. Yet the library is and must remain
an aggressively American institution, or fail in its patriotic
and educational function. By what means shall such a
library become an integral part of the community and yet
carry efficiently its vital message of Americanism?

Accurate knowledge of the people, their backgrounds,
social and human, is the first essential. By this I mean an
intimate acquaintance on the part of every member of the
library staff with the history, traditions, and literature of
each nationality that the library expects to serve. The
results of such a knowledge must always be a sympathetic
understanding, untouched by sentimentality. The arti-
ficial missionary spirit so lauded in the past will die, as it
should, a natural death in the vigorous atmosphere of
wholesome friendliness. One cannot patronize and still
hope to be accepted as a friend.

Our non-Jewish library assistants at Seward Park are
studying Yiddish and Russian literature. We hear lectures
from rabbis, educators—including public-school teachers—
Jewish newspaper men, workers in our neighborhood. One
of our Jewish friends from the neighborhood said one day:
"You have the Jewish spirit in this room. We feel it,
we Jews! And yet you are Christians!" Yet these
studies would have little value if they were not guided

by those who are intimate with the traditions, sentiments, prejudices of the people.

One of the most important results of our growing knowledge is the avoidance of mistakes in approach which would nullify future work. We have patriots of the ardent Jewish type, prompt to enlist and face any hazard for their country's sake. But we are also among pacifists of a dozen sorts. Our work is not to refute, but to persuade. We do not urge war or even patriotism, but we show, if we can, what patriotism really is, what our nation stands for, and what it demands from patriots in order that the ideals of America may be realized.

Nor do we fear the organization which seems wholly devoted to Jewish interests. Even the Literary Forum, conducted in Yiddish, and addressed by the young and prominent literary men of Jewish New York, an organization which offers to all Jews an opportunity of hearing the best Yiddish literature read in the original, is yet doing a service to what we call Americanization. It is teaching what is true and beautiful, and such qualities, wherever found, will contribute to the coming America.

During the summer we have held meetings twice a week in the roof reading room at Seward Park. These have been addressed by speakers of power and sympathy on subjects vital to the American Jew. Some of the subjects were "American Government," "The United States and Its Laws," "Naturalization, Its Responsibilities," "The Jewish Congress," "The Jew in America," "The Russian Revolution," "The Help That the Public Library Is Giving the Immigrant Throughout the Country."

Even the mothers' club conducted in Yiddish has its current-topics discussion. The origin of this club is an example of those natural contacts whose importance I have emphasized. During a visit to the Educational Alliance, across the street from the library, an institution famous for its practical work among the Jews and successfully reaching both young and old, I was invited to speak at a mothers' meeting. As I did not know Yiddish, I sent the head of my foreign department. Being an enthusiastic librarian and eagerly interested in the intellectual progress of her own people, she invited the mothers to visit the library on their only free afternoon—Saturday. At first, very few came to this unknown American institution, but soon others joined them, and a club was formed to discuss current topics and to read Yiddish literature. The first subject discussed, and it was suggested by one of the mothers, was the Gary system of education. We soon made these Jewish mothers feel at home by giving them the opportunity to cultivate their Yiddish folk songs—incidentally, for our personal gain, we heard for the first time a new and beautiful form of music. This did more than anything else to assure the success of the club. Topics connected with health and the home are most popular, but these East Side mothers are keenly interested also in political and economic matters, as, for example, the high cost of living and food values. Unexpected results of this work with the mothers have been free and unsolicited publicity in the Yiddish press, and a request for the organization of a men's club along similar lines.

The most serious problem with which we are grappling is that of the gulf between the older and the younger generations. As one of our foreign assistants said to me, "It is not a problem; it is a tragedy." Moreover, it has issues which are far-reaching and evil, twisting and distorting our growing American civilization. Of this menace the librarian is forced to ask two questions: How is the library affected, if at all? What can the library do about it? Without doubt the library is affected. In the first place it is a grievous fact that the library is generally avoided by the foreign-born adult. In some very foreign neighborhoods it is still rare to see a person over forty within the library doors, while the place swarms with children, and is welcomed by the youth at once as a social center and a graduate school. When I first went to the Seward Park library I had a distinct sensation of living on the surface of the neighborhood. I saw the child life, the school life, much of the political and intellectual life. Yet I saw nothing of those realities of heart, home, and religion from which these children came to view with eager, half-comprehending eyes the new civilization existing side by side with that of their fathers and mothers. I felt that our library, like our civilization, was failing to meet the difficulty in a way which could bridge the gulf. Yet we have now fully proved the library's possibilities in work with the adult foreign born.

Two years ago, when dwindling funds made it necessary for us to change the closing hour of our reference room from 10 to 9 P.M., the Young Men's Club prepared a remonstrance and petition. For this they secured the support of more than fifty organizations of the neighborhood. They carried the matter to city hall. They forced us to change back; and happy we were to do it, for they helped secure the money to make the longer hours possible. The incident showed the widening possibilities of public support, if we could only make our service understanding, sympathetic, and efficient.[1]

## COMPOSITE NEIGHBORHOOD CENTERS

Branch libraries are included in the park centers of Chicago. There is also an effort in that city, as yet unsuccessful on account of conflicting official interests, to co-ordinate the activities of school centers and park centers. This could be done more readily if school buildings adjoined parks, with branch libraries as the third unit in the scheme. In some places in California the park director and some of the workers live at the park, and in the Northwest resident "teacherages" are being somewhat developed. The

[1] Ernestine Rose (Seward Park Branch, New York Public Library), *Bridging the Gulf*, pamphlet, Immigrant Publication Society, New York.

adoption of these ideas would bring park and school into more intimate, sympathetic, and accepted relationship with the neighborhood.

Under these conditions, with funds supplied through public taxation rather than philanthropy, but with opportunity for extensions of one sort or another through local self-support, a very complete and promising type of neighborhood center would be provided. Co-ordination and co-operation would take the place of duplication and competition. Such a general center, by utilizing the combined experience and resources of each of its component parts, with their more or less distinct appeals and functions, ought to succeed better than the school, the park, or the library has yet succeeded or can succeed alone, in making itself an adequate center of immigrant neighborhood life.

# IX

## OTHER AGENCIES
## AND THE NEIGHBORHOOD PRINCIPLE

Some kinds of agencies of course have a merely geographical connection with the neighborhood in which they are located. This is true, for example, in the case of a jail, insane asylum, or home for the aged. Other kinds of agencies, while not primarily identified with the neighborhood round about them, may have a functional relationship with it. A hospital, for instance, though its work is not as a rule confined to the immediate district, usually draws from that locality in larger proportions than from elsewhere, especially in its clinical and out-patient departments. Thereby it necessarily becomes a real factor in the neighborhood and may form co-operative ties. A third kind of agencies consists of those which, while conforming to a general type and applying a standardized program as between one locality and another, also include functions and relationships adapted to local neighborhood conditions. The most important of such agencies, which are of a semi-neighborhood character, have been discussed in the preceding chapter. A fourth group, of which the social settlement is the most familiar example, but which includes others not yet considered, is made up of agencies which are concerned primarily and specifically with the particular neighborhoods in which they are situated.

In addition to forming connecting links between the local neighborhood and themselves, such agencies as those suggested above are sometimes able to link their own neighborhoods up with the larger community. Reference has been made, for instance, to the way in which this is brought about through leagues of settlement clubs and federations of parents' associations. There are some agencies, however, such as charity organization societies, whose interests are community-wide, to begin with, but whose activities may take on more or less of a distinctly neighborhood character in different districts. In so far as they form organic local connections, agencies of this sort are in a better position to link the different neighborhoods with one another through the medium of a common central motive. Finally, there are some organizations which have as their definite purpose to promote community of interest and action on a basis of local neighborhood units.

There is involved here what may be called the *neighborhood principle*. It is proposed in the present chapter to inquire how far this principle has been recognized and applied in immigrant neighborhoods, by agencies, in addition to those previously discussed, that are carrying on local activities. There is no intention of suggesting that agencies chiefly concerned with a wider area should be controlled by their immediate neighborhoods; nor that these neighborhoods should even take part in determining activities which are not localized. The present query applies only to such activities as have to do, or might have to do, with the immediate neighborhood.

## POSSIBILITIES GENERALLY UNREALIZED

Agencies whose activities extend over a larger area, such as hospitals, museums, and various educational institutions, interrelate themselves hardly at all with the neighborhoods in which they are located. Indeed, they do not think in neighborhood terms. They lump everyone together. Some regard it as undesirable to form definite neighborhood connections. This attitude is typified in the following reply of the superintendent of one hospital in New York, who was asked whether he made any effort to enlist "co-operation on the part of organizations representing immigrant groups in the neighborhood."

This is an American institution, nonsectarian. We do not make any discrimination. We are receiving and treating in the hospital as well as in the dispensary department, patients of all nationalities and do not co-operate with any special nationality whatsoever. Societies have occasionally favored us with donations, but it is not our purpose to recognize any special nationality. All we insist upon is that persons applying here for treatment or advice must be ill. The indigent are treated free; those able to pay must do so. We are not working with co-operating committees, appointed at our request or on the initiative of other societies, and in a general way mind our own business, the execution of which more than occupies the full attention of everyone connected with the institution.

In the estimation of this official, the hospital's minding its own business precludes securing organized assistance from the neighborhood in matters which pertain to the neighborhood. In an earlier chapter mention was made of a Bohemian society called Lidumil, which is composed of delegates from practically all the organizations of a large Bohemian colony, and contributes regularly to half a dozen hospitals in that neighborhood. Reference was made also to donations from other immigrant bodies, and to the fact that most mutual insurance societies systematically visit their members who are ill in hospitals. In such cases the initiative is usually taken not by the hospital, but by the immigrants. It does not appear that such co-operation is preventing the hospitals concerned from minding their own business. Indeed, it might be assumed to help them in that laudable endeavor, so far as their business and the natural interests of the neighborhood have anything in common.

A hospital located near the one just mentioned has a different attitude and policy. In co-operation with a city-wide association devoted to maternity care, it carries on intensive home treatment of maternity cases in the locality. Further to relate itself to the neighborhood, it co-operates with other local American agencies, and with some immigrant societies. Several of its officials serve on a community council, which includes several immigrant leaders.

I would like to see the day [writes the superintendent] when the hospital, while maintaining its complete integrity as a hospital, could still at the same time play a much larger part as a social factor.

A privately endowed trade school, situated among immigrants who would be greatly benefited by the practical education it provides, writes that it has no local connections, and only a comparatively small number of pupils from the locality. Might not this school attract many more young people from the vicinity if it had a co-operating committee, representing immigrant organizations, who would bring its advantages more fully to the attention of their people? A society whose function it is to distribute flowers and fruit to the sick and poor likewise states that it has no local affiliations. Might not a local visiting committee supply, with the society's kindnesses in the vicinity, just the touch of neighborliness that makes such gifts most acceptable?

### NEIGHBORHOOD ASSOCIATIONS

Nominally, "neighborhood associations" are bodies organized by the residents of a given neighborhood, on their own motion, to put through a program of social betterment. Actually there are few such associations in immigrant communities which are thus constituted.

Such associations have been inspired largely by the example of social settlements. They are an attempt to apply settlement motives in a less institutional, and, in their own estimation at least, a broader and more democratic way. But they are composed chiefly of social workers and social-service agencies, who carry on their work in the neighborhood or are otherwise concerned with it, and funds are obtained in the main from philanthropic sources. Though they render considerable service to their neighborhoods, only in very minor degree do they enlist co-operation on the part of the neighborhood itself. Even when their nominal membership includes an appreciable number of actual residents, the latter are not usually real partners in the undertaking, and include very few men. So that, in fact, these associations are much less representative than their name would imply.

This estimate is confirmed by the opinion of neighborhood leaders. One association in New York City, for example, is unusually active and efficient, especially in matters of health and education, in a district composed of half a dozen fairly large racial groups and scatterings of others. But it is directed and supported from outside. Its services are appreciated by the different racial elements, but the latter do not feel that they have any part in it.

It's the same old story [said a leader of one group]. They come here and tell us they want our help and co-operation. They call a meeting, and when we suggest anything they don't pay the least attention to it. How can anyone Americanize a Slovak unless he understands him? No outside agency can do it unless it gets the fullest co-operation from the Slovaks themselves. The same is the case with the Poles and others.

Said another, representing another group:

The trouble with the association is that it works from without and not from within. There are plenty of people here that are capable of working for local improvements and that are doing so, in their way. I know the neighborhood from beginning to end, and was eager to help in the beginning, but they thought no one but a social worker could do the job. They talk a lot, but don't get you anywhere.

### GOOD INTENTIONS BUT POOR RESULTS

Among a number of associations which were observed, the one which comes nearest to being representative of the neighborhood is in a district of New York City composed partly of the foreign born and partly, at one end, of well-to-do and wealthy native Americans. It has about a thousand members. These are divided about equally into the "West Siders," who contribute most of the money, but do not take much further part, the "middle class," who do most of the work, and the "tenement-house" people, who pay only twenty-five cents a year and come in mostly as beneficiaries of the services rendered.

These services have a wide range, including local studies, an information bureau, health conferences and clinics, pageants, block parties and other social gatherings, educational classes, lectures and excursions, and co-operation with the schools in conducting several school centers. A number of blocks have been canvassed and an advisory council has been formed, chiefly of workers from various agencies in the district.

So far, so good. But there is little accurate knowledge of the many immigrant organizations of the district and little effort to enlist their co-operation in any permanent organic way. Rather, the social workers who largely control the association regard these organizations as barriers which should be broken down, and strive to bring people together regardless of race. In this they have not succeeded very well so far as the large foreign-born element is concerned. "I should say that a very small per cent of our members are foreigners," states the secretary, and "no non-English-speaking person has been attracted" to become a member of the advisory council.

### IMPROVEMENT ASSOCIATIONS DOING BETTER

More promising results are being obtained by "improvement associations." These associations are confined, as a rule, to the business and taxpaying elements of the district, and concern themselves more especially with physical rather than social improvements. Within these limits they are representative of the district, in that they originate there and are composed of and actually directed by residents. Though they have doubtless been influenced by the settlement idea, they are not of the settlement fold, like the neighborhood associations, nor are they usually allied with settlements. They have a different and more "practical" point of view. The same kind of organization is sometimes called a business men's or taxpayers' association, but the other title is commonly selected as likely to make a wider appeal. These associations take up such matters as better streets, garbage collection, and lighting, and proceed largely by bringing local pressure to bear on the municipal authorities. Thus they involve a considerable measure of local participation in larger civic affairs.

### A GOOD EXAMPLE

They fall short of being wholly representative in their lack of members among the laboring people. Sometimes, however, they include workingmen as well as business men. This is true in the case of one association in Paterson, New Jersey, whose district is made up partly of native-born Americans and partly of Italian and other immigrants, and which includes all these elements in a membership of about two hundred men. It sponsors general neighborhood celebrations on the Fourth of July, and carries out a program of public meetings and lectures. Every year it distributes throughout the neighborhood an attractive calendar containing its schedule of events. Once a year it holds a big dinner, open to the whole neighborhood, to which all the city and county officials are invited to speak. It has obtained many local improvements by arousing and expressing a real neighborhood demand for them. To facilitate this, it has developed a simple plan of block organization, with designated workers for each block.

One of its principal objects was to get a new public school for the neighborhood. For several years some of its members took turns in attending every meeting of the board of education. They did not make a nuisance of themselves, but just sat there, to let the board see that they were sticking on the job. In the end they got their school, and this in spite of the fact that the party in power at the time was not the one to which the majority of the voters in this neighborhood belonged.

The following statement by one of the leading members of the association shows what a vigorous, self-directing body it is. No "neighborhood association" has been discovered which could lay claim to any such record as this:

We organized about ten years ago with a few men and have grown to a present membership of one hundred and ninety. All members are in good standing, being required to pay ten cents per month for dues, no arrearages permitted over six months.

The association has been most active in securing necessary improvements, including better sidewalks, lights, sewer, and improved streets. Through lack of suitable quarters no attempt has been made for real community work, except for a few lectures, but this condition will be eliminated upon the completion of the new school now under construction in our neighborhood, said building to cost about $300,000. The school, and the new Park Bridge which has been assured, the latter to cost $150,000, are improvements obtained directly through the efforts of our association. A ladies' auxiliary has lately been formed for the purpose of co-operation with the association, especially as regards community work.

The foreign-born residents are taking a lively interest in the work of the association and number about 60 per cent of the membership, among which are manufacturers, business men, and mill workers, and representing half a dozen nationalities. All members of the association are made to feel their responsibility to the uplift of the community and cheerfully respond to any calls for service. No favoritism is shown, each member being accorded like consideration with the next.

The neighborhood and improvement associations of different localities are sometimes affiliated, respectively, in federations covering the city as a whole, with a central council composed of local delegates. In the case of improvement associations especially, such federations sometimes have a good deal of democratic vitality.

## COMMUNITY-WIDE AGENCIES

Among agencies which combine community-wide interests with local activities, charity societies and organizations of the type of the Y. M. C. A., the Y. W. C. A. and Community Service, Inc., will be considered here in their relations with immigrant neighborhoods.

## CHARITY ORGANIZATION SOCIETIES

A charity society is interested primarily in the individual "case"—that is, the person or family in need of material relief or other assistance. As "case work" increased in thoroughness, however, it became evident that the problem presented by any given family was vitally related to the conditions existing in the locality where the family lived; to such conditions, for instance, as housing, opportunities for employment, health facilities, and moral dangers. It also came to be generally recognized that racial characteristics must be taken into account. These considerations led in due time to the employment of visitors and secretaries who were expected to become familiar with their assigned districts. These workers found the co-operation of local people and agencies essential, and as a result regular district committees were organized. Such local committees, at first exceptional, have now become the rule. Usually the districts are so large that they include a number of neighborhoods, but the personnel of the committees is supposed to represent the smaller areas and the different racial groups.

Thus the neighborhood principle is in a measure recognized and applied. To a large extent, however, the local committees are composed of social workers who carry on their activities in the district, but do not live there. This is due partly to the society's reluctance to lay before actual residents cases involving their own neighbors, and a natural hesitance on the part of such residents to undertake even advisory responsibilities in such cases. But sometimes committees do include actual residents. In one such instance in an outlying steel district, composed mostly of immigrants, a committee thus constituted gradually developed so much go of its own that it became a separate society, locally supported.

## CO-OPERATION WITH IMMIGRANTS

A number of charity societies report that they have established co-operative relations with organizations of immigrants. Such co-operation usually comes about in one of two ways. Either a worker of the society discovers the immigrant society in connection with some "case" and asks its help, or the latter may come to the charity society to seek assistance for some one who needs more ample relief than the society itself can provide.

The following letter from the secretary of a charity society in Boston indicates the chief lines which such co-operation takes:

We have had excellent co-operation from organizations of immigrants in four ways.

First: In furnishing money for special families regardless of their respective nationalities.

Second: Advice on difficult family problems.

Third: Consecutive friendly visiting.

Fourth: Interpreting.

A second letter, from Providence, Rhode Island, brings out the mutuality of such assistance:

In the largest of the Italian quarters, the Italian benevolent society (Instituto Italiano di Beneficenze) and the Sons of Italy are helpful in an advisory service which is thorough and enlightening both to us and to our families.

These societies give relief, and although, generally speaking, it is given by the societies directly to the family, their lists are open to us and occasionally the relief is given by us and paid by them. The Society for Organizing Charity has received contributions from individuals in these societies interested in us through their co-operation with us, but the societies have not made contributions as such. The members of these societies consult us as freely as we do them in making plans for their families, and in every way we feel we are mutually helpful.

Two societies, the Cape Verdean Mutual Benefit and Christian Relief Association and the Portuguese Benefit Association, are actively interested in this society's work in another district, and the latter pays a pension through our office. One member of the Portuguese Benefit Association has acted as friendly visitor for us and substitute worker as well. The Swedish Benefit Society and the American Women's German Aid Society have co-operated less frequently because they have fewer cases, but their advice and sometimes their contributions have been given with cordial feeling on both sides.

A third letter, from Cleveland, is especially interesting as showing co-operation with a Polish Catholic organization:

The most outstanding instance of co-operation, both in an advisory way and financially, that we have had with organizations of foreign groups is with the Polish Ladies' Aid Society. Primarily this group was formed as a relief agency for the largest Polish Catholic church in town. However, its activities extended beyond its own parish. They have many times given us money for families and we work with them very closely on Polish problems in that district. This relationship has extended over a period of twelve years and too much cannot be said in appreciation of the service they have rendered in interpretation and friendly counsel as well as in a financial way.

Last year, through the Hungarian newspapers, we secured

the names of all Hungarian lodges and church organizations. A letter of appeal was written in Hungarian and sent out to these groups, many of whom in return made contributions to go for the benefit of Hungarian families under our care. We have had financial assistance for special families from a Bohemian group, a Swedish society, and a Slovak organization

A fourth letter, from the superintendent of a society in New York City, goes into further detail:

I got reports from our district secretaries on the following agencies for dealing with foreign born, with which we had good co-operation: St. George's Society, St. Andrew's Society, St. David's Society, French Benevolent Society, Netherland Benevolent Society, German Benevolent Society. These societies co-operate with us constantly, the co-operation consisting mainly, however, in furnishing relief along lines suggested by us.

Other societies with which we have had recent helpful co-operation are the Armenian Colonial Association, which, in addition to relief, has furnished interpreters and will send in Armenian-speaking doctors. The same is true of the Syrian Ladies' Aid in Brooklyn. The Pan-Hellenic Union in America has co-operated well on one case. The Friendly Sons of St. Patrick paid the fare of one man back to Ireland. Casa Maria helps with employment, shelter, and occasionally with relief for Latin Americans. The Serbian Relief Committee through special action of their committee gave a weekly allowance to a family living in this country, which was referred to them by our society. The Slavonic Home has helped us in finding work for a woman, and the Society for Italian Immigrants gives allowances and also tries to find work for people we refer, and has helped in getting citizen papers.

### Y. M. C. A. AND Y. W. C. A.

The Y. M. C. A. has a good many local branches. Their activities, however, consist mainly of classes, which, even in immigrant neighborhoods, enroll mostly native-born young people. English classes reach the foreign born, as do the gymnasiums, especially in the case of Greek young men. Special events, such as community sings and outdoor "movies," attract them in larger numbers. But, great as its services are in instruction and enjoyment, the Y. M. C. A. has established remarkably few organic relations with immigrant groups and has enlisted comparatively little co-operation on the part of such groups. It has not, as a rule, developed teamwork with immigrant organizations as some of the charity societies have done.

One reason for this, of course, is that the Y. M. C. A. is regarded by Catholics as a Protestant sectarian body. The Knights of Columbus, which is the corresponding Catholic organization, conducts similar activities. Besides the English-speaking branches of this body, which include a good many members of foreign parentage, there are foreign-speaking or racial branches situated in immigrant neighborhoods and composed mainly of the foreign born. Various other Catholic bodies are undertaking kindred activities. Among the Jews, the Young Men's Hebrew Association serves a similar purpose. The chief reason for lack of neighborhood relations, however, is that the Y. M. C. A. has developed more along institutional lines than in the direction of identifying itself with neighborhood interests outside its own walls. Recently, signs of a change of policy in this respect have begun to appear.

Until recently, the Y. W. C. A. also has been chiefly institutional, and has done little to reach foreign-born women. One extension during the last few years, however, is unusually promising. This is the International Institute of Foreign-born Women. Its aim is to reach immigrant women, and it is doing this through home visiting, English classes, and informal little clubs. The remarkably rapid headway which this new work has made appears to have two causes. One is the employment of foreign-speaking, and in many instances foreign-born, workers, who are able to get inside the immigrant groups. The other is that the work is conducted on an intensive neighborhood basis. Home visiting is the entering wedge. Gradually classes and clubs are formed among women who already know one another, or who live near one another. Often these groups meet, at least for a time, in the homes of the women themselves; otherwise they gather wherever is most convenient for them, in one of their own neighborhood centers, the public school, or the local quarters of the Institute. The social motive is put first, and English is left to come along when the women want it. Thus the lines of least resistance are followed.

It is hoped that these little groups will prove the nuclei for neighborhood organization of foreign-born women on a larger scale. What such future developments may be, and to what extent the immigrant women will have a responsible share in the activities, remain to be seen, but at any rate a good start has been made. The women's department of the National Catholic Welfare Council and the Council of Jewish Women are taking up similar work.

A new agency in the field is Community Service, Inc. This is the successor of War Camp Community Service, and it aims to develop permanently activities that center about "the use of leisure time." The whole organization is still in such a formative state, and its programs and policies appear to differ so much from one locality to another, that it is difficult to discuss it definitely. Thus far, many of its activities are directed from the respective city headquarters with little neighborhood participation beyond enjoyment of the recreation provided, Funds are supplied mainly by philanthropic donation.

Some activities have been put partly or wholly on a basis of local direction and support. In some instances, broad neighborhood connections have been formed through committees which include representatives of local organizations and delegates selected by "blocks." Wherever such local groups have developed, they bear a close resemblance to Community Councils, which will be considered below. As yet, Community Service has enrolled mainly native-born young people, and comparatively few foreign-born adults. Instead of trying to enlist the co-operation of local immigrant organizations, it has in some instances regarded racial lines as barriers to be broken down as speedily as possible. By community singing, pageants, dances, and mass gatherings, it has attempted to bring people together regardless of race, but it has not yet produced much durable organization comprising adults of different races.

Recent developments indicate, however, that, no doubt as a result of actual experience, this organization is beginning to recognize the larger possibilities of co-operating with immigrant groups in a natural and organic way.

### COMMUNITY COUNCILS

Of organizations which profess as their principal aim to organize the local neighborhood for more effective action in the larger community, so-called Community Councils probably have the most ambitious program.

Community councils, in a general sense not identified with any particular organization or propaganda, have doubtless existed in one form or another ever since human communities have existed. Through leaders and organizations, as well as directly, people living in communities have always taken counsel together with regard to community affairs. In this way more or less permanent and representative community councils have naturally and almost unconsciously come into being. Practically all the people of the world have evolved such councils while still in a primitive state. The Russian *mir* and *artel* are present-day survivals of primitive types.

Excellent historical precedent is found in America in the tribal councils of peace and war, which the American Indians had developed to a high degree of perfection long before America was discovered and invaded by European civilization. The Anglo-Saxon immigrants who settled in New England organized councils which they called "town meetings." Our present-day immigrants form their own local councils of various kinds almost as soon as they land in the New World, and later combine these in city, regional, and national federations. In fact, more or less complete councils may be observed on every hand. They are a spontaneous and irrepressible growth. In order to be a council, a given organization need not bear that name, nor does the name make a council.

The particular movement which has been promoted under the title of "Community Councils" during the past few years is new only in its label and its particular form, but it merits careful consideration because it gives special expression to a general social principle. These councils are an outgrowth of the Councils of National Defense, which were organized by the Administration during the war to help marshal the resources of the nation. Organization of the National Council of Defense was followed by the formation of state and in some cases of county, city, and district councils. Though this was an emergency organization from the top down, it was successful in promoting the various war drives, especially through the local district councils.

## NEIGHBORHOOD PRINCIPLE

The idea was then conceived of making this plan of organization permanent as a means of more effective community organization in time of peace. The name "Community Council" was given especially to the local unit, but the plan in view was to link these local councils together in city, county, state, and national bodies. The framework and to some extent the personnel of the Councils of National Defense were taken over, but with the avowed intention of gradually reversing the process by which they had been formed and organizing from the bottom up.

### THE FORM OF ORGANIZATION

Actually, however, no such closely knit fabric has resulted, nor has there been any complete reorganization on a more democratic basis. Almost all the Community Councils extant are confined to several widely separated states and to a comparatively small number of cities and localities within these states. The great majority of councils which have been "organized" have survived their birth in little more than name, and many others, after a short and feeble lease of life, have gradually died out. Some have lasted; in New York City the number appears to be increasing and a rather impressive city-wide organization has been developed. The form of organization shows some variations in different states and in different local councils, but in general it is as follows:

# AMERICA VIA THE NEIGHBORHOOD

The official bodies within a Community Council are two, the Governing Board, corresponding to an executive committee, and an Advisory Board.

The Governing Board shall be made up of not less than ten members who represent various parts of the district. The Governing Board shall be elected by the members of the Community Council. *It may be provisionally selected, and, if desired by those attending the first general meeting of the Community Council, be ratified by a two-thirds vote.*

The Advisory Board shall be made up of official representatives of organizations, be they religious, municipal, political, war, or any other, which operate in the district of the Community Council. . . . The Advisory Board shall recommend to the Governing Board the establishment of necessary committees. These committees shall act as functional committees to . . . co-operate with various Federal, city, and semiofficial agencies. On each of these committees local representatives of the appropriate municipal, Federal, and semiofficial bodies shall be included.

The Advisory Board as such may advise, but its most important function shall be to present to the Governing Board plans prepared by its committees. Upon approval of each plan by the Governing Board, the committee in question shall devise means for carrying out its programs. At the request of the chairman of the Governing Board the Advisory Board itself may take entire charge of a particular activity.

Committees may, for a particular time or purpose, increase the number of their members within or without the Advisory Board. *Members of the Governing Board shall be ex-officio members of all committees.*[1]

Two passages in this quotation have been italicized by the writer because they are particularly significant in connection with the way in

[1] *Constitution and By-laws,* Community Councils of National Defense in the City of New York, pamphlet.

which councils have actually been organized. The announced intention of the original promoters was to organize from the bottom up, but as a rule this intention has not been carried out. In most instances the governing boards have been hand picked from above and have remained practically the whole council. Ratification by any more generally representative local body has been largely nominal.

## THE USUAL PROCEDURE

The procedure in the case of a given city is briefly as follows: A central promoting office and staff, usually carried over from the National Defense organization, are maintained by philanthropic donations. There is a central city committee, composed mainly of philanthropic persons and social workers serving at the invitation of the inner body of promoters. This overhead organization precedes any local councils, is not supported by them, and does not in any definite way represent them. It divides the city into districts, into which, usually without waiting for a local request, it sends organizers.

These organizers, with the assistance of local social workers and others who are presumed to know the district, select a number of persons to make up a local governing board. Later a more or less general invitation to a district meeting is issued, and at this meeting the board thus "provisionally selected" is ratified and becomes thereafter practically the whole council. Though there are some exceptions, where a considerable number of the people of the district are active, the procedure outlined above is the usual one. Such being the case, it is not surprising that there are comparatively few councils which really represent their districts.

## NOT REACHING IMMIGRANTS

The deficiency of Community Councils is especially pronounced in immigrant neighborhoods. They seldom include representatives of local immigrant organizations or labor bodies, two vital interests of the .foreign born, and naturally they do not become an organic part of such neighborhoods.

Significant in this connection are the following quotations from "inside" reports of meetings held to organize local councils in a certain central state. The comments are made by an organizer from the state office. In one instance "union labor and foreign groups" were not invited, on the ground that the "scope of the council was not really understood" by them. The immigrants in this community were referred to as "accustomed to keeping together to the exclusion of Americans." The native Americans thus excluded, however, announced at the meeting from which they excluded the immigrants that they would promote a "program that will absorb them (*i.e.*, the immigrants) into the life of America"! In another case the meeting was confined to "philanthropic agencies,

churches, and organizations for war work."
"Union labor, fraternal bodies, benevolent associations and neighborhood groups among the
poor" were not invited. Again, "foreign societies, union labor, and the like" were "not
asked to attend," apparently because "they have
always remained by themselves." Similar comments are made in many other instances.

In some cases labor bodies were invited to
the meeting, responded, and stayed with the
councils for a time, but gradually lost interest
when they failed to do anything vital. One
labor delegate explained that his patience was
exhausted when the council declined to help
an industrial school for working girls, but voted
to incur the expense of doctoring a tree in the
local park for a rotten trunk.

## SIGNS OF DEMOCRACY

Though philanthropic support and control
from above have prevented local councils in general from taking root in their neighborhoods,
there are some indications that in spite of these
handicaps the movement is becoming more
democratic. In New York there is now a city-
wide "parliament" made up of delegates from
some fifty local councils, most of which, however,
are still rather inchoate. The sessions of this
body are interesting. Though immigrants and
laboring people are not much in evidence among
the delegates, who are mostly of the "middle
class," there is a substantial proportion of men,

and professional social workers are in the background. There is also a measure of healthy local kicking against some of the proposals which originate in the overhead central office.[1] The local councils, though mainly at the inspiration of the central office, have also begun to concern themselves with such practical matters as regulation of local markets, reducing the price of milk, indorsing collective bargaining, and encouraging consumers' co-operatives. A real effort has been made to enlist the co-operation of labor unions. A resolution indorsing the councils, which was prepared in their own central office, was submitted to the labor federation of the city and adopted by that body, and a small scattering of labor men are serving unofficially on central and local committees. All this is at least moving in the right direction.

In a few instances foreign-born men and women are included in the personnel of local councils, but no council has been found in an immigrant neighborhood in which the foreign born have an active and responsible part. The nearest approach to such a case, and an example, at any rate, of representative local organization, is a council in a small suburban community near Chicago where the people, though mainly native born, are of German, Jewish, and Swedish, as well as American, stock. There are few recent immigrants in this community and no labor unions.

The present council there grew out of a pre-

_____
[1] The central overhead office has been in part discontinued since the above account was written.

vious Council of National Defense. Each of some fifteen local bodies, including a Swedish church and a Jewish synagogue, elected delegates to form the governing committee. The Catholic Church is friendly and is unofficially represented by a layman. The general membership is about two hundred, and there are active committees on ways and means and publicity. To get the neighborhood "warmed up" a big Fourth of July celebration was held, for which two thousand dollars was raised in small amounts, entirely within the district. A women's auxiliary furnished a small neighborhood club, intended particularly for the returning soldiers. Plans are now under way for a more ample community building.

## THE SOCIAL UNIT

The National Social Unit Organization is promoting an experiment in community organization in Cincinnati which has been the subject of widespread publicity. Recently this organization entered into a sort of working partnership with the Community Councils of New York City. The Cincinnati experiment is not taken up here for the reason that it is being conducted in a district composed largely of the native born and does not enlist immigrants to any substantial extent. The program to be applied in New York is at this writing still undeveloped, but it will probably take the form of more detailed and intensive local organization in connection with

the Community Councils. The question pertinent to this study is whether this more intensive
plan will enlist foreign-born adults and organize
immigrant neighborhoods on a democratic basis.[1]

## LINKING NEIGHBORHOOD WITH COMMUNITY

Besides Community Councils there are a good
many other organizations which have as their
object to link the different parts of a city together
in one united community. Such movements
usually call themselves leagues or federations,
and are frequently initiated by chambers of
commerce or women's clubs. In most cases,
the neighborhoods to be federated are not represented in the organization itself. In other
words, the members are self-appointed bene-
factors, who have no intimate knowledge of the
conditions with which they attempt to deal. No
organic connections are established with immigrant groups, and the immigrants themselves
are not consulted or included in directing the
enterprise. Consequently, small tangible results
are produced. Mention will be confined to two
such undertakings which are exceptions to this
general rule.

## AN AMERICANIZATION LEAGUE

One is in Syracuse, New York, a city which has a
large immigrant population, including Italians,

[1] The New York partnership of councils and unit has been
discontinued since the above was written.

Poles, Jews, Syrians, Greeks, Ukrainians, Armenians, and Albanians. Several years ago an Americanization League was organized to bring these different racial groups fully into the life of the community. The formation and development of this organization are due largely to the persistence and personality of one man, a man of large vision and rare sympathy and common sense. The League began as an Americanization committee of the Chamber of Commerce, but it soon became so active and important that it was made an independent body, and officially indorsed by the municipality, which also provided from public funds the major part of its remarkably modest budget. The fact that the League operates as a semi-official body has greatly strengthened its appeal to the immigrants, especially the men.

Instead of trying to impose a ready-made program, the original committee took time at the outset to consult with leaders of the different immigrant groups in order to ascertain their real problems and interests. Then they organized a larger committee on which leaders of all these groups were invited to serve. This representative committee co-operated with each racial group in organizing local branches of the League. Since then the local branches have elected delegates to the general committee. Thus, though started from the outside in and from the top down, as soon as was humanly possible the League was reorganized from the inside out and from the bottom up. In other words, the immigrant groups were really taken into partnership.

Some of the local branches are now conducting social and educational meetings on their own responsibility. The central representative committee, besides encouraging and as far as necessary supervising the branch activities, carries out a general community program. This includes largely attended public meetings at which each racial group interprets its own background and culture. The League maintains a general information bureau for immigrants and a speakers' bureau which works both ways—that is, which not only supplies native Americans to speak before organizations of immigrants, but also English-speaking representatives of the different immigrant groups to speak before American audiences. The response of the immigrant elements was illustrated in a naturalization contest run by the Italian branch of the League. Thirty-eight Italian societies took part, and as a result four hundred applicants for first papers and three hundred for second papers were registered in two months.

After two or three years' experience with this group plan [states the president of the League], Syracuse is convinced that it is founded on sound pedagogical and political principles. The reservoir of new power has been discovered. First-hand knowledge of the problems has taken the place of speculation. The initiative of our foreign-born people has been awakened. Americanization has followed the natural lines of group feeling. A real partnership between foreign born and native born has been established. The foreign born have become an integral factor in the movement and the trust imposed in them has been fully justified. It is another manifestation of the incalculable power of democracy.

## NOTABLE RESULTS IN LIBERTY LOANS

The League outlined above is confined to one city. But a notable demonstration of the effectiveness of a nation-wide organization based on the same fundamental principle is provided by the foreign-language division of the Liberty Loans. Perhaps it is not generally realized that this division capitalized racial coherence, taking each immigrant group into responsible partnership with the government, and through the nation-wide organization of each group enlisting every neighborhood of that race.

Fatefully enough it was an American citizen of German parentage, Mr. Hans Rieg, who conceived the plan and who guided it to this extraordinary result, which America may well commit to memory. Of the total number of individual subscriptions, the proportion obtained through the foreign-language division far exceeded the proportion of people of foreign birth or parentage in the nation's total population. Here, in the words of the man who was chiefly responsible, is the story of how this historic result was accomplished:

## HOW IT WAS DONE

When borne in mind that the Bureau of Publicity of the Treasury Department was organized May 7, 1917, and the campaign for the First Liberty Loan opened but twelve days later, it can readily be seen that time was most valuable. Within a period of three days I proposed the formation of a distinct Foreign Language Division, form-ulated a plan of activity and organization, obtained the approval of W. G. McAdoo, then Secretary of the Treasury, was placed in charge of this division, and started operation May 11, 1917.

Just as scarce as time was working material. Everything had to be dug up. Authentic and up-to-date lists of publications printed in foreign languages, lists of national organizations of all kinds, with members of foreign birth or extraction, statistics on the various racial groups show-ing where they predominated, how engaged, their leaders, etc. — all this had to be gotten, and gotten quickly. I did the best that could be done under the many adverse conditions and showed noticeable results in behalf of the First Liberty Loan.

Immediately after the first campaign steps were taken to organize more thoroughly this specialization along national lines. I was authorized to make trips to the various Federal Reserve centers, in each of which a Foreign Language Division was established. In addresses before racial groups, editors and publishers of foreign-language publications, etc., I drove home the exigency of organized and undivided support of the government, so that by the time the Second Liberty Loan was announced a nation-wide, highly specialized campaign in its behalf could be conducted, *which reached into almost every nook and cranny inhabited by foreigners.*

A special poster was designed for distribution among the foreign born. Special publicity material was prepared. *Some twenty-odd thousand organizations, both civic and church, were directly appealed to, and racial group leaders, pastors, priests, and presidents of organizations were enlisted in the campaign.* All these agencies responded most will-ingly, and seemed to welcome the opportunity of doing something for their adopted country. As a consequence the response to this loan from that part of our population was amazing. Subscriptions came not only from least expected sources, but in most surprising manner, both as to numbers and amounts.

The interval between campaigns was used to extend and intensify the organization of the existing Foreign Language Divisions throughout the Federal Reserve Districts, to steadily enlarge the lists of organizations of all kinds with a membership of foreign extraction, to keep the interest alive and increase it wherever possible—preaching loyalty, patriotism, and 100-per-cent Americanism at all times.

So that by the time the campaign for the Third Liberty Loan was launched contact had been established with more than *forty thousand organizations* and with every foreign-language publication in the United States. *Racial group committees* in Foreign Language Divisions of Federal Reserve Districts ranged in number from *eighteen to thirty-seven*, representing as high as *forty-three distinct nationalities*, their number depending upon the number of their kind within the district. Steps also were taken to provide facilities to record and tabulate the support of these various nationalities to this loan. This was done for a double purpose—first, to establish rivalry and thereby stimulate production; and second, to enable the Treasury Department properly to give credit where credit was due.

The tabulations of the subscriptions to the Third Liberty Loan, as reported to the Foreign Language Division of the Federal Reserve Districts, show that thirty-eight nationalities produced \$741,437,000, or 17¾ per cent of the total amount subscribed, and 7,061,303 subscriptions, or 41½ per cent of the total number of subscriptions.[1]

The showing in behalf of the Fourth Liberty Loan was even more gratifying. Of the total amount of subscriptions, \$1,114,536,350, or 16 per cent, came from those of foreign birth or foreign parentage, and the number of individual subscriptions was 10,614,632, or 46½ per cent of the total number.[1] The response to the Victory Liberty Loan, in proportion, came up to past achievements.

---

[1] Persons of foreign birth or parentage form 33 per cent of the population.

# AMERICA VIA THE NEIGHBORHOOD

Backing up most intensified organization among all these various races and nationalities, the Foreign Language Division prepared publicity material in *thirty-four different languages.* Special posters, pamphlets, editorials, feature stories, news items, copy, and cuts for display advertisements, and personal appeals published *over the signatures of racial group leaders* were given national circulation. Take just one item; a lithographed reproduction in colors of the "Americans All" poster, which had been especially designed for that part of our population, was circulated to the number of seven million copies as an art supplement through the foreign-language press.

From all this it is obvious that this specialized work was not only necessary, but most productive. The actual result should be measured not only by the amount of dollars produced for governmental purposes, but also by their benefits to the foreign born, which, I believe, are much farther reaching. It tied him to this country by a new bond and laid the foundation of a deeper, better citizenship. A Liberty Bond has nothing in common with anarchy, atheism, and soap-box Bolshevikism.[1]

### THE LESSON FOR AMERICA

Could the lesson of how to utilize the neighborhood principle in uniting immigrant groups with the common life of America be taught more convincingly or on a grander scale than by this achievement? Instead of disregarding or overriding lines of race, these lines were recognized and accepted as the natural foundation upon which the loyalty and Americanism of each

[1] Hans Rieg, chief, Foreign Language Division, U. S. Treasury Department, Washington, D. C., Address at Eighth Annual Congress of the National Safety Council, Cleveland, Ohio, 1919. (Italics are used here to emphasize the neighborhood aspects of the campaign.)

immigrant group must be built. This lesson, and the eventual outworkings of this principle by which we have sought to test the various activities described, could not be expressed better than in Mr. Rieg's own words:

> The unification of each race among its own people and of dozens of races in a great movement like this got them acquainted, blotted out racial and religious differences, and merged all in Americanism. It has made every native born, the so-called Simon-pure American, who has come in touch with this ground swell of foreign-born Americanism, have a deeper confidence in the future of our country and a holier appreciation of the liberty and democracy which those who were born here take as a matter of course. From these many peoples from many climes, now all under one flag, we now have an outward and visible sign of that inward and spiritual Americanism which is evidenced by our country's motto, "E Pluribus Unum."[1]

\* \*  \* \* \* \*

To the question of what native American agencies are accomplishing in the Americanization of the immigrant through the medium of the neighborhood answer has now been given, so far as certain kinds of agencies are concerned. Though in outward form the agencies thus far considered have included a wide variety, from the point of view of their inner significance in Americanization they are all alike in one vital respect. In the main, the working relations between these agencies and the immigrant are those of benefactor and beneficiary, of director

---

[1] From Address quoted above.

and directed, and sometimes of patron and patronized. In other words, these are philanthropic or governmental agencies, in the initiative and control of which, as a rule, the immigrant neighborhood group has comparatively little part.

Though significant exceptions have been cited, the facts show that in general the results obtained by such agencies are meager, when measured in terms of immigrant adults effectively enlisted and immigrant organizations and groups organically related to community affairs.

For such failure it appears that there are two underlying reasons. In the first place, the appeals held out by these agencies are not as a rule sufficiently virile and practical to interest and grip immigrant adults, especially men. In the second place, these agencies do not take the immigrant into a real and responsible partnership, and thus provide an adequate medium for his interest, his initiative, and his ability. Though rendering many services, particularly to individuals, which are very good as far as they go, these agencies, as they are usually administered, fall short as working examples of democracy.

But these are the agencies which are commonly regarded as the chief reliance of Americanization. Does the fact that when weighed in the scale they are found wanting mean that there are no native American forces which are really enlisting the immigrant in vital democratic ways, and bringing not only exceptional individuals, but organizations and groups of immigrants, into the full current of American life? Perhaps in other quarters there are motives which strike deeper and movements which bulk larger in these respects.

# X

## LABOR UNIONS

THE initiation ritual of the American Federation of Labor, recently made public for the first time, contains the following pledge: "You also promise . . . never to discriminate against a fellow-worker on account of creed, color, or nationality." In so far as this pledge is fulfilled, the unions stand for equality of foreign born and native born in the fellowship of labor.

Union membership, both under the A. F. of L. and other labor organizations, is based upon occupation rather than locality. Specifically, therefore, the labor union is not a neighborhood organization, and in general it makes no formal recognition of the neighborhood in its activities. But as a matter of fact, a union draws its members largely from one locality, informal neighborhood relations grow out of union affiliations, and under certain conditions unions become closely identified with neighborhood life. In this study unions will be considered only in their distinctly neighborhood aspects, and their consequent effect upon the Americanization of the immigrant. Their industrial significance is discussed in another volume.

## ORGANIZATION BY RACE

Some unions are composed almost entirely of one race, and conduct their meetings in the language of that race. Such organization by race is contrary to the traditions and professed principles of the A. F. of L., and these unions form only a minor proportion of the total number in the United States. A concession to actual fact, they are regarded not as a permanent part of the union scheme, but as practical makeshifts to be eliminated when they cease to be necessary.

Except for German unions, formed in the earlier period when German immigration began, there were not many racial unions up to about 1880. Until then the unionized element among non-English-speaking immigrants was so small that it could be absorbed without separate organization. From that time on the rapid increase of immigrants in American industries, combined with the constant extension of the labor movement, made it practically impossible to combine the numerous races immediately in the same unions. In order to make it possible to reach the various immigrant groups, separate racial unions were sanctioned.

Such one-race unions often amount to neighborhood affairs, for the simple reason that most of their members live in one immigrant colony, and so have either known one another as neighbors before or form neighborhood relationships through the union. In their bearing on Americanization, however, unions of this sort differ in this essential respect from the organizations of the immigrants themselves, considered in earlier chapters; though their membership is composed of one race, they are integral units of an inclusive American organization.

Through them, the conception and ideals of this nation-wide organization are infused into the immigrant colony neighborhood, and the immigrant unit is bound up with the organization as a whole. Their delegates to the larger bodies keep the racial unions in close touch with the general movement, and the members, through free discussion in their own language, are able to become familiar with the issues involved.

Where there are a number of racial unions in the same immigrant colony, there is an increasing tendency for these to federate among themselves, while still maintaining separate relations with their respective craft organizations. In the case of the United Hebrew Trades, this plan has been carried out on a national scale.

An interesting example of how such federations work out is given by the large Bohemian colony of New York City. About a dozen Bohemian unions draw their membership mainly from this colony. These unions have a central council, in which all are represented, to act upon matters of common concern. Besides promoting union organization among the Bohemians, this council collects and distributes relief in connection with strikes and helps to settle strikes. For instance, in a local strike of butchers and bakers, in which both employees and employers were Bohemians, the council acted as mediator, and performed this function much more intelligently than outsiders could have done.

Each separate union, as for example the butchers, is an integral part of the general union organization of that craft, from the district up to the nation. Its representatives sit in the district council of the crafts with the representatives of similar unions of other races and of native Americans. The district is in turn represented in the craft council for the city, while this craft, along with others, is represented in the general labor federation of the city. The members of the local unions attend district and city meetings, and are elected as delegates to conventions. So it goes up the scale, through the larger territorial divisions, culminating in the country - wide organization. Thus, through the local Bohemian unions, the Bohemian neighborhood is tied up with the larger community, and ultimately with the nation.

### A UNIFYING FORCE

Beyond the temporary expediency of separate racial unions, the aim of the A. F. of L. is to unite individual workers of whatever race, both native and foreign born, in one and the same union. This is so much a matter of principle that some crafts make no concession from it. The United Mine Workers of America, for example, although probably including a greater racial variety than any other union organization in the country, sanctions no separate alignment by races, but stands squarely on a platform of one union for all.

Though in general racially mixed unions are not so distinctly neighborhood affairs as are unions of one race, they have something of a neighborhood character. Except where the membership of a particular craft is so limited, or the community itself is so small that a single union suffices to cover the whole city, each craft is organized in a number of local unions, each of which is districted. Though the membership is not rigidly confined to district lines, and frequently a man retains membership in the same union after he has moved elsewhere, a majority of the members live in the locality, and ordinarily those who move away are transferred to the unions in their new localities.

Though the districts are usually larger than single neighborhoods, they of course include in their membership men of the same craft who live in the same neighborhoods within the district, and thus the union serves as a common interest which tends to draw these men closer together as neighbors.

In a certain section of New York City, where a dozen or more races live near one another, a longshoremen's union is the only body which unites men of these diverse races in one organization.

We are meeting here on the basis of common understanding and good-fellowship [said one of the officials, himself of Irish extraction]. We understand one another, whatever the nationality, and we have about every nationality except Chinese and Japanese. Our meeting place is open all the time and the men come here at any time when waiting for work. They read and discuss everything. Card playing is not allowed, because this is business and there can't be any fooling around. I know many a boy who has learned English because he had something to say at our meetings and he wanted everybody to understand him. We do not compel immigrants to become citizens, but we always make a point of finding out whether they have taken out their papers. I have taken many a fellow up to naturalization court myself, and helped to put him through.

Union members of various crafts living in the same neighborhoods form there, though as yet potentially more than actually, a sort of labor brotherhood. They embody a certain morale, due to their training in organization, which, though difficult to trace, is from its very nature a vital factor in uniting different racial elements and in developing neighborhood solidarity.

One manifestation of this tendency is the increasing demand in neighborhoods which contain a considerable union element that the local stores sell goods bearing the union label. As this is urged by union members irrespective of craft, taken up by their families and made a subject of local discussion, it tends to become a general neighborhood motive. More impressive still is the leading part which union members have taken in the organization of local co-operative societies. In neighborhoods composed predominantly of laboring people, as are most of those where laborers and immigrants live, such solidarity of labor amounts to solidarity of the neighborhood.

## UNION TOWNS

While unions in general have the distinctly neighborhood aspects suggested above, there are certain conditions under which the union and the local community are far more closely identified. This is the case especially in mining towns—communities which center about mines of some kind.

The population of such towns is composed almost entirely of mine workers, practically all of whom belong to the local unions of the United Mine Workers of America. Sometimes a mining town is so small that it is virtually a single neighborhood. In that case there is usually only one union. Where the town is larger there are branch unions with a central council. In either circumstance, the unions, though specifically labor bodies, are neighborhood organizations as well. As a rule, they include a great variety of races. They therefore provide a demonstration *par excellence* of the effectiveness of the union as a racially uniting force.

Racially, most of the miners' unions are very much mixed. In some cases one race happens to be predominant, and naturally takes the lead. A majority of the leaders are native-born Americans. But throughout, in principle and in fact, members of the various races stand on an equal footing, share equally in the initiative and responsibility, and generally pull together. So successfully have the United Mine Workers met the problem of uniting different racial elements in common action that they are now recognized as one of the strongest union organizations in the country.

These unions also promote the use of English as the common tongue. Under the requirements of the national organization, no matter what the racial make-up of the union, all meetings are conducted officially in English, with translation into other languages as far as may be necessary. In this way most of the members learn to understand and speak English well enough for practical purposes. The unions do much to encourage naturalization. They conducted vigorous naturalization campaigns during the war, and were active in Liberty Loan and other drives.

## LABOR TEMPLES

Many of the local unions have built good-sized halls, in which they hold not only their regular business meetings, but also informal sociables, entertainments, and educational talks, which usually include the women and children. In some places small reading rooms and libraries have been started.

In Staunton and Collinsville, two small mining towns of southern Illinois, the unions have erected buildings, so-called labor temples, the equipment and present use of which suggest large future possibilities. In both cases these buildings, the larger of which, a fine three-story structure, cost $139,000, stand out as the central feature of the community. Both, in addition to various meeting rooms, contain theaters which are far more attractive and better equipped than the commercial theaters usually found in towns of this size.

The larger theater has a seating capacity of over thirteen hundred. The curtain is decorated with a symbolic scene painted by one of the local union members, and bears this inscription: "United we stand; divided we fall. We believe in organization—education—justice." One of the theaters is leased, on a profit-sharing basis, and the other is conducted by the union itself. Though thus far only ordinary movies and vaudeville have been given, at least the local demand is being met in this way, and the theaters are available for higher forms of entertainment, such as educational motion pictures and plays dealing with the labor interests, whenever the community desires it.

Both theaters, because they provide the largest seating capacity in their towns, are used by the schools for graduating exercises, by the war veterans' association, and for other public gatherings. Recently a bankers' convention met in one of them. A union official explained that the local bankers were "nice men," and were very kindly disposed toward the unions because the latter had large deposits in their banks. One

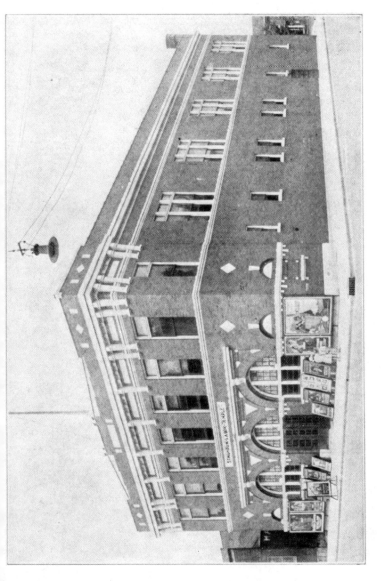

A LABOR TEMPLE AND THEATER

This building, erected by the labor unions of Staunton, Illinois, contains a well-equipped theater hall. Community gatherings of many kinds are held there.

of these labor temples donated space for the public library of the town, and maintains shower baths which are open to any one. The four miners' unions which own this building jointly are composed of native Americans, Italians, Lithuanians, and small proportions of other races. Both the Italians and Lithuanians take an active interest, and the former are especially well represented among the officers.

### A UNITED COMMUNITY

The fundamental effect which the fusion of different races in the union may have upon neighborhood and community life is revealed in the case of another mining town, Nanticoke, situated in the anthracite region of Pennsylvania. This town is larger, having a population of about 25,000.[1]

Welsh miners and other immigrants from the British Isles first settled there. Then came some Germans. The town remained small till about 1880, when a new and rapid influx began. This was mainly Slavic, though a substantial flow of English-speaking and German immigrants continued. To-day over 35 per cent of the townspeople are of foreign birth, about 50 per cent are of foreign parentage, and only the remaining 15 per cent are native born of native parents.

The most remarkable thing about this town

---

[1] Much of the information about Nanticoke has been supplied by Capt. Stanley P. Davies, who has made a special study of this community.

is its fine spirit of amity and co-operation. So
naturally and heartily are the different racial
elements living and working together that racial
lines seem hardly to exist. To be sure, each
racial group, as, for instance, the Poles, Slovaks,
or Lithuanians, has its own churches and societies, and there are two "colonies" in the
town's outskirts; but for the most part native
Americans and immigrants of the various races
are living as next-door neighbors. Even "Quality
Hill" has its foreign-born residents, who are
fully accepted in the inner circles.

The business men of the city represent practically all the racial stocks, and the employees of
the stores and banks run the whole racial gamut.
Nor is the town government in the hands of one
or a few groups. On the contrary, it represents
them all, not as the result of militant insistence
on the part of each group, but as a natural
outworking of the spirit which prevails. The
present burgess, for example, is an Englishman,
the tax collector a Pole, the president of the
board of health a Welshman, the executive
health officer a Lithuanian, one of the appraisers
a Slovak, another official an Irishman.

Through such interracial team play a fine
town has been built up. A handsome high
school, rising from the crest of a hill, is the most
conspicuous landmark. The local schools rank
among the best in the state. There are many
other substantial public and business buildings,
the streets in the main district are well paved, and
a majority of the townspeople own their homes.

# LABOR UNIONS

The Americanism of the community is manifest on every side. English is the common medium of speech. On patriotic holidays American flags are displayed everywhere. The response to the Liberty Loan, Red Cross, and other war drives was excellent. A thousand young men of the community rendered military service during the war, and two-thirds of these were of foreign parentage. The names of those who gave their lives, soon to be inscribed on a memorial tablet, epitomize the story of the union of many races in one all-American community.

How is this remarkable evolution to be accounted for?

In seeking the answer to this query, the writer talked with leading representatives of practically all the different elements in the town. First certain business men, leaders at the "top," were questioned.

"What organizations have you had which have brought the different races together?" "Well, we have had a sort of board of trade, but only intermittently, for a few years each time." "Why hasn't it continued?" "Oh, a few men were doing most of the work, and after a while they got tired."

Then the leading educators of the community were approached.

"You have had a community forum at the high school?" "Yes, we did have one, which was very successful for several years, but recently it hasn't been kept up." "Why not?" "Well, it wasn't really an organized affair, and a few men had to bear most of the burden. Then, too, some of the speakers, who were mostly outside men, said some unfortunate things which affected racial sensibilities. So it couldn't very well be maintained."

It seemed as if some strong solvent must have operated to bring the various elements so fully together. Eventually the right answer was found. It was the labor unions.

These unions were organized nearly twenty-five years ago, when the immigration to this mining town was reaching its height. At first, they were composed mainly of the native-born or English-speaking miners. But when a strike for better wages and hours was declared, in 1902, it became necessary to take in the Slavic and other foreign-speaking groups, in order to win. With men of many races standing shoulder to shoulder in the common cause, the unions were victorious, and the sense of common victory greatly furthered their solidarity from that time forth. To-day the unions include practically all the mine workers, and as the latter make up all but a small portion of the town's population, they come close to being an all-inclusive community organization.

There are nine local unions, each of which is virtually a neighborhood body, in that it draws its members from a small living district and holds its meetings in that vicinity. In each case the racial make-up of the union is as variegated as that of the neighborhood. Without exception, the meetings are conducted and the minutes kept in English, but such explanations as are necessary are made in other languages. Inquiry and assistance regarding naturalization are on the regular order of business at every meeting. Members are encouraged to attend evening classes at the public schools. In the Liberty Loans and other war drives the president of each local served as chairman of the drives for that district. It was stated that in addition to bonds purchased by the unions from their treasuries, some of which have accumulated surpluses of over $10,000, 95 per cent of the members bought bonds individually.

Local meetings are held weekly. In connection with each local there are joint grievance committees, and joint conciliation boards of miners and employees, for the adjustment of disputes. No strike has been necessary since 1902. Each local elects five members, who must be able to speak English, as its representatives on the central council, which meets every two weeks. Several times a year there are general meetings of all union members, at which addresses are made by officers of the national body, the United Mine Workers of America.

During the war a public welfare committee, representing all races, was organized by the central council to stimulate production. Great mass meetings were held, especially on holidays, such as Labor Day and John Mitchell Day, at which local and outside speakers explained in English and the different native tongues the nation's war-time needs. A movement to build a well-equipped labor temple, to serve as the center for the union activities of the community, is now under way.

By bringing men of all races together without discrimination in a united cause the unions have been the fundamental, constantly growing influence which has fused this community and its many elements in a common Americanism. As a young American banker who was born in the town and grew up there expressed it:

The part which the labor unions have had in bringing about the fine spirit of this community has been a big one.

### NEIGHBORHOOD UNIONS IN CITIES

Though it is in mining towns that unions acquire the strongest neighborhood character, there are also conditions in large cities under which the neighborhood aspect is strongly pronounced. This holds true wherever laborers live in concentrated communities in the immediate vicinity of the industrial plants where they are employed, a situation which is by no means uncommon.

The stockyard district of Chicago supplies an example. There, in an area approximately three miles square, live some 250,000 people, all of whom, except the tradespeople who serve local wants, are dependent upon work in the yards. The Poles are the largest group, then come Lithuanians, Bohemians, Slovaks, Negroes, and various others.

In the main, each group lives in a section of its own, with its own churches, societies, and activities; but the unions, under a new plan of organization, are doing wonders in bringing all these racial elements into a community of interest. Formerly, though different groups of workmen, such as the butchers, had unions of their own, the various crafts did not pull together, and in consequence were not able to accomplish much. The recent adoption of the so-called federated plan has resulted in effective team play.

There are between twenty-five and thirty local unions, ranging from those of ordinary laborers up to those of workmen whose tasks require the highest skill. The unions of so-called miscellaneous laborers are by far the largest, contain the greatest proportion of recent immigrants, and represent the rank and file of the people living in the district. There are eight of these—four of men and four of women. Though each of the other unions draws from the entire area, the laborers' unions are districted, and the membership of each is confined in the main to one local division. As a member moves from one locality to another, he is transferred from one union to another. This was done to regulate the size of the laborers' unions, but the effect is also to identify each union with a particular part of the whole district, and in so far to promote neighborhood unity.

Language difficulties are of course serious, but they are being overcome. While most of the skilled unions are English-speaking, all but two of the laborers' unions are Polish-speaking, a considerable majority of their members being recent Polish immigrants. The business of the meetings is translated from these major languages into as many others as is necessary.

This is a concession to the facts of the situation. In the earlier attempts to organize the yards the American leaders discountenanced the use of any language other than English, either at meetings or in printed propaganda. Consequently they failed to get or to hold the recent immigrants in sufficient proportions, and so lost their strikes and suffered disorganization. Profiting by experience, they now use the method which yields the best results.

Referring to the necessity of recognizing the many languages of the yards, for practical purposes, a labor leader said that at one union meeting a particularly important motion had to be put in seven languages before an intelligent vote could be taken, while on another occasion the substance of an address which he made was translated on the spot into thirteen languages.

Only English-speaking delegates may serve on the central council, through which all the unions in the yards are federated, and the meetings of this representative body are conducted solely in English. When mass meetings are held some of the addresses are always in English. Thus the use of English is gradually extended, and this purpose is kept constantly in view, as it is apparent to the leaders that a common language would greatly facilitate union activities.

The unions have grievance committees which take up with the employers complaints made by members. They also assist members or their families from their treasuries in cases of distress, and a substantial amount of relief is thus provided. One of the officials spoke of the difference in the attitude of the men in accepting such help and in taking assistance from the charity society.

> They feel that here the money comes from themselves and their fellow members, and that others may need the same kind of help sometime. It's all done together. It isn't a charitable hand-out, and no one looks down on a fellow when he happens to be in trouble.

Much attention has been given to naturalization, especially during the war, when batches of fifty to seventy-five men were taken to the court every week as declarants. The members are encouraged to attend English classes in the public schools.

Looking beyond these present activities, some of the leaders have in view a larger program of community betterment. This was outlined to the writer by the general organizer for the yards. This man was born in Poland, but came to America as a boy of twelve, and speaks English fluently. He is a big fellow, forceful rather than rough, simple, definite, and straightforward. One gets from him an impression of honesty of purpose combined with a large grasp of the situation. This man is generally recognized as having the complete confidence of the workers and as being a power among them.[1]

---

[1] John Kikulski; since the above was written he was killed by ruffians who have not been apprehended.

Just as soon as things quiet down a bit [he said] we're going to tackle the housing situation here. First we'll call the landlords together and we'll say to them: "Now it is up to you landlords to put in bathtubs and make repairs. If you do it, we'll see that your rent is increased a fair amount. If you don't, then we'll build houses ourselves and our competition will force you to do the right thing." After that we'll call in the tenants and tell them that it is only reasonable to pay enough more rent to cover actual improvements. I think we can work it out that way, by fairness on both sides.

Then as soon as possible we intend to organize co-operative stores, starting with one, but working toward having a number of them located in the different sections, with office quarters and meeting places overhead, where we can have sociable gatherings and educational work. In fact, we're going to take care of the whole situation. The unions represent the people of this district, and the people are going to do these things themselves.

In this same district there is a so-called community council, known as the Community Clearing House. It is supported by the packers. It is composed mostly of social workers. Although, as has been said, all but a small fraction of the population is made up of laborers and foreign-born immigrants, neither labor unions nor immigrant organizations are really represented on this council. On the other hand, the central council of the labor unions contains delegates of some seventeen different races. It represents the great mass of the people and their most vital interest—livelihood. Which of these two bodies is more truly a community council? There can be no doubt that the unions are by far the deepest, broadest, and strongest influence in developing interracial neighborhood relations and community consciousness among the people of the yards.

A substantial proportion of the total number of immigrants in the United States live in mining towns or in concentrated industrial communities similar to that of the stockyards. The results which labor unions accomplish under such conditions in uniting different races and foreign and native born may therefore be set down as an outstanding contribution to the cause of Americanization. These results are achieved through the fusion of union and neighborhood. But in view of the fact that under other conditions unions are not primarily or specifically neighborhood organizations, it may be asked whether they are likely to develop neighborhood activities more generally in the future.

Apparently the neighborhood motive has not yet entered consciously or definitely into the union movement as a whole. Union representatives whose views were sought have seldom expressed this motive themselves, though some of them have recognized it as a factor when it has been suggested. Thus far the separate crafts have figured most prominently in the union movement, and each craft has been concerned chiefly with its own organization and interests, often to the extent of disregarding the interests of other crafts. This has retarded the development of neighborhood solidarity of labor irrespective of craft.

Gradually the different crafts have come to recognize their interdependence, and a constantly increasing measure of union solidarity has resulted. This solidarity is now beginning to penetrate down to the neighborhood, at least in some small measure. This tendency is noticeable in connection with the less formal activities of unions, those having to do with recreation and education.

The so-called educational "shop meetings," now becoming common, are steps toward neighborhood coherence. These meetings bring together all the workers in a given shop or industrial plant, irrespective of the craft union to which they belong, and are educational in the sense that they discuss questions of common interest. They are usually held immediately after working hours, in a hall near the plant. Often a majority of the workers live in the vicinity, or at any rate it is usually those who do live near by that remain for these meetings. As a result the latter have a heightened consciousness of being neighbors, as well as of working in the same place.

Some unions, most of whose members live near a single plant or group of plants of the same kind, are developing sociable and educational activities in a local headquarters. This is more often true of unions which are composed largely of women, who naturally prefer to meet near their homes. The extensive educational

work of the International Ladies' Garment
Workers is carried on in local "Unity Centers."

Our activities [states an educational director of that
organization in New York City] were conducted in such
very large labor groups — and those so homogeneous in
racial composition, residence, habits, and customs—that
the neighborhood group was the industrial group for the
most part.

In one case in Chicago a joint board of five
garment workers' unions is planning a series of
family meetings in different localities, for sociability combined with informal educational talks.
It is significant that women union leaders, as
a rule, take more interest in such activities than
men, and that the neighborhood motive is
most in evidence in activities which have something of a family character.  In other words,
as unions have occasion to reach not simply
their individual members, but the laboring home,
the whole labor constituency, they show a
greater tendency to relate themselves to the
neighborhood.

If the educational activities are finally conducted for all
trade unions under the same direction [states the same
official quoted above], the neighborhood group in working-
class neighborhoods is practically coterminous with the
industrial group.

How far this tendency will go among unions
in general remains to be seen, but it is probable
that as unions gain their ends sufficiently to
advance beyond the stage of incessant struggle,
and have more time and resources to devote to

recreational and cultural activities, they will find it both practicable and desirable to utilize the natural neighborhood unit.

THE UNION'S LIMITS

The adequacy of labor unions as a neighborhood and community force is sometimes combated on the ground that, in their very essence, they are not unifying, but divisive; that they cannot represent the whole community, since they are limited to one "class" or "interest"— namely, labor.

According to estimates based upon the figures of the United States Census, approximately two-thirds of the people of America gainfully employed belong to the so-called laboring or wage-earning class. In the case of immigrants the percentage is still higher. In many neighborhoods and communities "labor" comprises approximately 100 per cent of the residents. Under these circumstances, while labor unions may be "class" organizations, the class to which they pertain practically includes the whole neighborhood.

When unions are further decried as class affairs because they are organized and supported by laboring people, and represent their interests, labor counters by asking why the various philanthropic agencies discussed in previous chapters may not be called class affairs, too, in that they are organized either by the capitalist and leisure class or by persons employed by them, are sup-

LABOR'S SELF-EDUCATION

One of the "Unity Center" groups of the International Ladies' Garment Workers of New York City.

ported by this same class, and represent its
interests, even though these interests be philanthropic. It is for this reason, says labor, that
it is not enthusiastic about affiliating with such
agencies, and is not much influenced by them.
This attitude, usually taking the form of indifference, is sometimes expressed vehemently, as
when "Mother" Jones, in addressing a mass
meeting of steel workers on strike at Gary,
Indiana, shouted, according to newspaper reports:

We don t want any welfare workers, sympathy, Y. M.
C. A.'s, churches, and charity brigades. These institutions
are built on our backs. We want justice.

Furthermore, "labor" appears to be a constantly broadening term. Now that musicians,
clerks, and teachers are organizing unions affiliated with the A. F. of L. the term can no longer
be restricted to those who labor with their hands.
The logical outcome of this broadening process,
indeed, would be to include in "labor" all
workers whose income consists of payment for
service rendered. Whether practical developments will ever reach this culmination cannot
be predicted, but it is evident that labor's own
conception of "labor" is a broader one than it
used to be, or than is admitted by those who
view the labor movement narrowly.

When all is said it remains true that the unions
draw a line between the great bulk of the country's population ranged as "labor" on the one
side, of which the unions or "organized labor"
are the most effective representative, and the

small minority set over as "capital" on the other side. But it is because of this very element of struggle that the labor movement grips the workers as strongly as it does. Struggles of one sort or another have always been necessary to arouse the mass of the people, just as the World War aroused so many subject nations to strike at last for their freedom.

So the labor-union movement has deeply aroused the working people of America. It has moved them to action, to self-directing participation in American life, on a more extensive scale than any other single influence. It has been a factor sufficiently powerful to unite different races, and native Americans and immigrants, in common interest. It has worked to Americanize the immigrant by enabling him to take part on an equal footing in a great and vital American movement.

# XI

## CO-OPERATIVES

Is there anything which goes beyond the labor union as a medium through which, under existing conditions, Americans of all classes and races may come together and work together on a common basis?

The answer to this question is suggested by the following statement, made by one of the strongest union leaders in the central part of the country:

I should never have remained in the union movement until now [said this man] had it not been for my belief that it would eventually lead into co-operation. "Why are you not satisfied with the unions in themselves?" he was asked. "Simply for this reason," he replied, "the more labor organizes the more capital organizes—and the fight goes on, with no end in sight. But the co-operative movement offers a way out."

Co-operation, or at any rate consumers' co-operation, is in its very nature involved with the neighborhood. Any co-operative scheme, no matter how large or elaborate, must rest upon the neighborhood unit as its foundation. Why this is so will be apparent from a brief explanation of the subject. Although the main features of co-operation were mentioned in describing the group activities of the Finns, it is advisable to go into the matter more fully, especially since the co-operative movement is not very generally understood by native Americans.

### WHAT CO-OPERATION IS

Co-operation, technically speaking, is the union of a number of people, in the capacity of either consumers or producers, in an undertaking in which each has equal rights and equal voice. Though this union may be for any object in any field of activity, and has in fact extended into many fields, the immediate motive is, as a rule, economic, and the effect is to substitute co-operation for competition.

People may co-operate as producers, in order to produce and sell something, or as consumers, in order to buy. The purpose of producers' co-operation is to secure greater returns to its workers, that of consumers' co-operation is to reduce the net cost of necessities. Consumers may co-operate for production; both in theory and practice, however, consumers' co-operation in production follows and serves their co-operation in distribution.

That is, the co-operators first organize a store, in order to buy what they need in the general market at a saving to themselves. The conduct of a store initiates them into the business of supplying staples and the art of successful collective action. In order to effect a still greater saving, they may then enter into manufacturing, agriculture, mining, or transportation, and thus produce a supply of their own. The operatives in these industries may not be co-operators themselves, but simply employees of the co-operators. This is not producers' co-operation, therefore, but the co-operation of consumers for production.

There are variations of detail in working out the form of organization, but in general the procedure follows the so-called Rochdale plan. Shares are sold at a price ranging usually from five dollars to fifty dollars, low enough to be within the reach of people of small means. The number of shares which one person may buy is usually limited to five. Voting power is distributed not one vote to each share, as in stock companies, but one vote to each person, regardless of the number of shares he owns.

The shareholders elect a board of directors and, as a rule, a treasurer and a secretary for a specified term, usually a year. The board of directors, as the executive body, elects a president to preside at all meetings, and a manager to have charge of the practical details of the undertaking. The manager is immediately responsible to the board, and the board is fully responsible to the shareholders. Regular and special meetings of the shareholders are held frequently, and if any of them is dissatisfied with the conduct of affairs, he may readily present his grievance for discussion and action.

The unit of consumers' co-operation is the

retail store, conducted and patronized by the co-operators. At these stores goods are sold at current prices, but the profits, which in a private store go to the proprietor, are periodically distributed among all the co-operators, in the form of rebates or dividends paid to each shareholder in proportion to the amount of his purchases. A similar, but as a rule a smaller, rebate is made to customers other than the co-operators, in order to get their patronage and arouse their interest. Before distributing the profits, and as a cost of operation, interest at a fixed rate is paid to the co-operators on their original investment in shares.

### HOW THE NEIGHBORHOOD COMES IN

Co-operation for production, whether of producers or consumers, need not have any neighborhood character, because it may be carried on at industrial plants by workers coming from various localities. But consumers' distributive co-operation, which is the most prevalent form, is necessarily developed in close relation with the neighborhood. The co-operative retail store, in order to be successful, must be near to its customers, so that the saving it offers will not be offset by car fares, loss of time or inconvenience. If a main store is located in the general shopping district, there are usually neighborhood branches, as in the case of the Finnish co-operative at Fitchburg. It is here that the neighborhood enters in.

As a rule it is people who are already neighbors that come together to establish such a co-operative store. Indeed, it is highly desirable that there should be a previous close relationship making for solidarity. Once organized, the store itself furthers the neighborhood motive and tends to become an integral part of the neighborhood's organization. This being true of the retail store, the co-operative unit, it follows that the whole superstructure of co-operation rests on a neighborhood foundation.

### SPREAD OF MOVEMENT IN EUROPE

The present-day co-operative movement had its beginning in Rochdale, England, in 1844, when a group of twenty-eight weavers established a store to supply some of their wants. At first this little store carried only four commodities, kept open only in the evening, and was served by volunteers. The form of organization which they adopted is the one outlined above, which has come down in history as the standard "Rochdale plan." From that humble inception a great co-operative system has spread all over Europe. In different countries it has taken on somewhat different aspects and excelled at different points.

Along strictly economic lines its most impressive development has taken place in the British Isles. There to-day some fifteen hundred co-operative societies include as their constituents fully a third of the total population, and their rate of growth has been five times faster than that of the population as a whole. The saving to their members, through profits distributed as rebates, amounts to a million dollars a year.

This co-operative system includes, besides retail stores, a central wholesale, with many branches; thirteen great warehouses; eight flour mills, the largest in Great Britain; sixty-five factories of various kinds; many farms and dairies; extensive wheat lands in Canada, tea plantations in Ceylon, palm groves in Africa, and vineyards in Spain; coal mines; banking departments whose combined business ranks next to that of the Bank of England; insurance departments which write one-half of the total life and accident insurance of Great Britain; and printing plants adequate to the demands. The total products are five times greater than those of all the private manufacturers included in the Manufacturers' Association. The British co-operatives maintain their own fleet, and engage in international trade with the co-operative organizations of other countries.[1]

In Germany, the co-operative societies number about four million members. Although mainly agricultural at first, the movement has recently taken on much the same form as in England. In what was Austria-Hungary the total membership is well over three million. In France and Italy co-operation is less advanced, but still very extensive. In Switzerland one out

[1] Agnes D. Warbasse. *The Story of Co-operation*, pamphlet.

of every ten persons is a co-operator. Denmark leads the world in proportion to its population, for in that little country one person in every five is a member of a co-operative. If it is assumed that each membership represents an average family of four, then fully four-fifths of the Danish people are comprised within the co-operative system. In Belgium the outstanding feature of the movement is that the savings are not distributed in money, but are devoted to a broad program of social betterment, a phase of co-operation which will be discussed later in the chapter.[1]

The situation in Russia is in many respects the most remarkable of all. In the last fifteen years, during which the rapid disorganization of the old order has compelled the people to work out their own salvation, the number of co-operative societies has leaped from 5,000 to 50,000, and their total membership is now about twenty million, representing a family constituency of from seventy-five to a hundred million people.[2] These figures apply to Russia as constituted before the war, and include Finland and other countries which are now independent.

In point of numbers, the Russian movement is the most extensive in the world. Economically, its development is as many-sided, though not yet so advanced, as England's. Socially, it is deeper and broader. It embraces political

[1] Agnes D. Warbasse. *The Story of Co-operation*, pamphlet.
[2] Alexander J. Zelenko. *What the Russian Co-operatives Do for the Social Uplift of Their Country*, pamphlet.

conservatives and radicals in its membership, but it is itself an economic movement—not to be confused, of course, with the soviets. Many observers who have visited Russia recently report that the co-operatives stand like a solid rock in the midst of all the turmoil.

### FAILURE FIRST IN AMERICA

In the United States the co-operative movement has sprung from three main sources—labor unions, farmers' organizations, and immigrant groups.

The earliest attempts were made by labor unions, and considerably antedated the Rochdale store in England. But, unlike the Rochdale demonstration, these attempts did not establish themselves upon sound principles, and therefore figure only as experiments along wrong lines. Co-operation for production was here tried independently, to supply union members with work, and thus maintain wages during periods of depression and unemployment.

Eventually labor realized that co-operative efforts as producers to keep wages up must be supported by organization as consumers to keep prices down. But the consumers' co-operatives that were afterward started by labor unions, and later by farmers' societies, notably the Grange, were not organized along the essential lines of the Rochdale plan. They were mere joint-buying propositions, lacking any adequate conception and morale, and loosely managed, so most of them came to naught.

## CO–OPERATIVES

In the last few years the labor unions have got on the right track, and are putting their shoulders to the wheel of co-operation with good results. But in the meantime a new factor entered into the situation and showed the way to success.

### AN IMMIGRANT CONTRIBUTION

That new factor was the immigrant.

The new life came into the movement [states the president of the Co-operative League of America], with aggregations of immigrant people from countries which had well-established co-operative societies.[1]

The immigrant group which has made the most outstanding contribution has already been mentioned in this connection:

A group of people who have done more than any other nationality to promote co-operation in the United States are the Finns. They have the intelligence, the solidarity, and the traditions necessary for success.[2]

Lithuanian, Ukrainian, Polish, Italian, Scotch, and English immigrants have also been especially successful in their co-operative undertakings.

Although this chapter is concerned mainly with racially mixed co-operatives which bring immigrants and native Americans into immediate working relations, the relation of the racial co-operatives to the whole co-operative movement in America is so important that they must be considered somewhat further at this point.

[1] James P. Warbasse. *The Co-operative Consumer's Movement in the United States*, pamphlet.     [2] *Ibid.*

# AMERICA VIA THE NEIGHBORHOOD

The following quotation from the address of a Finnish delegate at the National American Co-operative Convention, held in 1918, indicates the attitude of the Finnish co-operatives:

We do not think of co-operation as a Finnish movement. I do not want you to think that we Finlanders do not know what you are doing. We know almost everything you are doing. And we are always looking for you to do something. We know we are a very small group of people in this country. Therefore we cannot do very much alone. Everything that the workingmen should do and should want in this country has to be started by the workers. It has been my job for the last five or six years to work in the co-operative movement, doing educational work among the Finnish people. We take almost every one of your co-operative journals, from England, Canada, and the United States. We translate almost all of the articles from those papers into the Finnish language, and distribute them among the Finns. I am free to say that we have the first Finnish co-operative journal in this paper, which I show you here. It is the largest co-operative journal in the United States in any language. You have very good co-operative journals, quite a few of them. But, comparing the groups of people, I think we have done very well. In conclusion, I will say that we, as the Finnish people alone, cannot expect the full benefit from co-operation unless you, the Americans, will help us. We believe in co-operation in its fullest extent. We want to see that every consumer who is buying the necessities of life with his or her money, earned by hard labor, shall join the local stores, and those stores join in their territorial, national, and international unions.[1]

Here is a letter from a Bohemian co-operative, which was read at the same convention:

---

[1] Report of Proceedings of First American Co-operative Convention, 1918.

# CO–OPERATIVES

The Bohemian Workmen's Co-operative Mercantile Association hereby extends to your gathering fraternal greetings and sincere congratulations. We regret that we are not able to be represented. However, we pledge our support to your recommendations and decisions you may make in behalf of the co-operative movement. Our association, consisting of five hundred members, has in its last meeting approved a resolution to apply for membership in the Co-operative League of America.[1]

These quotations imply that, although different racial groups are to a large extent organized in co-operatives of their own, they are not separatist in their tendencies, but consider themselves an integral part of the general co-operative movement in this country, as in fact they are.

Though the co-operatives of some of these immigrant groups are united in regional federations of their own, most of them are affiliated also with the regional and national organizations of the general American movement, and buy their supplies from the same co-operative wholesales. At the general conventions, the co-operatives composed of immigrants are represented by delegates who have an equal voice with native American delegates in the proceedings. For that matter, they are frequently the ones to whom the native Americans look for practical guidance.

Racial co-operatives, like racial labor unions, are usually situated in immigrant colonies, and are for that reason even more closely identified with their neighborhoods than are co-operatives

---

[1] Report of Proceedings of First American Co-operative Convention, 1918.

in general. They constitute a strong tie between such neighborhoods and the American community, through which broad community motives may gradually make themselves felt.

The process of uniting foreign born and native born is going on more directly and speedily in local co-operatives which bring both elements together in their own membership. Due largely to the labor unions, the number of such co-operatives is steadily growing. To some extent officially, but for the most part through their individual members, unions have got strongly behind the co-operative movement in the last few years. Their support has helped to bring about in co-operatives a mingling of races similar to that achieved in the unions, but with this vital difference: that for the motive of class struggle, with all its inevitable, though incidental, wastage, is substituted the motive of working together constructively.

The American Federation of Labor, at its annual convention in 1917, unanimously adopted resolutions indorsing co-operation, with the proviso "that central labor unions and local trade unions, as such, shall not form co-operative societies, but shall appoint committees from their membership to act in co-operation with other citizens who are in sympathy with the trade-union movement in assisting in the upbuilding of a general co-operative movement."[1]

[1] Proceedings, Annual Convention, A. F. of L., 1917.

# CO-OPERATIVES

Plans are now under way for establishing a department of co-operation in the Federation, to educate the union membership and help to put the foregoing resolution into effect. The Railway Brotherhoods, the Postal Employees, and other large labor groups have also entered the field. The United Mine Workers of America, following substantially the plan indorsed by the A. F. of L., have probably done most thus far to get co-operatives actually started, especially in the mining districts of Pittsburgh and Illinois.

## UNITING THE RACES

The Tri-State Co-operative Association, which extends from Pittsburgh as center, and includes adjacent portions of Ohio and West Virginia, and the Central States Co-operative Society, which reaches from Illinois into Iowa, Missouri, and Wisconsin, represent the two largest groups of co-operatives in this country, and it is from these two that most of the examples cited below, of co-operatives which unite different races, are taken. Most of these co-operatives are situated in communities which are so small as to be practically a single neighborhood; or, if they are in larger communities, they usually have branch stores in different neighborhoods. Under these circumstances, the co-operatives are virtually neighborhood organizations.

Regarding the extent to which the co-operatives in the Tri-State district have successfully combined many races, the president writes as follows:

# AMERICA VIA THE NEIGHBORHOOD

The Tri-State Co-operative Association has connected with it from forty to fifty retail co-operative stores. These stores are located in various parts of the Pittsburgh district and their membership includes nearly every nationality. I think we have few, if any, stores that cannot be called cosmopolitan. In some stores we have as many as six to ten nationalities represented in the membership.

I am glad to say that these various nationalities work together quite harmoniously. It is our experience that when you can unite people on the basis of common interest they blend and work together amiably. It is our personal conviction that the co-operative movement in general, and the Tri-State in particular, is one of the greatest Americanization agencies in the country. The Tri-State is doing much in this section of the country to harmonize the various foreign elements and inoculate them with American ideals and standards of life.[1,]

A former president of this association, who is now in Chicago as organizer for the National Co-operative Wholesale, states that in his experience it proved entirely practicable, with the assistance of the labor unions, to organize racially mixed co-operatives.[2]

In one case mentioned by him the membership includes Scandinavians, Bohemians, Poles, and Russians; in another Hungarians, English, and Italians. In one town an organization committee, preceding the formation of the co-operative itself, was made up on the basis of two delegates from each racial group. The result was a steady broadening of interest. At the first public meeting only fourteen persons were present; at the second there were thirty; but at the third, which was held after three months

---

[1] William A. Prosser.    [2] D. R. Tanner.

of community education, and immediately preceding the opening of the store, over seven hundred, representing all races, crowded the hall.

The Central States Co-operative Society includes some seventy co-operatives, most of which, according to the secretary, are racially mixed.[1] In order to get detailed information, the writer communicated with sixty co-operatives in Illinois, asking certain questions regarding their racial make-up, and how the various races got on together. About a fourth of them, apparently a representative assortment, replied, and the facts thus supplied are exceedingly interesting.

The proportion of foreign born in these particular co-operatives ranges from 10 per cent in one case up to 98 per cent in another, but in most cases it is reported as being from a half to two-thirds of the membership. The number of different races comprised varies from three to nine, and includes Italians, Poles, Slovaks, Russians, Lithuanians, Hungarians, Germans, Scotch, English, Finns, French, Belgians, and Negroes. As to representation on the board of directors, a practical test of the degree of participation and equality of the different racial elements, four co-operatives failed to specify, but in all cases where this question was answered the boards likewise are racially mixed.

As a rule, however, the number of native-born Americans elected to the boards is large in proportion to their quota of the membership. For example, in one case where the membership

[1] Duncan McDonald.

361

consists of seventy-five Slavs, twenty-five Germans, and fifty-nine Americans, the board is made up of two Slavs, two Germans, and eight Americans. Even in the case previously mentioned where 98 per cent of the members are foreign born, and only four American members are reported, two of the latter are included on a board of nine.

As nearly all the racially mixed co-operatives conduct their meetings in English, it is desirable to elect to the board persons who speak English fluently, of whom, naturally, the largest quota are found among the native born. Beyond this consideration, however, there appears to be an assumption of leadership on the part of Americans, and more than willingness on the part of the foreign born to defer to such American leaders because of their assumedly better acquaintance with American conditions. In short, co-operatives which include different races and both foreign and native born in their membership and management are being developed under American leadership and the influence of American standards.

To the question of how the different racial elements got on together, one co-operative answered "fairly good," but all the others said "good," "very well," "fine," "splendidly," "in the co-operative movement there is no difference in nationality."

Several typical replies are quoted below:

1. We have thirty-six Italians, ten Russians or Slavs, two Austrians or Hungarians, and sixty-two Americans.

# CO–OPERATIVES

Our board of directors consists of four Italians, one Austrian, two Russians, six Americans.

2. We have in our association about one hundred and ten members, made up of different nationalities: French, German, English, Scotch, Austrian, Italian, and American. The different nationalities agree very nicely and everything moves on in harmony.

3. Total membership one hundred and thirty-one. About half the membership is Italians, the other half is composed of Americans, English, Russians, and Lithuanians. Board of directors is chiefly composed of Americans and Italians. However, we elect new board every six months in order to give all a chance to serve. In general the foreign born are the most active in the movement. Harmony exists among the various nationalities. More literature is necessary to get the people interested in the co-operative movement.

A quarterly meeting of shareholders, which the writer attended in an Illinois town, exemplified the co-operative spirit in the way it was conducted. It was held in the labor temple. The members began to come before the meeting was called to order, and stood out in front of the building, chatting with one another, or lounged on benches in the "common" across the street. It was a slack period in the mines just then, and they talked about the prospects of work increasing, and about the way prices were steadily going up.

After a while they all went inside, and the meeting began, with the president and the secretary on the platform. Among those present were native Americans of English and German descent, and Polish, Lithuanian, Bohemian, and

Italian immigrants. The most impressive thing about the proceedings was the complete absence of "railroading" and "slates," those two little devices so common in ordinary business meetings. The president went almost to an extreme in inviting discussion from the floor on every question that was brought up.

In the selection of a committee to edit the by-laws no names were suggested by him as coming from the board of directors, but nominations were requested. Some one moved that a committee of three be "appointed." "No," said the president, "that is not the way we do things. This committee must be elected by the members." Eventually, three persons were nominated by as many different members, and were unanimously elected. As various other matters were discussed, the president, or at his request the manager, explained and emphasized the basic principles of co-operation.

## CO-OPERATIVES IN CITIES

Up to the present time racially mixed co-operatives are found mostly in small communities, where either the labor unions or some other influence has previously brought the different racial elements into close relations. In larger cities, where each race is usually segregated, co-operatives are far more likely to be confined either to one race or to native Americans. Even under city conditions, however, there are already a number of instances in which a few

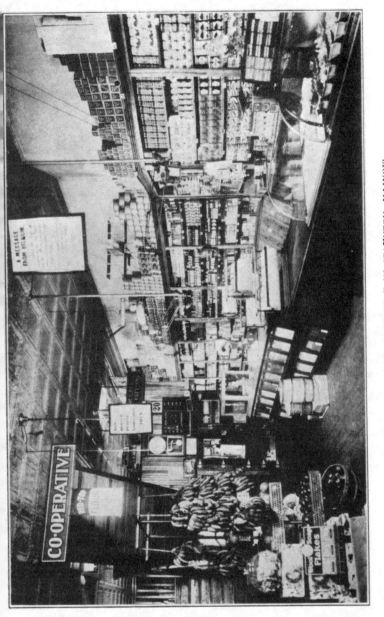

AN INTERRACIAL CO-OPERATIVE IN STAUNTON, ILLINOIS

This successful store, conducted by members of the United Mine Workers, represents half a dozen races working harmoniously together.

# CO-OPERATIVES

Americans are joining Finnish, Lithuanian, or other racial co-operatives in their neighborhoods, or in which a few immigrants are being drawn into American co-operatives. There are also some cases in which different races, and both foreign-born and native-born, combine forces at the outset, just as they do in the mining towns.

In a cosmopolitan neighborhood of Chicago, for instance, is a co-operative practically all the members of which are English-speaking American citizens, but about three-quarters of whom are of foreign birth, chiefly Swedes, Dutch, and English. Of the board of directors, only one member is native born; the others have had some co-operative experience in Europe of which they are now giving the American community the benefit.

The way in which this particular co-operative was launched is typical. The rising cost of living was the incentive. First a few people familiar with co-operation met in the house of, one of them, and issued a call for a general meeting of the neighborhood to discuss starting a store. This first public meeting was well attended, and in turn called another, at which several hundred people, mostly home owners in the vicinity, were present. At this meeting a provisional board was elected, to sell shares at $10 each, and only one share to a person, the desire being to get as many individual members as possible. The response was good and four hundred shares were sold, giving a capital of $4,000.

# AMERICA VIA THE NEIGHBORHOOD

A private store in the neighborhood was
bought out. The enterprise prospered, and a
little later a second membership canvass enrolled
four hundred additional members. The difference between the attitude of the shareholders
toward their own store and the way they felt
when it was run privately came out in their
queries and comments. "Well, how are we
coming along?" "We're doing nicely, aren't
we?" "Our dividends certainly come in handy."
It was decided to set aside 5 per cent of the
profits for education in the principles of co-
operation. For this purpose the whole neighborhood is invited to meetings, at which well-
equipped speakers make addresses, followed by
general discussion.

## SOCIAL AND EDUCATIONAL FUNCTIONS

What has been said up to this point has dealt
with the immediate economic object of co-
operatives. The economic foundation of co-
operation is the solid rock bottom upon which
it is established. But that is only the beginning.
Upon this foundation is being reared a broad
superstructure of social and educational activities. Here again, as this development of the
movement has been carried farthest in Europe,
reference to European experience is necessary
to an adequate appreciation of similar possibilities in America.

In England activities of this sort have been
promoted by the Co-operative Union, a central

organization to which each local society contributes.

For many years, through its annual co-operative congress, the Union has exerted a big influence on the general movement. It has published many hundreds of tracts interpreting the work of the co-operative; has established scores of libraries and reading rooms; has conducted thousands of courses on co-operation and civic problems; has exerted considerable pressure on political bodies to insure that rights of co-operatives were not invaded; has organized lectures and entertainments.

An indication of the way in which the retail store at times may provide the rallying place for the social and intellectual activities of the neighborhood is seen in the case of the Edmonton Society. Organized in connection with this store are numerous men's, women's and junior guilds, comrade circles, and dozens of propaganda clubs—in fact no less than fifty organizations, each with its councils, lectures, socials. Every night the attractive meeting rooms are filled with the animated faces, young and old, of the loyal co-operators of this North London suburb.[1]

**In Belgium the chief characteristic of the co-operative movement is the attention it devotes to social betterment.**

The surplus savings are not returnable to the members in the form of cash, but are used for social-welfare purposes. This money is used for doing for the members of the co-operative societies what the socialized state does for the people in Germany. Old-age pensions, life insurance, insurance against sickness and unemployment, maternity benefits, and medical and nursing care are provided. Those beautiful buildings in Belgium, called the houses of the people, are owned by the co-operative societies. They are community centers, used for meetings, dramatic presenta-

---

[1] Harry W. Laidler. *The British Co-operative Movement*, pamphlet.

tions, schools, and recreation. About some of them are parks where fine music is rendered, mothers sew, fathers talk, and children play.[1]

## RUSSIAN CO-OPERATIVE CENTERS

It is in Russia that the social betterment program of the co-operatives is most closely linked with the neighborhood.

Probably no people have been so trained in co-operative association. Since the dawn of history the Russian workers have associated themselves together in *artels* which are purely co-operative working or living associations. Russia is a network of *artels*, and such association is almost instinctive with the Russians. Likewise they have held their lands in the *mir* in a community of ownership and occupation. If any nation was prepared for co-operation it was such a people.[2]

The extent to which the local co-operatives in Russia have become neighborhood social centers, and the many ways in which these local activities are promoted through the regional co-operative associations, is described by a Russian who is now in America fostering closer relations between the co-operatives of Russia and the United States, and studying American life for such suggestions as it may have for his own countrymen:[3]

The village co-operative store is the beginning of it all. The peasants say, "That is our store," and it is no wonder that the store is a sort of clubhouse. In the morning

---

[1] Agnes D. Warbasse, *The Story of Co-operation*, pamphlet.

[2] Emerson P. Harris. *Co-operation, the Hope of the Consumer.*

[3] Alexander Zelenko, Managing Director of the American Committee of Russian Co-operative Unions. *What the Russian Co-operatives Do for the Social Uplift of Their Country*, pamphlet.

farmers, on their way to the cities, stop to purchase something for the trip; in the afternoon boys and girls, returning from school, laugh and chat over new books, or some cheap ornament to attract the girls; in the evening the housewives gather, and groups of somewhat sinister old men, with long hair and beards, appear in homespun overcoats and heavy boots. Now and then the schoolmaster drops in for school supplies, or the clergyman to see the people, for usually both of these village notables are members of the local co-operative board. There politicians spin their small village meshes, radicals throw their heated arguments, conservatives grumble about young soldiers who have brought home so many new ideas from the war front, and new propositions for social uplift are met, discussed, and planned.

Next enters the wholesale union, a union formed by all the local co-operatives in a given district, to supply themselves with such commodities as they need, and also such specialized guidance in their social activities as they could not afford with their separate resources. There are some five hundred such unions in Russia. Each has its own staff of traveling instructors, about five thousand altogether, who are constantly going about among the local co-operatives.

The instructors are not satisfied with their contracts and publications, but they are also trying to introduce more intensive social and educational training among their groups. If a local society decided to start a village library, the members ask the district wholesale union to send the material, and the latter in turn addresses the central wholesale union, which prints its own books and buys whole editions direct from private firms. Not less than a hundred thousand books and ten million pamphlets have been printed by the unions during this last year, to be resold in the small co-operative societies.

Besides material on the principles of the co-operative movement, and its history in Russia and other countries, these publications include such pamphlets as *Rules for a Village Educational Circle, List of Readings with Lantern Slides for People's Houses, Children's Literature for Kindergartens, How to Organize a Community Chorus,* and *Children's Kitchen Gardens.*

The instructors try to satisfy the needs of all generations. The older people want mostly solid information, the younger ones material for their social, literary, and theatrical clubs. Sometimes the unions keep special instructors who go into the villages to show the people how to start their dramatic ventures. The plays produced are, for the most part, of very good social and cultural value, and with the aid of the instructors the best classical works are introduced. Very good guidebooks for the People's Theater are written by the co-operative instructors, and the best dramas and comedies are published in very inexpensive form for from five to fifteen cents apiece.

Assistance from regional headquarters is given especially to the less developed local communities. In many places the local co-operatives are carrying out equally varied programs on their own initiative and resources.

In very many villages the Russian co-operatives have established what are called people's houses, similar to what are known in America as social or community centers. When the war broke out and the Russian central government prohibited the sale of liquors, many houses run by the liquor dealers were taken over by the co-operatives, and thus the problem of transforming saloons into club-houses, of which there is now talk in America, was practically solved in Russia as long as five years ago. I think that no less than three or four thousand tea houses are already in operation in Russia. There are many small libraries run by the co-operatives, and when such a library is joined to a tea house a hall for meetings and theatrical performances is assured, and soon a regular social center established. Separate committees are appointed to have charge of chorus drilling, orchestra practice, agricultural courses, lectures on various social subjects, juvenile clubs or kindergarten.

Educational stereopticon and motion pictures are widely utilized.

The central unions have begun to establish their own shops in order to produce films showing the usefulness and advantages of the co-operative movement.

Going still farther in co-operative education, the regional unions have established special extension courses and schools. These include brief local courses, summer and winter courses in the larger towns and cities, advanced courses of college grade, and half a dozen so-called peasants' universities.

There is a new movement on foot to establish new types of elementary and high schools for children where the whole system is based upon co-operative principles. I found in the small town of Mariynsk, in Siberia, a wonderful school of the intermediate type which had been established by the local union. In this school the bookkeeping of the establishment is taken care of by the pupils, and they run a magazine on the co-operative shareholders' scheme. The discipline of the entire school is maintained on the self-government principle, and the system of training in languages, mathematics, history, and geography is based upon the co-operative idea. They also conduct a co-operative savings bank. The school is co-educational, and the children have not only conducted their business successfully, but have included in their working plan the children

of all other city schools which are run by the local municipality. In the cities of Charkoff and Chita are other
high schools which are run on the same co-operative basis.
Many other unions have begun to follow the new plan of
education, which should be introduced in regular municipal
schools.

The cultural life of Russia is now supported mainly
through the co-operatives because they not only control
to a great extent the productive, consumptive, and credit
activities of the Russian peasants, industrial workers,
small officials in state activities, and city folk, but also
because they pay so much attention to the social uplift of
their people. The twenty million members do not include
all that are reached, for behind each member is his family,
which in Russia is usually composed of at least four or five
members, so that a population of not less than one hundred
million is influenced by the co-operative movement. Every
day some new activity spreads its network in response to a
crying need.

### SIMILAR ACTIVITIES IN AMERICA

In the United States co-operative developments of this broadly social character are still
in their infancy, but the seeds are being planted,
modest beginnings are appearing, and the possibilities of the future are coming more and more
into view. Here again it is the immigrants
from Europe who are showing the way. In fact,
the Finnish Workers' Educational Associations,
which are essentially co-operative organizations,
have worked out in America a scheme of educational and recreational activities, previously
described in connection with the community
in Fitchburg, which in its completeness stands
comparison with similar local activities in Europe.

American co-operatives are entering this

broader field through the educational approach. Every local co-operative that has any real "go" is doing something in an organized way to educate first its own members, and then the neighborhood, in the principles of co-operation. Public meetings are held from time to time, at which different aspects of the subject are explained and discussed, and these occasions usually wind up with refreshments and informal sociability.

The manager of one co-operative said that at a recent banquet of this sort, to which members were permitted to invite friends, the number of people was several times larger than expected, and some close reckoning was necessary to make the "banquet" go around. In summer a good many educational picnics are held. One of the most vigorous co-operatives in Illinois, whose members are of eight different races, reports as sociable and educational features "dances, lectures, picnics, shows, literature, and education committee work."

Women's auxiliaries are being organized to promote activities of this kind. The following quotation from the address of a woman co-operator at the American Co-operative Convention of 1918 shows what such a women's auxiliary did in one case:

I went out to get the women together, to organize them for social and educational work. One of the first things I discovered was that there was no library; so we had two meetings; one was a mass meeting and the other a general meeting, in which we discussed the possibilities of a library. We had a member of the state commission of education tell the people how they might get a library. Right next to their store there was another store; this they rented and cleaned out for clubroom purposes. This week they are opening their library. This is one thing they have done, and it is really doing good work in so short a time. The women of the organization did the papering of the clubroom; and they did a splendid job at that. The women put up the shelves and did the painting and got the room ready; and it is really in fine condition. That was all done gratuitously and during the spare time of the members.

Then we had a number of picnics in the summer. One was on a Sunday, so that the men could attend, and the women and children. By this means the people got to know one another. Considering the percentage of people that usually turns out when people are not acquainted or in the habit of getting together for social purposes, we had a big success. We have tentative plans for a busy winter this year. We have been meeting once a week at the different homes. The manager of the store feels it has been helpful to him in the store to have the women come together, especially right next door to the store. I think the library will be another attraction to the center where the women will congregate. When they come to make their purchases at the store they will always find other women in the clubroom next door, where the library is. This should help along in promoting interest.[1]

The Co-operative League of America is circulating a pamphlet on *Recreation and Education in Co-operative Societies,* and addresses dealing with this subject were included in all the programs of the half-dozen regional conferences on co-operation which were held in the autumn of 1919.

### CO-OPERATION VERSUS PHILANTHROPY

As distinguishing the point of view of co-operative social work from that of philanthropy, the fol-

----

[1] Report of Proceedings.

lowing quotation from another address made at the convention of 1918 is of significant interest:

One of the things that drew me to the co-operative movement is the fact that it bases its democratic ideals upon an economic foundation. It thus gets away from the well-meant meddlesomeness of the professional worker. It is upon this sound economic basis that the community centers of Europe are founded, and it is this fact which gives them their effectiveness and freedom.

If community organization is ever to be anything more than an academic attempt to uplift the poor, if it is ever to be anything more than a device by which professional social workers and reformers can ply their trade of manipulating other people, it must concern itself with something more vital than organizing the leisure time of the masses. It must organize the vital needs of the people. It must socialize their common economic interests—that is, their interests as consumers—and socialize them in their local applications. It must put people in an economic position to buy and pay for their own cultural and recreational goods. Anything else is charity, I care not how we may disguise it with the name of democracy. The community-center movement, of all things, ought not to have to solicit contributions from socially minded business men to finance its work. You may be very sure that any kind of social work belongs to the people who pay for it.

Co-operation would enable the community center to be its own boss, and to become a significant force in the progressive reconstruction of democratic society. It would make it economically possible for the organized people to escape the tutelage of wealthy and official patrons. It would give them the economic advantages of co-operative buying. It would make them masters of their own social activities, and it is the only way. With the present high cost of living it is impossible for wage workers to support by voluntary contributions taken out of their small means any large and significant educational or recreational activities of their own. The larger part of such support

must come from wealthy donors or from public funds raised
by taxation. In either case what the people get is almost
sure to be what some one else thinks they ought to have.
I for one am absolutely sick of this business of arranging
social philanthropy to appear on paper so that it will sell
in Wall Street. Let the community center take up the
co-operative movement and any small community, on a
small portion of the profits now going to private dealers,
could build its own community house; it could have its
own theaters, forums, orchestras, and lectures.[1]

### CO-OPERATIVE HOME OWNING

No limits can be set to the range of social
activities which co-operatives may undertake.
They are capable of becoming complete centers
of neighborhood life. But there is another
possible relationship between the co-operative
movement and the neighborhood which strikes
still deeper as a constructive force. That is
the relationship between the co-operative ownership of homes and neighborhood stability.

Though in smaller cities and the suburbs it
is still possible for people of modest means to
have individual homes, in the inner districts of
large cities this is no longer feasible. Land
values are too high to permit it, and people have
to live as tenants. Tenancy means imperma-
nency, and a probable attitude of irresponsibility
with regard to the neighborhood. Constant
moving out and in renders impossible the stability and continuity of neighborhood life that
would exist under more settled conditions. At

[1] Everett Dean Martin, Assistant Director of the People's Institute, New York. Report of Proceedings.

the present time the situation is further aggravated by the rise in rents and the acute shortage of housing accommodations.

Under these circumstances, it would appear that the only practicable way out is the co-operative way, as demonstrated by the Finnish co-operative apartments described in a previous chapter. These Finnish co-operators, no one of whom could have afforded to buy a home in that locality, obtained good homes of their own at a cost much below what they would have had to pay in rent, by the simple process of co-operation. Now they can remain in that neighborhood contentedly and their interest in its affairs will be that of people who have a permanent stake there. Is there any sufficient reason why this example set by the Finns cannot be followed by others? In fact, so distressing has the housing problem become that it will be difficult to understand if this solution does not become one of the main features of the co-operative movement in America.[1]

Co-operative home building has already made great strides in England.

Thousands of semidetached houses for workers, on tree-lined avenues, surrounded by pretty gardens, scattered throughout England, are also evidence of the enterprise of many of the co-operative societies. By 1907, over 400 "co-ops." had expended nearly $50,000,000 in building or acquiring something like 50,000 dwelling houses, most of them to pass ultimately into the ownership of the in-

---

[1] In New York especially a large number of apartments are now being taken over by the tenants on a partly co-operative basis.

dividual members. A number of building organizations, formed by co-operators, have also aided in this direction.[1]

In so far as such co-operative home-ownership develops in America it will tend to counteract the instability of residence which is now so pronounced under city conditions, and which is such a serious obstacle to the continuity of neighborhood life. This increased stability will in turn provide a firmer foundation for the development of co-operative activities based on the neighborhood unit.

## UNIFYING INFLUENCES

In comparing the value of co-operatives and labor unions as racially unifying factors it may be said that although the unions are uniting the races in degree equal to that of the co-operatives and at present reach a much larger number of individuals, the co-operatives are working along more inclusive and constructive lines. Co-operatives are not inherently confined to one "class." In Europe, where for the most part co-operation originated among the working classes, it has gradually made headway among the middle class, and to some extent people of these two classes are members of the same local co-operatives.

In Great Britain there are many instances of bourgeois and wealthy people, even among the nobility, having united with the co-operative movement and displayed an interest

---

[1] Harry W. Laidler. *The British Co-operative Movement*, pamphlet.

which has made them highly valuable and respected. The same may be said of the membership of many societies on the Continent.[1]

As a rule, however, the different classes are separately organized locally, but are brought into working relations through the various regional and national associations and conventions.

In the United States the situation is about the same. Though the co-operative movement here has been especially fostered by labor unions and groups in sympathy with labor, and though the most successful co-operatives are those of working people, here, also, there are middle-class co-operatives, and in some measure, small but nevertheless significant, co-operators of all "classes" may be found working together in the same local organization.

In one co-operative in Chicago, for instance, a number of contractors and professional men are combined with manual workers. There are also instances of bankers joining co-operatives under similar circumstances. Such cases are as yet exceptional, for co-operation in its basic economic aspect appeals primarily to people of limited means, who are hard pressed by the cost of living, while for the very reason that it distributes among its members the profits which would otherwise go to private merchants it is usually opposed, rather than welcomed, by private business. But in principle and potentially it is all-inclusive, and it will doubtless

---

[1] James P. Warbasse, correspondence.

become inclusive in fact as it demonstrates its practical success and attains the dimensions and momentum, as it has in Europe, which will enable it to compete with "big business" in appealing to the type of men whom "big business" attracts.

### THE FUTURE IN AMERICA

What can be said, in conclusion, of the present strength and future prospects of the co-operative movement in America? How large and promising a factor is it in our national life?

As a movement organized on a national scale, it is still very young. Notwithstanding an early beginning, co-operative efforts in this country remained sporadic and only loosely related until within the last four or five years. Then, thanks to the many sturdy co-operatives organized by immigrant groups, and the vigorous way in which labor unions, especially those of the miners, entered into the movement, it began to liven up and subsequently moved forward rapidly from one end of the country to the other. There are now co-operative societies in every state in the Union.[1] The entire number of such societies is probably about two thousand.[2] As yet, however, not even an approximate estimate is available as to their total individual membership.

Substantially two-thirds of all these co-operatives have been organized by immigrant groups of one race or another.[3] This fact clearly shows in how large a measure co-operation in America

[1] James P. Warbasse, personal statement.  [2] *Ibid.*  [3] *Ibid.*

is an immigrant contribution. The other one-third consists of racially mixed societies and those composed of native Americans. The number of producers' co-operatives, outside of the farmers', though comprising an interesting variety, is still small. The great majority are consumers' co-operatives, including some restaurants, boarding houses, and credit unions, but mostly stores. The small local retail store, virtually the neighborhood store, is the root from which co-operation in the United States is sprouting.

To bind all these local co-operatives together and help in starting others, six or eight regional wholesales are now in operation, and recently a national wholesale association has been established. These wholesales not only supply the local stores with goods, at a considerable saving, but assist in the organization and management of retails and branch wholesales, and in fostering extension work through publicity and otherwise. As the general educational and promoting body, concerning itself mainly with research, propaganda, and the arrangement of conferences and conventions, rather than with business management, stands the Co-operative League of America. The American movement is related to the same movement in other countries through the International Co-operative Alliance.

Thus, while co-operation's foundation is the neighborhood, its reach is world-wide. The co-operative movement is uniting different races in the same neighborhood, binding different neighborhoods and communities together with a common democratic motive throughout the nation, and moving toward the establishment of a solidly grounded international neighborhood of all the peoples of the world.

# XII

## POLITICAL ORGANIZATION AND GOVERNMENT

TIME was when the neighborhood and the political unit in America were one and the same. That was in the days of the New England town meeting, which was in its prime about the time of the American Revolution, and which had itself fostered the spirit of self-reliant patriotism which made the Revolution inevitable in face of the denial to the Colonists of representation in the control of their own public financial affairs.

The town meeting was the coming together of all the freemen of the town, at least once every year and on other occasions as needed, to elect the "selectmen" and other officials and to settle all the common political concerns of the community. One man was as good as another in his right to be heard.

There, face to face, the citizens threshed out their differences and reached their agreements. There, the town elected its delegates to the provincial assembly, before the Revolution, and afterward its representative in the state legislature. In those early days few local communities had grown beyond the size of villages which were so isolated and so homogeneous in their population as to be single neighborhoods. The town meetings were therefore neighborhood gatherings; local political affairs were conducted on a "face-to-face" basis, and the state was a federation of neighborhood units.

In the towns, and even in some of the smaller cities of New England, the town meeting still survives and, though not all important as of yore, retains a good deal of its inherent vigor. It is still the neighborhood assembled for political purposes. This is manifest in the fact that although only legal voters of the town may vote at the meetings, any resident, women and minors as well as men, may attend, ask questions, and take part in the discussion, and that many nonvoters participate in these ways.

In towns where there are immigrant residents it is not uncommon for immigrants, who are not yet naturalized, but own property and pay taxes, to attend and sometimes to join in the discussion. The measure in which the town meeting enlists immigrant residents corresponds with the measure in which they are an accepted part of the neighborhood. In towns where their status is that of an alien "clan on the town's outskirts"[1] they hardly figure in the town meeting. But as they come to have a share in the general life of the community they also take an active interest in the town meeting.

Outside of New England, the town meeting never became general, and in New England it has in the main fallen into disuse as towns

[1] Paul Harlan Douglas. *The Little Town.*

384

have grown to be cities. The reason is obvious. A general meeting, bringing together all the people, is practicable only in small communities. In cities it would be unwieldy. The passing of the town meeting, and the absence of any adequate substitute for it under present-day city conditions, is often lamented. But notwithstanding the fact that officially the neighborhood is no longer the political unit, the neighborhood motive is so fundamental and persistent that informally it has never ceased to figure in politics; and to-day, even in the hurly-burly of city conditions, it finds some measure of real political expression.

### INITIATIVE OF IMMIGRANTS

In the case of the immigrant, political expression through the neighborhood is an early development. Immigrant groups usually display an interest in politics which, though it may later be sorely disillusioned by the manipulation of "politicians," is in the beginning ingenuous and wholesome. To the newly arrived immigrant America is the land of freedom and promise. What more natural than that he should want to learn how this land is governed and have some part in its government?

Immigrant societies of many kinds encourage and assist their members to become naturalized citizens. But naturalization is an arduous undertaking, beset with many practical and technical difficulties which are often outside the immigrant's control. Therefore the political interest of any immigrant group cannot be measured wholly by the extent to which its members become naturalized citizens. Their interest is more adequately evidenced by their efforts to establish some sort of political connection with their new environment.

Nearly all immigrant groups have specifically political organizations of their own. These are of two kinds. The first is the nonpartisan organization, which is political in the broad sense. It aims to educate the members of its group politically; to prepare them for, and in some measure engage them in, civic and political activity. A number of examples of this type of organization, including Italian, Russian, and Syrian political societies, and Polish and French-Canadian citizens' clubs, were cited in an earlier chapter. The second type of organization here involved is political in the more ordinary partisan use of the term—that is to say, affiliated with a political party. Inasmuch as political affairs in America are organized on a party basis, this type of organization is more immediately and practically effective than the other.

Various factors, many of them purely casual, determine the immigrant's first party affiliations. As between the two old parties, it is often simply an accident whether he enrolls as a Republican or a Democrat, depending on how his friends advise him or which politicians get him first.

The party labels in themselves have had some influence. Sometimes immigrants assume that the Republican party is the one which stands for a free republic instead of for a monarchy, like those of the countries from which they came. More frequently, however, the name "Democratic" catches the immigrant. "Many of our people join the Democratic party," said one immigrant leader, "because they think that means democracy." "We love the word 'democracy,'" another explained, "and so we are Democrats."

Partisan societies or clubs whose members are of one race, and which are identified with single immigrant neighborhoods, sometimes originate through the initiative of the immigrant group itself, and at other times are the result of encouragement and fostering care on the part of politicians outside the group. All such clubs, however, are real organs of the immigrant neighborhood, in that they serve as a local center and medium of expression, particularly for the non-English-speaking element. Some are ephemeral, or are active only around election time, but others are permanent and have regular meeting places.

Some devote considerable attention to assisting immigrants to learn English and become naturalized. All of them bring their members into contact with political affairs, and serve as a connecting link between the immigrant neighborhood and the community at large. They introduce the community's larger political motives and issues into the neighborhood, and thus draw the neighborhood out of its purely local concerns. As this interrelating process advances, the racially separate party clubs are often discontinued or merged with the English-speaking political clubs of the locality.

A desire on the part of immigrant groups to increase their own voting strength and improve their political status in the community is, of course, a foremost incentive in leading them to organize. But this motive is altogether natural and wholesome; and if it is effective, as in fact it is, in influencing members of these groups to become citizens, and to take an interest in the political affairs of the community, surely it is to be encouraged rather than objected to as "clannish." Here, again, this is clannishness of a sort which eventually links the immigrant group with the whole body politic. Experience shows, furthermore, that after becoming voters immigrants divide on general party issues, in the main, and do not stick strictly to racial lines.

### NEIGHBORHOOD UNIT IN POLITICS

In approaching the political life of America the immigrants themselves take the first steps, within their own colony neighborhoods. In the absence of any official "town meeting" in which they may take part, they provide their own town meetings by organizing and taking counsel among themselves. But how far are they included in the general counsels of the leading political parties of America? Do the general party organizations substitute anything for the town meeting which enables the immigrant neighborhood to function democratically in political affairs?

## ORGANIZATION AND GOVERNMENT

In general, political parties have recognized and capitalized the neighborhood as a very human and fundamental factor in politics. The ways in which the Democratic and the Republican parties build upon the neighborhood unit are substantially the same. The Democratic party, however, includes immigrants in larger numbers, and has gone farther in developing neighborhood organization.

For party purposes, a city is divided into districts and subdistricts. Though these divisions differ a good deal in size and in the names applied to them in different cities, they usually conform to legally established election districts. Sometimes the larger divisions are the city wards, from which aldermen are elected; or they may be the districts used in electing members of the state legislature. The subdivisions are sometimes called precincts. The latter approximate the size of a neighborhood. In each of the larger divisions there is a district leader This district leader, in turn, appoints a captain for each precinct or subdivision.

### ORGANIZATION BY PRECINCTS

It is at this point that recognition of the neighborhood begins. Practically always an old resident of the precinct, and not an "outsider," is selected as captain. Personal popularity and influence in the locality largely determine the selection. What is wanted is some one who is a "mixer," a "good fellow," and who "represents the neighborhood." Before making appointments, the district leader usually sounds out the different neighborhoods to make sure of picking the right man.

In immigrant neighborhoods it is customary to select a member of the predominant racial group, provided one can be found who has the requisite qualifications. It is the function of these captains, and of the helpers whom they usually appoint, to know their precincts thoroughly, to become acquainted with all the local members of the party, and to be of as much service as possible to them individually, and to the neighborhood as a whole, by rendering personal assistance and favors and by promoting local improvements.

Any party member, or, for that matter, any resident of the precinct, understands that he may go to the captain for advice or help, or to discuss some local need. Each captain serves as a medium between his precinct and the district leader, interpreting the neighborhood to the district leader, on the one hand, and on the other transmitting back to the neighborhood such political favors or requests as the leader may issue. All the captains and their helpers, meeting regularly with the district leader, make up a district committee. These committees often include immigrant leaders representing half a dozen or more racial groups. They bring these leaders into working relations with one another and with native Americans, and bind the different precincts or neighborhoods together through the common party interest.

## ORGANIZATION AND GOVERNMENT

In states which have adopted woman suffrage, the form of organization which has been outlined above is beginning to be paralleled by a similar one of women, with women district leaders and precinct captains.

### GRAFT AND BOSSISM

Now it is in connection with just such party machines that graft and bossism have flourished. But it does not follow that either of these abuses is inherent in such a plan of organization, which in fact simply follows the lines of efficient organization in any field, including that of business management. Graft and bossism are now generally recognized as products of the inertia and complaisance of the community with regard to political affairs.

However this may be, such an intensive scheme of organization, with the precinct as its unit, makes for increased political participation, amounts itself to participation, indeed, on the part of the local neighborhood. To appreciate this fact it is only necessary to contrast the widespread interest in politics, and the proportionate vote cast, in a well-organized Tammany district, with the cynical indifference and feeble vote of many a respectable middle-class or wealthy district whose residents regard close contact with "politics" as besmirching.

The very foundation of a democracy is faith in the rank and file  Granting that the ideal to be striven for is general interest and activity without graft, there can be little question that

more progress toward the ideal is to be made
with intensive organization than without it,
even if such organization helps to distribute
graft more widely and lower down; for without
local organization there is little local participation, and the graft is simply concentrated
higher up.

With respect to bossism, while it is obvious
that local organization makes it easier for the
boss to have his orders carried out, the fact of
most significance is this—that the orders which
the boss issues are not solely his own personal
and arbitrary commands, but are in considerable
measure the crystallization of popular demand.
In short, the successful boss must be largely governed by the people whom he bosses. Through
his organization, which reaches into every home,
he finds out what the people want, and then
proceeds to give this to them.

This sounding-out process often takes place
so automatically and unconsciously, that to an
outsider the boss seems to be running things
according to his own sweet will. But the best
proof that in the long run he gives the people
what they want is that he holds their votes for
the party and thus keeps himself in power.
Competition between the parties also plays its
part. Neither party can afford to be asleep on
the job or continually to neglect or go against
the wishes of the voters. If either does, the
other seizes the opportunity to strengthen its
hold in the locality at the expense of its rival.
Every now and then the voters assert their

final authority by kicking over the traces and going directly against attempts of the bosses to hold them in line.

A striking illustration of this, in the case of an immigrant group, occurred in a recent municipal election in New York City, where the Italians, a large proportion of whom were closely affiliated with the Democratic party, voted solidly for a Republican candidate. The fact that this candidate was a popular young man of Italian parentage, who had made a fine record in the American army during the war, had something to do with the swing-over. The chief reason, however, was the incensement of the Italians against President Wilson for his stand in the peace-treaty dispute over Fiume, which they regarded as anti-Italian, and their enthusiastic reception of the more favorable stand taken by Senator Lodge.

They therefore registered their feelings by voting almost solidly, in every locality, for the Republican candidate, who was elected against seemingly impossible odds. This incident is not cited with any suggestion that an international issue should influence a purely municipal election in America, but simply to show that when the voters are really aroused, rightly or wrongly, they vote as they feel, no matter whether the boss likes it or not.

### RELATES POLITICS TO DAILY LIFE

The local effect of intensive political organization is to relate politics to the daily lives and the practical needs of the people and the neighborhood. Three of the traditional services which local politicians render are supplying jobs, providing relief of various kinds, and helping people out of difficulties with the authorities. For example, a man who used to be a local contractor related how, when he needed men in his work, he would go to the district leader; the latter would send word around to his captains to find the men who were most in need of work, and in this way the number desired would be supplied. In another instance, a woman district leader told of a considerable fund kept by her father for people who were hard up. Sometimes rents or funeral expenses were paid, and Christmas dinners given. Said another leader:

We are helping at least a hundred families who are in need of assistance. These people don't like to go to the charity societies or the settlements. There everything has to be investigated and in the meantime it may be too late. We never bother about that, but do the best we can right away. They come to us for all kinds of help, especially when they get into some difficulty or other with the authorities that they don't understand. A good many of them are not voters yet, and some are not in our party, but we help them out just the same.

Such assistance becomes generally known in the neighborhood, these politicians say, and as a result there grows up a confidence on the part of the neighborhood that the political leaders are real "friends of the people." This sort of thing "warms the neighborhood up" and makes it feel that politics is not something altogether removed and impersonal.

Our Democratic organization in this city [said a prominent Tammany chieftain] has for more than a hundred years been doing for the people what settlements and community centers claim they are doing for them now. All these social-service agencies think they are "scientific" and want to investigate everything. The same thing is true of all the plans to "Americanize" the poor foreigners. The best way to Americanize is through human kindness, understanding, and willingness to give every one a helping hand. That is what we have always done. We're not "scientific" and we have no formalities, and any one who wants to see us is welcomed and no questions asked. Any one elected by the people must be of service to the people.

### THE LOCAL CLUB

Where neighborhood participation in party organization appears most plainly is in the local party clubs. Usually there is a central district club, where the leader, captains, and helpers meet and any one is welcome, and often there are one or more clubs in different parts of the district which draw from a smaller area and are still more distinctly neighborhood affairs.

One of three Democratic clubs in a certain district of New York may be cited as typical. It occupies an old brick dwelling, which has been altered for club purposes, containing a general meeting room, smaller committee rooms, pool and game tables, newspapers and magazines. The basement is set aside for the women, who meet separately. This clubhouse is open all the time, but is frequented mostly in the evening and on Saturdays and Sundays.

It has five hundred members, membership being open to any one in the district who wishes to enroll with the Democratic party, including immigrants not yet naturalized. Something over three hundred of the members are native-born Americans, mostly of Irish descent; the rest are foreign born, and include Jews, Italians, and smaller contingents of Greeks, Bohemians, and Germans. All, however, speak English at least well enough to get along with their fellows. On any evening a group representing all these races may be found at the club chatting, smoking, playing pool or cards, and having a general good time together, all on a plane of equal good-fellowship and everybody feeling "at home."

Dues, to defray upkeep, are fifty cents a month. Business meetings of the full membership are held monthly. Besides the usual officers, an executive committee of fifteen is elected, of which the district leader customarily serves as chairman. This leader and the club president are Irish, the vice-president is a Jew, the financial secretary an Italian, and the executive committee contains members of several races. The captains of this district, of whom there are twenty-one, likewise represent all the leading racial groups who live there.

There is a naturalization committee, which keeps tabs on the men not yet naturalized and assists them either directly or through the local captains or the district leader. Every year, it was stated, from three hundred to four hundred men are helped to secure citizenship papers. A good many are referred to English and civics classes in the public schools, and some informal instruction is given at the club.

Frequent smokers, card parties, and picnics are held, and also dances and entertainments which usually take place in a theater near by, and for which an admission fee is charged to defray expenses. The larger gatherings are often attended by fifteen hundred to two thousand people, drawn from the different racial groups in the locality.

In the Liberty Loan drives captains served on the local campaign committees, made house-to-house canvasses of the party members, and held local rallies. The same method was followed in the Red Cross and other war drives. At the time of the Spanish-influenza epidemic the captains took charge of assisting party members in their respective neighborhoods, as they did also in the fuel-saving campaign. In these tasks they called upon a good many others in the neighborhood to help them.

There are a great many political clubs such as this, ranging in size from small ones which meet in a single room up to some considerably better equipped than the one just described. Some bestir themselves only around election time, but others keep on the job the year round. In all cases they are centers of political interest and participation on the part of the neighborhood, which, though informal and rather casual, are none the less real. Here the people of the neighborhood gather to discuss political affairs. In combination with the scheme of district organization previously outlined, such clubs do a good deal to bring people of different races, and native born and foreign born, together in common action. Thus they are important factors in the promotion of neighborhood amity and unity.

### RELATING THE DISTRICT TO THE CITY

Nominally, at least, the district leader is elected by the party voters of the district, at the primaries. As a rule a considerable number of committeemen are similarly elected by districts to form a general party committee for the city. These committeemen include representatives of the various racial elements. The district leaders for the whole city are frequently called together, as a sort of upper council; gatherings of all the captains sometimes take place, and the entire membership of the city committee is convened more or less regularly for discussions of party policies. Under this scheme of organization, not only are the local precincts bound together within their respective districts, but the districts in turn are related to one another and to the community at large.

So much for the two old parties. It remains to report what several of the newer parties— namely, the Labor party, the Nonpartisan League, and the Socialists—are doing to unite the races through the medium of the neighborhood. Here the writer wishes it clearly understood that he is not discussing the platforms of these parties or passing judgment either for or against their general principles. He is simply reporting certain instances of activity on their part which make for neighborhood solidarity and initiative.

### THE LABOR PARTY'S AIMS

The Labor party, at this writing, is still so embryonic that little or nothing in the way of local results, but only its general status and aims, may be mentioned. It stands for a departure from the traditional policy of organized labor in America to keep out of politics, and proposes to organize laboring men and women as a polit-ical party. It had its origin among a group of labor leaders in Chicago in 1918, but it has not yet been recognized or sanctioned by the American Federation of Labor.

The launching of this party in America was largely inspired by the rapid growth and success of the Labor party in England. The motives and ideals of the English movement have been voiced by its secretary, Mr. Arthur Henderson, who is reported by the papers as saying in a recent address:

The development of political institutions has not kept pace with the growth of democracy, which is awake and conscious of its power, but unable to obtain any real control of the machinery of government. The possessing classes contrive to defeat the popular will on every first-class political issue in which the rights and liberties of the peo-ple are involved. . . . The main problem now [he con-tinued] is to restore popular confidence in representative institutions and to guide the movement of the masses along the path of constitutional changes and to enable democracy to become master in its own house without violence.

As the American Labor party develops, it will attempt to reach every working man and woman, whether unionized or not, by means of local organization even more intensive than that which has been built up by the old parties. In Chicago, where the new party is most fully organized, it has in view such enterprises as community laundries and kitchens, and co-operative stores and clubhouses. Its intent is to put into definite, regular, and fully democratic form the constructive neighborhood service which the old parties have fostered in more or less casual, paternalistic, and sometimes questionable ways. As the great mass of immigrants are laborers, they will be reached by the appeal to all laboring people, native born and foreign born, to unite on a basis of political solidarity. The party expects to enlist immigrant workers, and in Chicago, for example, the personnel of the ward chairmen, secretaries, and committee members includes representatives of a dozen or more immigrant groups.[1]

### THE NONPARTISAN LEAGUE

The reasons for the organization of the National Nonpartisan League in 1915 are explained as follows in one of its official leaflets:

[1] Since the above was written the Labor party has entered into a combination with other elements, which has taken the name of the Farmer-Labor party and put a national ticket in the field.

## ORGANIZATION AND GOVERNMENT

The need in response to which it came into existence was this: Everywhere politics was corrupt and partial. Everywhere politics was used to enrich the business class—bankers, lawyers, and middlemen—land sharks, and speculators in the necessities of life. All of these were becoming rich at the expense of the farmer and the wage earner. Farmers saw this everywhere. But farmers in their efforts to remedy the situation simply butted their heads against a stone wall. They tried petitions to Congress and the state legislatures; they tried to control the politics of the Democratic party and make it clean and honest; they tried to control the Republican party and make that clean and honest; they tried in every way they could to have clean and wholesome laws passed to bring a little of justice into the lives of the common people. Everywhere they failed. Always the class that profit upon the wages of the wage earner and the product of the farmer controlled the machinery of politics and enriched themselves at the expense of the producers.

The League as yet operates mainly in North Dakota, but is spreading into adjacent states. By its constitution it is restricted to farmers and farm hands, but it has co-operated with the labor-union movement and with the Labor party, and has in turn been indorsed by the State Federation of Labor of North Dakota and other labor groups. Developing along these lines, it has begun to organize in towns as well as in the rural districts, and has developed certain distinctly neighborhood activities which are bringing immigrant residents into fuller relation with these town communities. As the population of North Dakota includes German, Scandinavian, Russian, Icelandic, Slavic, French-Canadian, and other immigrant groups, the League has ample opportunity to serve as a racial solvent.

## UNITING IMMIGRANTS AND AMERICANS

A correspondent living in a small town writes as follows:

The way this League seems to be tying up the immigrant more closely with the American life is that it is arousing an interest in public life, showing them the power of the ballot, as well as their privilege in the ballot, which we know is our strongest democratic weapon. If I remember rightly, this is the very first time in the history of our country when laws have been referred back to the people, giving them the opportunity of expressing their minds as to the value of said laws to the common people.

Another correspondent from the same town says:

The different nationalities here are easily mixed, for the simple reason we teach them to think and act for themselves as soon as they get located among us.

Another correspondent, living in another town, makes this exceedingly interesting report:

We have therefore taken the education of the foreign-born citizen into consideration in the Nonpartisan League and its auxiliary, the Woman's N. P. L. The foreign-born population in our particular vicinity is principally Russian, with a sprinkling of Scandinavian, Bohemian, German, and so forth; but that does not make a great deal of difference, as most of the Russians speak German and many read it, so that with the German edition of our League paper we can reach both German and Russian. The Scandinavians learn to speak and read English very quickly and Americanize in a short time. We have both

English and German-speaking lecturers in the field, and hold picnics with speaking, and debates during the winter. At these meetings some local men talk a little before the traveling speaker begins.

Our laws provide for compulsory school attendance for the young, so the matter of acquiring American ways will take care of itself in a generation or two. Whether they cook by American recipes or wear hats in lieu of the little shawl, we consider of very little importance beside learning to speak and read English and taking an active and intelligent interest in affairs of the state and nation. It would seem that about the best way to create a spirit of Americanism in either foreign or native-born citizens is to make the conditions—social and economic—in this country come somewhere near approximating their preconceived ideals of the "sweet land of liberty."

A particularly significant piece of Americanization work in this same town is thus described by another resident:

Three years ago several foreigners asked Miss —— to teach them English, and, as there was no other place, we gave her the use of our home. Some weeks later a Federal naturalization agent came to the city to urge the commercial club to start a night school. The commercial club agreed that they would supply the place, providing twenty pupils would attend. I went immediately to the president of the club and told him that we had a night school of twenty-five people, and asked him to come up and see it. He was astonished that there were so many people in town who did not know the English language. We had two illiterates over fifteen, who had grown up in ——. In about six weeks we were given an unused basement room of one of the schoolhouses.

The teachers were volunteers, and students progressed rapidly. The night school formed a social nucleus and gave several entertainments in their schoolroom, and rented a hall for dancing. Some of the teachers invited the school to their homes and the young people said they have never had such a delightful winter in their lives. The school superintendents were at no time in sympathy with the school, though they supplied us with books, but no janitor service and frequently with no heat. The school board did not employ teachers and we could not close it so long as there was so much interest. We had an average attendance of over twenty, five nights a week. These difficulties led to the passage of the bill giving state aid to night schools. Our school is now under the supervision of the city superintendent.

As many of the pupils walked fourteen blocks to night school, this gave us the means for agitation for a school in the foreign part or the "south side" of town. The residents of this part circulated their own petitions, appeared before the school board, forced through two special elections to vote on school bonds; then the school was named for the man who had opposed it for three years. The agitation they made for the school building was done by the foreigners themselves. I merely suggested. They built the school within two blocks of the city dump and now we are trying to have that moved.

These are the principal things that have been done. I believe that the chief value lies in the fact that they have done these things themselves—really managed their own campaigns, and appeared before the school board, the commercial club, and the city commissioners.

### ORGANIC PLAN OF SOCIALISTS

The Socialist party, now well established in nearly every country of Europe, is still new in the United States as compared with the Republican and Democratic parties, but not as compared with the Labor party and the Nonpartisan League, and the Communist, Communist Labor, and numerous other small political groups which have recently sprung up and which at present figure so conspicuously in the newspapers and in governmental attempts at repression.

These later and more or less revolutionary groups now regard the regular Socialists, with their belief in orderly evolution through the electorate, as altogether too slow and patient. In fact, the country at large, now that on the one hand it is learning something of the platforms and proposed methods of the more drastic groups, while on the other hand it sees Socialists in city and state offices behaving in a rather matter-of-fact and responsible way, is beginning to look upon the regular Socialists as comparatively conservative. Reference is made below solely to the evolutionary Socialists—that is, to the Socialist party proper—which depends upon the peaceful and nonrevolutionary methods of the ballot.

The relation of the Socialist party to the Americanization of the immigrant is exceedingly important in that from a third to a half of its dues-paying membership, and a large percentage of its total voting strength, are composed of immigrants. Though the total number of immigrants enrolled is much larger in the case of the two old parties, the ratio of immigrants to native born is far larger in the case of the Socialists. This means that the problem of developing party unity out of diverse racial elements is more serious among the Socialists than in either of the old parties. Facing this problem, the Socialists have worked out a definite and complete plan of party organization to co-ordinate and eventually amalgamate the, different racial groups.

## FOREIGN-SPEAKING FEDERATIONS

This plan of organization, which in effect reaches down into the neighborhood, and indeed starts from the neighborhood, is provided for in the following sections of Article XII of the national constitution and platform of the Socialist party, entitled "Foreign-speaking Federations":

Sec. 1. Five branches of the Socialist party working in any other language than English shall have the right to form a National Federation under the supervision of the Executive Committee.

Sec. 2. Such National Language Federation shall have the right to elect an officer known as Translator-Secretary, who shall be conversant with his own language as well as the English language, and whose duty it shall be to serve as a medium of communication between his federation and the National Organization of the Socialist party.

Sec. 3. When such National Language Federations shall have at least 1,000 members, their Translator-Secretary shall be entitled to necessary office room in the National Office.

Sec. 5. (a) Branches of Language Federations shall be an integral part of the county and state organizations, and must in all cases work in harmony with the constitution and platform of the State and County organizations of the Socialist party.

Sec. 9. Each national federation shall be entitled to elect one fraternal delegate to the National Conventions of the party. . . .

In accordance with Section 3 of these provisions, there is now assembled at the national headquarters of the Socialist party, in Chicago, a group of translator-secretaries who represent all the main racial elements in the party, and who are in constant intercommunication with their respective groups, the general officers, and one another. Prior to the summer of 1919, the number of immigrant groups thus represented by translator-secretaries numbered about a dozen. Then came the split which resulted in the expulsion or secession of two left-wing elements, who have become the Communist and Communist Labor parties. The leading racial federations which stuck to the evolutionary principles of the Socialist party and remained identified with it are the Finnish, Jewish, Italian, German, Bohemian, Slovak, and French.

These translator-secretaries are not appointed by party managers, but are elected annually by their respective federations. The general executive committee of the party, consisting of fifteen members, is also elected by the individual members of the party, voting annually in five territorial districts. Other things being equal, the disposition is not to re-elect the same persons, but to distribute the experience and responsibility involved by changing the personnel.

Explaining this form of organization in relation to Americanization, the national executive secretary of the party makes the following statement:

The purpose of these foreign-language federations is not to keep alive their spirit of nationalism, but is entirely one of practical organization work. Such a large percentage of the foreign-speaking population cannot be reached through the medium of English speakers or papers that it is absolutely necessary to carry on our propaganda in their own language. Since this could not be done in mixed locals, the language-speaking locals, and hence the federations of the language locals, were a logical development. We have, however, tried to encourage the Americanization and naturalization of the foreign-speaking Socialists, and for that purpose have published and widely circulated the inclosed booklet, *How to Become Naturalized.* Several of the state organizations also have a provision in their state constitutions requiring unnaturalized foreigners to make application for citizenship within a given period after their admission to the party. The recent convention held by the Socialist party adopted an amendment to the application for membership reading as follows:

Section A.—Upon the acceptance of my application for membership in the Socialist party I promise within three months, wherever possible, to make application for citizenship.[1]

## RACIAL BRANCHES

What has been said should not be taken to imply that all the immigrant members of the Socialist party are included in these one-race local branches and federations. A large number, who have been in America longer, are members of racially mixed English-speaking locals. As a rule, however, the one-race locals partake most of neighborhood character. The obvious reason for this is that their membership, being confined to one race, is usually drawn from a compact colony of that race. The Finnish Workers' Educational Associations, which are

---

[1] Otto Bronstetter, correspondence.

branches of the Socialist party, represent the fullest development of the educational and social activities of locals composed of immigrants of one race. The activities of other racial locals follow similar, but less generally developed, lines. Educational work in a strict sense has probably been carried farthest by the Jewish locals, of which the open forum and class instruction are the most characteristic features.

Frequently several locals representing different races will meet in the same place, and sometimes, under such circumstances, they will form a working alliance under a joint board. Such an arrangement is a sort of transition stage between the one-race local and the English-speaking local in which different races are united. An interesting example is had in the case of such an alliance in an Eastern city, which recently took over a building long occupied by a Democratic club. By a coincidence, this change closely followed a city election in which the Democratic vote was greatly reduced, and the Socialist vote, though still less than one-third of the Democratic, substantially increased.

In this case a Bohemian Socialist local wanted to get larger quarters and expand its activities. The members discovered that the Democratic club building, of four stories, could be bought cheap. But as they could not finance the undertaking by themselves, they got a Slovak, a German, and an English-speaking local to join with them. About a hundred persons representing these groups formed an operating corporation and bought the building, the money being secured within the membership.

For official purposes, each of the four locals will meet there by itself, but for social and educational activities they will all meet together. A number of local labor unions will also meet there and share in the social features. There are bowling alleys and pool tables; but a bar and disappearing roulette table in a rear room, which saw service formerly (the cutting off of the bar receipts by prohibition was said to account in part for the departure of the previous occupants), have been discarded.

We're not much for drinking and we don't gamble [said one of the officers]. We have other and better things to think of.

## THE ENGLISH-SPEAKING LOCALS

The goal toward which all Socialist locals tend in their evolution is the union of different races and native and foreign born in one English-speaking organization. The following example may be cited as typical.

This particular local, situated in New York City, maintains a four-story headquarters building, and has a full membership of some three hundred adults of both sexes, a women's auxiliary of about forty, and a young people's society, whose members graduate into the adult group, of a hundred or more. There is also a Socialist "Sunday school" for the children. The organization includes native-born Americans, of varied descent, and foreign-born members of half a dozen races.

The officers emphasized two characteristics of organization which, they said, distinguished local Socialist clubs from those of the old parties. One is that the Socialist society runs its local affairs in its own way. Only questions of general party policy are taken up with the central Socialist committee of the city, and that committee does not attempt to interfere. This, they said, is the general rule. The second distinct feature is that every effort is made to decentralize and distribute the responsibility for local management and initiative among the rank and file of the membership. There is an elected executive committee of fifteen members, and there are various special committees on upkeep, finance, propaganda, entertainment, education, and other activities. A regular program of educational lectures is conducted through the winter, and a good deal of informal assistance in naturalization is given. Though as yet the building is used mainly by Socialists, it is open to any one, and the aim is to make it increasingly a neighborhood center.

Several Socialist officials expressed a deep scorn for the ordinary type of Democratic or Republican club.

They do little or nothing that is really constructive [said one], but are more or less cliques of politicians whose chief interest is to get jobs for themselves or their friends, and who bestir themselves very little in the interest of the neighborhood except around election time. A real political

club should act as a forum for free discussion of current
political events, proposed legislation, and local improvements in such matters as housing, sanitation, and recreation.
Thus far, most of the Socialist locals have been thinking
chiefly of propaganda, and have not accomplished so very
much in the way of enlisting active interest and participation
in neighborhood affairs, but nevertheless there is a general
tendency for these locals to develop into real neighborhood
centers. Neither have we yet worked out any such complete district organization as the old parties have, but we
will gradually do that, too. But there will be this difference between their clubs and ours—that ours will be run
by the people themselves and not by politicians.

## NEIGHBORHOOD PARTICIPATION

What conclusion may be drawn from the facts
presented as to the measure in which the neighborhood enters into party organization? It is
evident that even in the confusion of city conditions the neighborhood functions and finds
expression in substantial degree. The political
motive is strong enough to interest the neighborhood and to stimulate it to action. This
motive and the political organization to which
it leads are effective in bringing native-born
and foreign-born Americans together on a basis
of genuine fellowship and co-operation.

The kind of local participation elicited in party
affairs corresponds roughly to the kind of political
food upon which the neighborhood is fed. In
the case of parties which are long intrenched in
power and patronage, local party activity runs
largely to the voicing of personal wants and the
distribution of personal favors. This reduces

412

politics to "human" and "practical" terms, which reach the understanding and enlist the interest of a large element whom more impersonal and abstract appeals might fail to move. But while the practical success of such methods demonstrates that to be most effective politics must be brought close to the individual's daily life, they can hardly be said to represent the highest political standards.

The newer parties, who are still fighting their way, and who have comparatively little patronage to dispense, rely more on militant denunciations of abuses, and upon appeals expressed in general terms of social welfare. The vigor of neighborhood response to the political motive depends mainly upon the scope allowed to local initiative. Here, again, the parties which are newer and less institutionalized call forth a larger measure of self-directing local activity.

## LOCAL UNITS OF GOVERNMENT

Party organization thus provides some political outlet for the neighborhood. But of course parties are partisan, and they also lack governmental authority. They are, therefore, only a partial substitute for the town meeting, in which the neighborhood spoke with finality, and settled its own affairs. In what measure does the neighborhood still figure as a unit of actual government? To what extent has the town meeting survived or been replaced by some adequate governmental substitute? How far, by such means, has the immigrant American been enabled to bear a responsible share in governing the community of which he is a member?

Part of the answer to this question lies in the fact that, since the days when the town meeting was all-embracing and all-sufficient for the affairs of its little village, a great number and variety of voluntary agencies have developed which attend to many concerns of the community on a basis of private initiative and control. In the case of immigrant neighborhoods, the numerous organizations formed by the immigrants themselves play a large part in meeting their special needs. Labor unions, co-operative societies, improvement associations, women's clubs, social centers, churches, settlements, charity societies —these and other private bodies conduct local activities which considerably relieve the demands upon the municipal government.

More definite attempts to supply a substitute for the town meetings are represented by Community Councils and the Social Unit. The latter, by organizing the people of a district into various occupational councils on the one hand, and a general citizens' council on the other, proposes to develop a working scheme which, its advocates hold, might eventually suffice to meet the whole range of local needs.

Such extra-governmental organizations and activities, as far as they go, provide the people of a neighborhood with opportunity to direct their own local affairs. In varying degree they enlist foreign born and native born in common action. In the total, they fill a considerable sphere. But, like political parties, they lack final governmental authority. They can go only so far on their own motion, and then they have to stop and await or adjust themselves to the motion of constituted government. They can petition the government, and they can bring the influence of public opinion to bear, but government itself has the last word and the final decision. Nothing can be a full substitute for the town meeting which does not possess equal authority.

With regard to the measure in which the neighborhood unit still figures in government itself, it must be said that, while in small towns the neighborhood and the body politic are necessarily one and the same, under city conditions the prevailing movement has been away from the local unit to a city-wide scheme. Under the slogan of "efficiency," this movement has embodied itself especially in the commission and city-manager plans. Increasingly, cities have given up boards of councilmen and aldermen elected by local districts and have substituted boards or commissions elected by the community at large. Municipal government has become highly centralized. It is urged that thus officials of higher caliber can be secured, petty local politics displaced, and the quality of public service enhanced.

Recently, however, a reaction has begun in the direction of restoring some measure of initiative and self-government to the local district. Thus far, this countertendency has taken form mainly in the appointment of local advisory boards to co-operate with city officials. A borough president of New York, for example, organized a number of such district boards in his borough, and states that he found them of much help. New York has gone farther than this in establishing forty-eight local school boards, for as many different districts, which have legally constituted and final powers in the regulation of certain school affairs.

Our experience shows [states a school official, referring to the effect of these boards in calling out local initiative and promoting common interest among different races] that, so far as school matters are concerned, the local school boards tend to unite the various racial elements that may be present in a given school district.

Mere numbers make it impracticable for cities of any size to carry out the town-meeting idea in its original form. But some New England communities which have long outgrown their village days still cling to the town meeting in modified form. The case of Brookline, a Massachusetts city of about 35,000 people, may be cited as an example. This city is divided into nine precincts. Each precinct elects annually nine delegates, to serve for a period of three years, making a constant representation of twenty-seven. The whole body of two hundred and forty-three delegates for the nine precincts, together with a hundred or more city officials and board members, constitute a town meeting of delegates. This plan works out very satisfactorily.

Our attendance and interest are the same as in the old days [writes a citizen], and no effort is needed to bring out

far more than a majority. To be elected a member of the
town meeting one must be a voter, but any one who is a
resident may attend and speak. At the last annual meeting, in fact, there were as many behind the rail as inside.

Town meetings [observed de Tocqueville] are to liberty
what primary schools are to science; they bring it within
the people's reach, they teach men how to use and enjoy it.[1]

The difference in scale and complexity between
the governmental problems of a village and
those of a city, and between those of a small
city like Brookline and those of a metropolis, is
of course very great. Whether or not it would
be possible or helpful to introduce into large
cities this or any other modified plan of local
"town meetings" is a problem which involves
many considerations. But that the elements
of local initiative and responsibility shall be
conserved and developed, whether by this means
or some other, is of vital importance to the
future of American democracy.

The neighborhood is at once the core and the
epitome of American life. The town meeting
has been called the "primordial cell of our body
politic."[2] In so far, therefore, as the city neighborhood of to-day can be utilized as the unit of
political organization and of government it will
be possible to say, with reference to both foreign-
born and native-born Americans, what de
Tocqueville said of the typical citizen of the
township-neighborhood of New England:[3]

---

[1] De Tocqueville. *Democracy in America.* Part i, chap. v.

[2] James K. Hosmer. *Samuel Adams, the Man of the Town Meeting.* Johns Hopkins University Studies.

[3] De Tocqueville. *Democracy in America.* Part i, chap. xiv.

# AMERICA VIA THE NEIGHBORHOOD

. . . his co-operation in its affairs insures his attachment to its interest; the well-being it offords him secures his affection; and its welfare is the aim of his ambition and of his future exertions; he takes a part in every occurrence in the place; he practices the art of government in the small sphere within his reach; he accustoms himself to those forms which can alone insure the steady progress of liberty; he imbibes their spirit, he acquires a taste for order, comprehends the union or the balance of powers, and collects clear, practical notions on the nature of his duties and the extent of his rights.

The township serves as a center for the desire of public esteem, the want of exciting interests, and the taste for authority and popularity, in the midst of the ordinary relations of life; and the passions which commonly embroil society change their character when they find a vent so near the domestic hearth and the family circle.

In the United States the inhabitants were thrown but as yesterday upon the soil they now occupy . . . the instinctive love of their country can scarcely exist in their minds; but every one takes as zealous an interest in the affairs of his township, his county, and of the whole state as though they were his own, because every one, in his sphere, takes an active part in the government of society.

# XIII

## THE OUTCOME

Account has now been taken of the Americanizing forces at work within the immigrant groups, of various attempts at Americanization from without, and of such basic interests as bring immigrants and native Americans together on an equal footing. These different sets of factors have been considered separately, each with respect to its particular line of effectiveness, but all with reference to the local neighborhood. Organizations and specific activities have received chief attention, as distinguished from the informal features and general development of neighborhood life. It will be profitable now to consider how the immigrant's Americanization works out from the point of view of the neighborhood process as a whole, including informal "neighborly" elements as well as definite and organized factors.

### 1. THE NEIGHBORHOOD PROCESS IN HOPEVILLE

This neighborhood process may be discerned most clearly in the case of a small and rudimentary community, where it is not obscured by the complexities of city life. Though such a simply constituted community lacks many of the particular forms of activity which have been discussed, it contains the basic ingredients. The process, once observed under such elementary conditions, may then be recognized under any conditions.

A rudimentary community which answers the present purpose is available in a village of Massachusetts in the Connecticut Valley, which, for convenience in reference, will be called Hopeville. Hopeville is the largest of several village centers within a township of small farms. The population of the whole township is about three thousand, and that of this village is about twelve hundred, which brings it within the size of a single neighborhood. The community, more than two hundred and fifty years old, is still in a comparatively simple stage of development. The town hall, a memorial hall, and a grammar school are the only public buildings. Besides these, there are three churches, an academy which serves as high school, and half a dozen little stores.

Scattered about here and there are a score of shops where tobacco leaves are dried, sorted, and packed. There are also a number of shacks in which onions are stored pending shipment. During the first century and a half of its existence the community depended on general farming. Then for about fifty years it took to raising broom corn and making brooms. But since the time of the Civil War the tobacco crop has been its chief dependence and it is now one of the chief tobacco-raising centers of the region in which it is situated. Onions are the crop of next importance. These industries figure vitally in the history of the community, and particularly in the story of its later immigrants.

### THE YANKEES

The original settlers of Hopeville were the native Americans whom Columbus discovered and called Indians. The first immigrants, however, were a dozen or so English families, who had left England and two earlier settlements in America in protest against restriction of their religious liberty. They founded Hopeville in 1659 in order to enjoy complete religious freedom. The church was their first interest. All were Congregationalists. For many years they held services in one another's homes, later in the town hall; not for a long time did they feel that they needed or could afford a separate church building.

The beginnings of the English colony of Hopeville thus correspond very closely with the beginnings of many of the present immigrant colonies in America, which have grown up around the church. The parallel applies still further, as in Hopeville the church and the community were at first no less closely identified than is the case in many French-Canadian, Polish, or Greek colonies to-day. In fact, the situation was substantially the same as that which now exists among Greek immigrants, where the Orthodox Greek Community establishes and maintains the church.

Until well into the last century the community of Hopeville supported its church from township funds, and regulated church affairs through the general town meeting.

Town meetings began almost as soon as the colony itself. The first one was called to discuss a very practical detail—namely, the building of a village fence. There were plenty of details of this sort in the pioneer community, and town meetings were held nearly every month. Protection against the Indians, who were disposed to regard these English colonists as "foreigners," was one of the chief concerns.

Church affairs, as has been said, were another, and these also took an intensely practical turn. How much to pay the minister; who should be sent as a delegate to close the bargain when a new one was engaged; how this delegate's farm work should be taken care of during his absence; who should chop the minister's wood and store it in his shed—such were some of the questions relating to religion which were thrashed out in town meeting.

Grants of land to newcomers, the laying out of roads, and the schooling of the children were other subjects of discussion. All the men attended the meetings regularly. Not to do so was almost as bad as not to go to church. These meetings were like gatherings of the family circle in their intimacy and interplay of personality.

At first they were held at different houses, and later at the village store. Many years elapsed before money was set aside for a town hall.

During the pioneer period of the community, and in fact until within the last fifty years or so, school education was subordinated, as it is among immigrants to-day, to the winning of a livelihood by hard work. Most of the children stayed in school only a few years. One of the oldest men in the village to-day, who was born about 1840, and who has held many offices, written a history of the community, and is generally revered by its people, says he went to school only four years in his life.

At first the village hired a sort of peripatetic teacher, who had to get his pupils catch-as-catch-can. It was many years before a little wooden schoolhouse was built, and the present brick building is very recent. Meanwhile, in 1872, a private academy was built through a bequest, and this has served as a high school, the town contributing toward its support.

To-day the "Yankee" descendants of the original English immigrants constitute a small minority of the population, less than a tenth in the township, and not more than a fifth in the village. In each generation many of the young people have moved away, and the birth rate has declined until instances of more than two children to a family are rare. There have been almost no intermarriages with other stocks, and now the Yankee families of the village are all more or less related to one another, so that, as a later comer remarked, "one must not say anything to any one about anybody else, because every one is some one else's cousin."

The Congregational church is still the center of organization of the Yankee element. Connected with it is a "Men's Club," and two organizations of women, one calling itself the "Real Folks," which was formed to promote foreign missions, and the other known as the "Book Club." There is also a rather literary "Village Improvement Society," composed of Yankees; a rather inactive library association is similarly made up; and the academy is run by a self-perpetuating board of Yankee trustees.

The tradition of deference to the descendants of the original settlers still survives in elections to the state legislature. Only straight Yankees have thus far been elevated to this honor. Yankees are still the largest landholders, and show a disposition to keep their holdings "in the family." Many of the present owners are living on inheritances.

### IRISH, FRENCH CANADIANS, AND GERMANS

The development of industries other than general farming—first broom-making, then tobacco and onion raising—produced a demand for additional labor and eventually attracted several groups of immigrants. The first to come were those who had the shortest road to travel, the French Canadians. At the outset they were mostly single men, who stayed only during the summer, returning to Canada after the harvest. But this transiency soon led to permanency, and about 1850 upward of fifty families settled in and about the village, working mostly in the broom shops.

As laborers, these French Canadians were welcomed by the Yankees, but they were at first regarded and treated as "foreigners." They could not speak English, most of them were illiterate, and, being Catholics, they were outside the Congregationalist fold. As the Yankees would sell land to them only in the less desirable spots, they formed a little colony by themselves. Few of the first immigrants became citizens. But they got ahead rapidly, built homes of their own, and their children mingled with the others at the village school. The French-Canadian immigration, never large, came practically to a stop at the time of the Civil War.

Not long after the streamlet of French-Canadian immigration began a small number of German immigrants arrived. The first one happened to be a Protestant from Saxony. He was taken into the Congregational Church. Most of the others, however, were Catholics from Bavaria, and formed a somewhat separate colony.

Beginning about the same time, but coming in larger numbers and over a longer period, Irish immigrants settled in Hopeville. Those who came first were men who had been employed as laborers in laying out a street-car line which ran near the village. In the course of this employment they brought their families to Hopeville and established themselves permanently. They, too, were welcomed by the Yankees as an economic asset.

The French Canadians, though excellent broom-makers, had not taken kindly to breaking uncleared land and thus increasing the acreage available for crops of broom corn, onions, and tobacco. The number of German immigrants was not large enough to help much. The Irish, however, were willing to tackle the rough land, and the Yankees were so willing to let them that for some time they declined to sell them any land other than that which had to be cleared. Like the French Canadians and the Germans. they were looked upon as "foreigners." Though they spoke English, it was hardly with a Yankee twang, and besides they were Catholics. Also like the others, they worked hard, bought land and sent their children to school.

### THESE THREE GROUPS UNITE

Quite naturally, these three immigrant groups, being thrown together as workers, "foreigners," and Catholics in this little community, combined for mutual aid and comfort. Led by the Irish, they united in organizing a Catholic church. At first they went to the church in a near-by town, and later they held services in the Academy Hall, but eventually they built a church of their own. As the Congregational church was the center for the Yankees, so the Catholic church became the rallying point for these later immigrants.

# THE OUTCOME

Gradually the three elements among the latter became amalgamated. To-day the pure French-Canadian stock has almost disappeared through intermarriage with the Irish, and both have intermarried more or less with the Germans. In numbers, this composite group is now more than twice as large as that of the Yankees, both in the township and in the village.

Meanwhile the incorporation of these immigrant elements as a part of the village community went on apace. Economic factors played a fundamental part in the process. In the beginning, as has been said, the Yankees would sell the newcomers only the less desirable land, and took particular pains to exclude them from the most select sections of the village. If property in these sections was offered for sale, well-to-do Yankees would sometimes buy it themselves simply to keep the "foreigners" out.

But Yankeee thrift had also to be reckoned with. As the "foreigners" accumulated substantial savings by hard work and became able to pay good prices, they found it possible to buy homes almost anywhere. Thus their colonies gradually dissolved and they were distributed through the village. To-day only one little section of the main street remains uninvaded. It is the Yankees' "last stand."

### NEIGHBORLINESS

Human neighborliness also developed naturally. The mingling of the children at the village school, and the childish gossip which they brought home about each other's family affairs, first aroused mutual curiosity and interest. This interest was deepened by the time-honored Yankee custom of visiting and offering friendly assistance at times of illness, birth, or death, and of attending funerals. This custom, on the assumption of *noblesse oblige*, was extended to include the immigrants, and the latter readily responded.

Lending farm implements was also part of the neighborly routine. The employment of Irish girls as servants helped the latter to take on American ways. A German immigrant recalls how he learned English from the daughter of the household where he first worked as "hired man." In the evening the little girl would play at "school" with this green German as her pupil. Later he bought a home of his own near by.

"Most of us Yankees don't think of them as foreigners any more," said one of the oldest inhabitants. "They are our neighbors and friends." This remark tells the story of what has taken place. When the Catholics built their present church, about thirty years ago, Yankee Congregationalists contributed toward the building fund, and when the twenty-fifth year of service of a generally beloved Catholic priest was celebrated all the leading citizens attended a testimonial meeting and the Protestant minister presented a gift from his congregation. The men's and women's clubs of the Congregationalist church frequently have Catholic friends at special meetings and entertainments, while the women's endeavor society of the Catholic church is equally cordial in inviting Protestants to its affairs.

Industrially, educationally, and politically, these immigrant groups, especially the Irish, not only have become an integral part of the community, but have in large measure come to hold its leadership. They own some of the largest farms, and most of the tobacco shops, and are generally more enterprising than the Yankees.

Though the immigrants themselves were mostly illiterate, most of the first generation born in Hopeville went to school till they reached working age, and many of the second generation, now reaching maturity, have completed the high-school course, and a substantial number have gone on to normal school or college. With the exception of one young woman, who is straight Yankee, all the teachers in the grammar school to-day, including the principal, come from this immigrant stock.

In local politics, the change which has come about is still more pronounced. The most influential office, that of moderator of the town meeting, has been held for the last fifteen years by a man of Irish parentage, and the later comers outnumber the Yankees on the town's boards and committees. Although there is a good deal of nonpartisan voting on purely local issues, nearly all the Yankees belong to the national

Republican party, while the other elements are consolidated as Democrats.

Notwithstanding the generally friendly relations which now prevail, the Yankees cannot help feeling somewhat resentful at being elbowed out. This undercurrent of resentment toward the Irish-French-German element helps to explain their hospitable attitude toward the group of recent immigrants now to be considered.

### THE POLES

Polish immigrants began to settle in Hopeville about thirty-five years ago, but came in largest numbers from about 1905 up to the outbreak of the war. With the development of the tobacco industry, the demand for additional labor greatly increased. Farm hands were needed during the summer, to expand the acreage, and shop hands during the winter, to prepare the tobacco for shipment.

The leaders in Hopeville's chief industry appealed to labor-recruiting agents in that region to help them out. These agents were accustomed to go to New York City, or Boston, and "persuade" newly arrived immigrants to return with them. The first Pole who came to Hopeville was thus persuaded. Soon others came through the same channel. They found industrial opportunities so satisfactory, especially work in the tobacco shops, that they sent back favorable reports to their relatives and friends, many of whom later joined them. To-day

# THE OUTCOME

Poles form more than a third of the population of the whole township, and about half that of the village.

As in the case of the French-Canadian, German, and Irish immigrants before them, Polish immigrants were welcomed as laborers, but regarded as "foreigners." Similarly they formed, in the beginning, a distinct colony. Within this colony they set about to organize and to get a foothold in practically the same way that the earlier groups of immigrants and the original English colonists had done as pioneers in their day. The church was likewise their first interest. But as the Catholic church was already on the ground, the Poles attended that at first, and continued to do so for some years. This arrangement did not prove satisfactory, however, and eventually they formed a church of their own.

## PIONEER ORGANIZATION

Meanwhile they organized several societies which provided mutual insurance against sickness and death, and also met, in part, the need for self-directing religious organization. These societies served virtually as town meetings for the Poles, where they could thrash out in their own tongue the numerous practical problems, akin to those of the original English colonists, by which they were confronted in their new environment.

The first of these societies was called St.

Michael's. Its membership was confined to men, and it was distinctly a religious society formed to preserve the allegiance of its members to the traditional church. Meetings were held on Sundays. One of the society's first investments consisted of two flags, which were displayed side by side, one the historic flag of Poland, the other the Stars and Stripes of America.

For a number of years the regular meetings, as well as dances and entertainments, were held at the town hall, such early use of which has doubtless helped to interrelate the Poles with the community. Five or six years ago St. Michael's bought an acre and a half of land on the main street of the village at a cost of $1,500, as a reservation for a Polish church. When a few years afterward a church was established the society sold it this land as a site for $1,000, thus contributing $500 toward the building fund.

Some years later a similar society, called St. Casimir's, was formed. It also met in the town hall. Several years ago the society purchased a piece of land with the intention of putting up a good-sized hall of its own. But finding that the expense would be too large, it modified its plans and built a block of seven small tenements. These living quarters, which were badly needed, were rented to Polish families, and the income was used to pay off the loan for construction. A room in the basement, reserved as a meeting place for this society and the others, has become the Polish center.

A third benefit society, including women, but

otherwise of less importance, was organized later, and also two local branches of country-wide associations for promoting the freedom of Poland. All these societies have continued to use the town hall for entertainments and special occasions. The disposition of the Poles to identify themselves with the community is further evidenced by the name given to a band which they organized to play at weddings and entertainments. They called it "The Hope-ville Town Band."

### ADJUSTMENT THROUGH THE CHURCH

The story of the Polish church in Hopeville is significant as illustrating how the adjustment of an immigrant group to the general community may be brought about most easily along the lines of least resistance—that is, the lines of race. At first it seemed a happy circumstance that an American Catholic church was at hand to receive and assimilate these Polish Catholics.

But it did not work out so happily. The Poles say that the members of this church did not welcome them as cordially as they might have, and were disposed to look askance at their gawky, "greenhorn" ways. The church members intimate that the Poles were unwilling to bear their fair share of the parish expenses. At bottom the trouble was obviously that the Poles could not understand what was said and did not feel at home. After a while they petitioned for a Polish priest, to hear confessions

433

and hold special services. When it appeared that the priest in charge was not inclined to grant this request, several Poles appealed over his head to the bishop of the diocese, and when he also proved unsympathetic, they went to see the cardinal. The latter was so slow in replying that they took matters into their own hands, withdrew from the church, met in the town hall for services of their own, and engaged temporarily a priest of the so-called "Independent" Polish Catholic Church.

We thought this would bring the regular Catholic authorities to terms [said one of the leaders], because we knew they would not want to lose our church.

This stratagem succeeded, and the bishop appointed the Polish priest of a near-by town to conduct masses for them until they could get a church and priest of their own. Meanwhile they continued to use the town hall.

At once the situation improved. The Poles themselves were much happier, and the community noticed a general improvement in their attitude. Previously the frequency of Polish religious holidays and their too convivial celebration had provoked complaint, especially on the part of employers. The Polish priest was able to reduce these holidays to six a year, and to tone them down considerably. With his sympathetic encouragement, the group began to raise a church-building fund.

By that time the community saw the practical common sense of their attitude and all the leading

citizens contributed to this fund. Now · the
Poles have their own church, standing on the
main street. It cost $16,000 and seats four
hundred people, but has already proved inadequate, as the principal services are crowded
to the walls with people standing. A Polish
priest has been installed who devotes his whole
time to this parish. Far from criticizing this as
a "clannish" development, the community has
welcomed it as a distinct forward step in group
morale. The general respect for the Poles has
been enhanced by their own demonstration of
self-respect and self-dependence.

### STEADY PROGRESS

Like the immigrants who preceded them, the
Poles have made rapid economic headway.
When they first came most of them worked as
hired men at low wages, but not for long. The
wages paid in the tobacco shops kept increasing
till now they stand at $3.50 to $4 a day. Men,
women, and children worked in the shops, and
the earnings thus accumulated have been put
into farms and homes in the village.

Unlike the Germans and Irish, the Poles have
not been content with cheap uncleared land, but
have bought some of the best farms in the township. Owing largely to their bidding up, the
price of such land has doubled during recent
years. They have developed onion culture particularly. Being able to pay good prices, they
have become the owners of homes in almost every

part of the village. Though in certain spots, particularly the block of tenements previously mentioned, there are remnants of the earlier Polish colony, the Poles to-day are generally distributed throughout the community.

Most of the Polish immigrants were illiterate, though some had been to school several years in the old country. The illiterate element showed innate progressiveness by engaging an instructor to teach them to read and write Polish, and the town officials co-operated by granting them the use of an old schoolhouse for this purpose. About the same time an evening school was started by the town, at the request of the state educational authorities. The younger Polish men attended in substantial numbers, but after one year the thrifty school committee decided that the enterprise was too expensive and stopped it. The Poles also made use of a small supply of books on "English for foreigners" which the village library got from the state library, but which it failed to replenish. Most of the Poles now speak passable English, however, having picked it up in their association with other villagers.

According to the principal of the grammar and high schools, Polish parents are showing much more interest than formerly in the education of their children. There is no parochial school, and all the children attend the village school at least till they reach working age. At that time the "big money" paid in tobacco shops, and the efforts which employers make to recruit workers from the young people, constitute a strong temptation to quit school. As one girl remarked, when a teacher was urging her to stay:

Why should I? I can't see how education will help me much. I can make more now in the tobacco shops than you can make by teaching.

But the teachers report that parents are beginning to ask their co-operation in persuading children to remain in school. In one instance a father who very reluctantly gave consent to let his son enter high school came back at the end of two years to seek the principal's help in urging the boy to remain and graduate. Polish children are reported to be fully as bright as any of the other pupils, and to make more use than others of the village library, preferring, interestingly enough, books of poetry.

### GROUP ATTITUDES

Though the Poles are still to a large degree looked upon and treated as "foreigners," there is a very interesting difference between the attitudes toward them of the Irish-led element on the one hand and the original Yankees on the other, and a corresponding difference in the attitude of the Poles toward these two elements.

The Irish, though appreciating the value of the Poles as laborers and admitting their thrift, persistence, aggressiveness, and honesty in money matters, are resentful of the general progress they are making, their rapid increase in numbers and the prospect that before long they will become a determining factor in local politics. This attitude was naïvely expressed by one of the political leaders:

The American farmers need labor and the Poles should supply it. That's what they're here for. They should not have gone ahead so rapidly. I am not interested in their becoming citizens.

Others said:

These Poles are altogether too independent. The rest of us should take a definite stand against them.

The Irish have gone farther than the Yankees in attempting to keep Poles out of the best residence sections. The following little incident shows strikingly how the tables have turned. A certain choice piece of property, which was offered for sale by its Yankee owner back when the Irish were "getting in," was bought up by another Yankee to keep an Irish bidder out. The latter eventually succeeded in buying it from this Yankee, by paying a good price. Now the Irish owner, in his turn, recently bought up an adjoining piece of property to keep a Pole out! It is realized that such expedients can have only a temporary effect, but, as several property owners expressed it:

We'll keep the Poles out for a while, anyway.

The Poles, on their side, say that the Irish farmers and proprietors of tobacco shops simply want to exploit them as laborers and work them to death.

> No wonder the Irish get rich so quickly [said one]. To them we Poles are like the young Western horses that I just bought. I will work them hard. They will be good for five years. That's the way the Irish want to work the Poles. The Poles do work hard and give their best because they have to and they are used to it, but it makes them old before their time.

However, the Poles are making such steady advances and are so confident of the future that they are as much amused as resentful at these efforts to hold them down.

> Just wait [they say, with a shrug and a smile], our day is coming, all right.

Toward the Yankees, or, as they call them, the "English," the attitude of the Poles is quite different. In fact it approaches a sort of reverence. They say they would rather work for them than for any others.

> The English want a full day's work, but they're satisfied with that. They don't swear at us and they treat us like gentlemen. They have been kind in helping us to learn English. They invite us into their homes and they always come to our christenings and weddings.

Yankee employers speak more highly of the Poles than do those of Irish stock, and in general get along with them better.

It is not unnatural that the earlier immigrants, having passed through the pioneer period and succeeded in establishing themselves as "Americans," should be jealous of these later comers and regard them somewhat as interlopers and rivals. Under these circumstances the Yankees, who first resented the earlier immigrants as "foreigners" and later accepted them as neighbors, with some reservations, now find themselves functioning as a solvent to unite these still more "foreign" Polish immigrants with the rest of the community.

## COMING TOGETHER

The town meeting and local politics are helping to promote such union. Owing to the fact that only a few of the Polish immigrants can read and write English and that few of the Hopeville-born generation have reached voting age, there were before the war only about a dozen registered Polish voters in the town. But some who are not voters have attended the town meetings, feeling they had a right to do so because they own property and pay taxes. Thus far only one Pole has held a town office. He was appointed constable and assigned especially to take care of disputes and disorder among his own people. The Polish group appreciated this recognition and the arrangement has had good results.

The Irish element are Democrats in politics, but most of the Poles prefer to affiliate with the Yankees as Republicans. Recently one of them was made a member of the Republican committee of the town. He was so impressed by this "responsibility," as he called it, that he even withdrew from the Polish benefit society to which he belonged, and took out insurance in a regular company instead, in order to be a full-fledged "American."

"It won't be long before we have plenty of voters," the Poles say, "and then we'll vote with the English and give them all the offices they want."

Another medium which is enlisting participation on the part of the Poles is a so-called board of trade, which is really a sort of community improvement association working in close cooperation with the town officials. One of the Polish leaders was elected a vice-president, and through him others became interested and have served particularly on committees in charge of local celebrations during the war. The prejudices of this little village, however, have cropped out even in this organization.

Two Irish members who have been criticized as "political bosses" have rather dominated it, and because of this the Yankees and Poles have not taken hold as enthusiastically as they otherwise might. The Poles became suspicious also because a committee, which included no Polish representatives, was organized to see if boys could be obtained through the state farm bureau as summer laborers. They saw in this an attempt to undermine their industrial position. The Irish element, on its side, criticizes the Yankees for not taking a more active part in the organization, alleging that they want their Congregational Men's Club to be the "whole thing."

The same sort of informal neighborliness, however, which played so large a part in blending the earlier immigrants with the community, is working to the same end, if more slowly, in the case of the Poles. Polish children mingle with the others at the village school and take part in public entertainments given by the school children. An increasing number of Polish parents attend these affairs. A Polish boy was recently elected captain of the soccer and basketball teams. A troop of Boy Scouts was organized several years ago and Polish boys were included.

The old custom of friendly visiting and assistance in time of trouble is practiced toward the Poles and reciprocated by them. The principal of the village school told how, when illness and death afflicted her home, Polish families called to express their sympathy and give practical help. Polish girls employed as domestics become a connecting link between the prior residents and the Poles. When these girls marry and go to live in homes of their own neighborly relations with their former mistresses often follow.

People generally call one another by their first names, and the Poles have quickly fallen in with this custom. There is a good deal of neighborly chatting and visiting at the gate or on the piazza. The first Pole who came to the village tells how pleasantly he remembers being invited into American homes to hear their new victrolas. One Yankee woman plays accompaniments two evenings a week for Polish girls who sing in their church choir, and has also had these girls at her home for Christmas dinner. Another Yankee said there was really no one he enjoyed chatting and smoking with more than a Polish friend who frequently came to see him. The rest of the community takes a real gossipy interest in the christenings, weddings, and other family affairs of the Poles, and are more and more coming to regard them no longer as "foreigners," but as "neighbors."

### UNITY THROUGH THE WAR

The war brought us all together in united action and made us realize more fully than ever before that we were really a neighborhood.

This is the testimony of scores of different people regarding scores of different neighborhoods throughout the country. Most of the neighborhoods of which this has been said are parts of large cities, in which the shifting of population and the cross currents of general community movements more or less confused and obscured neighborhood identities, until the patriotic appeal of the war caused them to surge into conscious expression. Such self-revelation is strikingly illustrated by Hopeville's reaction to war demands for unity of action. This little village shows in simple form the kind of neighborhood response which in varying measure took place throughout the nation.

In Hopeville the war put what may be regarded as almost the finishing touch upon the union of the Irish element and the Yankees. The "Real Folks" of the Congregational church combined with the Women's Endeavor of the Catholic church to form a single auxiliary of the Red Cross, and the wife of the son of a German immigrant was made president.

The local events of the war also did much to advance the incorporation of the Poles in the village life. Poles served on the committees for all the Liberty Loans and canvassed their people with good results. They shared in the Red Cross drives. They turned out for community singing. Polish women helped in the food-saving campaign. At the Welcome Home celebration for returned soldiers, a Pole made one of the addresses. Following the armistice, the town officials planned a celebration. They had not thought of including the Poles in any special way, but the latter had been making some plans themselves and came to ask if they might join in the general demonstration. Their request was granted gladly.

But we did not expect them to make the splendid showing that they did [said one of the villagers]. They got up a big parade. Their societies, about which we had not known very much before, marched in uniform, with American flags. They got out every one—men, women, and children. It was fine. Really, we were proud of them. We'll always think differently of the Poles hereafter.

The day's celebration culminated in a mass meeting in front of the Memorial. Polish young people were members of the chorus which sang patriotic songs, and Polish leaders were among the speakers. In the evening there was a dance at the Academy. Formerly such purely social affairs had not included the Poles, but Polish young people attended this dance and mingled naturally and freely with the others. Since then they have attended other village dances, and have been cordially received. A marked change of attitude has come about. Many Polish men of foreign birth are now citizens by virtue of their service in the war. The first generation born in Hopeville is beginning to contribute voters and leaders.

## THE FUTURE

Forecasting the future from the lessons of the past, the outcome of what is now taking place may readily be anticipated. Before many years the Poles will pass entirely beyond the "foreign" stage. They will be as much an inner part of the community as the children and grandchildren of the earlier Irish, French-Canadian, and German immigrants are to-day. As the latter have in many ways outstripped the original Yankees, so will they in turn be outstripped by the Poles.

The children and grandchildren of the Polish immigrants will become leaders in industry and political affairs, and for a while will play the foremost part in the community. Then, perhaps, will come another invasion of immigrants of some other race, whom the Poles will look upon as "foreigners," but who, with the hardiness and enterprise of pioneers, will in due time establish themselves as firmly as their predecessors.

## 2. AS IN HOPEVILLE, SO EVERYWHERE

In the little village of Hopeville it has been possible to trace very clearly the neighborhood process through which the immigrant is united with the American community. Essentially this same process is working itself out in every neighborhood in which the immigrant is a factor. It is a process which is altogether so natural as to be inevitable, but the conditions under which it goes on, its rate of progress, and its stage of advancement differ from one locality to another.

In separate immigrant towns, like those described in an early chapter, this process takes place mainly within the immigrant group. Through its own inner tendencies, and with a minimum of immediate association with native Americans, such a community becomes American in spirit and in fact, while at the same time it tends to dissolve by infusing its native-born young people into the American community at large.

At the other extreme, where only a few immigrants are scattered through a predominantly American neighborhood, the process must take place chiefly through association with Americans, in both informal and organized ways, and group activities of the immigrants figure incidentally or not at all.

# THE OUTCOME

The Hopeville situation is about midway between these two extremes. There colonies or clusters of immigrants immediately adjoining the American neighborhood were soon broken up and scattered through the community. On the one hand, Americanizing forces inherent within the immigrant groups, and on the other the influences growing out of close association with native Americans, have worked closely together and contributed jointly to the final outcome.

### THE COLONY'S EVOLUTION

In the case of the most usual type of immigrant neighborhood, the racial colony in the midst of a large city, it is obvious that there cannot be such close contact with the surrounding American population as is not only possible, but practically unavoidable, in such a place as Hopeville.

The colony itself is far larger in numbers and its centripetal influence is far greater. Owing to the bigness and busyness and sophistication of the city, the Americans living round about the colony, if not entirely indifferent to its existence, take only a casual interest in its people. Neighborly association between immigrants within the colony and Americans outside is conspicuous chiefly by its absence. Under these conditions, the colony is thrown back upon itself, and compelled to work out its Americanization through its own resources, with the help of such American agencies as may be operating there.

At the same time the colony, being within the boundaries of the city, is not isolated geographically as is a separate immigrant town, and for this reason cannot develop, under the present scheme of municipal government, anything like the civic self-direction that obtains in separate towns. In the towns the responsibility of self-government is one of the most vital factors in their self-Americanization. The colony is cut off from authoritative self-direction on the one hand, and from neighborly contact and association with native Americans on the other. Its Americanization must be brought about in the face of both these obstacles.

Earlier chapters described some of the ways in which, under colony conditions, immigrant groups undertake to solve their own problems and relate themselves with the surrounding community and American life. The previous account may now be supplemented by indicating briefly how these inner forces eventually affect the colony as a whole.

### ZONES OF SETTLEMENT

Though there are many variations, the history of a typical racial colony is as follows: A few immigrants of a given race arrive in a given city, where, let us assume, no others of their race have settled. Being under the necessity of finding the cheapest living accommodations as soon as possible they naturally seek out or are directed to that section of the city which has come to be the chief quarter for newly arrived immigrants.

Most cities have such a quarter. In New York, for example, it is the lower East Side. Though the Jews are colonized there in largest numbers and it is popularly known as the Ghetto, the lower East Side has been the first abiding place of nearly every racial group in that city. It is a great incubator, so to speak, in which these colonies are hatched, and in which they gather strength sufficient to push their way out.

The immigrants whose colony history we are tracing find living quarters in such a section. If possible, they locate near another group akin to themselves in race or language, with whom they feel some affinity and from whom they can get information. They write ere long to relatives and friends in the old country and in other cities, telling them where they are. Fellow countrymen come to the city and locate in the same locality. Thus the first colony of this racial group begins to grow and take form. At first the immigrants who make it up may be rather scattered, but as their numbers increase they tend to get together on the same streets, and even in the same tenements, and the colony becomes compact.

Almost as soon as it begins to crystallize, however, this first colony begins to dissolve. Its living accommodations, as has been noted, are the cheapest procurable. Often only one or two rooms must suffice for a family. As the members of the colony find work and get ahead, they are quick to move into somewhat better quarters in a somewhat better locality. They may move only a block or two away, but even so it is a move toward betterment and publishes the fact that they are getting on. The more progressive members move first; others follow as soon as they can. Some are left behind and are lost in a residue of many races.

The majority, however, form a second colony some distance farther along. As other immigrants of this race come to the city, those whose savings permit locate in this second colony at the outset. Then the pushing-out process begins again. The more successful immigrants move on to a still better district, others follow and a third colony takes shape. If the stream of immigration continues, the second colony is larger than the first, and the third may be larger than the second.

Whether the onward movement keeps up and forms further successive colonies depends on many circumstances. As a rule, it does not stop till a section is reached in which there is not so much pressure of population from other quarters but that the group can settle down there and expand. As the craving to own homes is characteristic of most immigrants, migration usually lands the group in an open district on the outskirts of the city where homes can be bought within the means of its members.

The Bohemian colony in New York may be cited as an illustration. This colony had its beginning in the lower East Side and became fairly well developed there. About thirty years ago it began to move northward, but two intermediate stops were made before its present location in the upper East Side became the center of concentration, to which all society headquarters, previously established downtown, were transferred. Though the present site of the colony is a tenement district of the better grade and property values preclude home-owning by the rank and file, a good deal of property is owned by Bohemian landlords who rent to their fellow countrymen on favorable terms, and this has been an important factor in holding the colony where it is. It is now moving farther north as the Italians push in from the south.

As the onward movement develops, the colony may split into several parts, each of which becomes a smaller separate colony. Thus the Italians in New York, starting likewise in the lower East Side, now have one colony there, another in the upper East Side just south of the Bohemians, a third still farther north in Harlem, others on the West Side, and still others in the outlying boroughs and the suburbs.

Besides dividing up in this way, the colony tends gradually to diminish in size, especially in the later stages of its development, because many of its more prosperous members move into American neighborhoods. Sometimes, in order to retain old associations, a small number of families who migrate thus will cluster together in their new location, but frequently single families go into neighborhoods where there are no others of their own race.

One of the chief reasons which lead immigrant families away from the colony is their desire to rear their children under more immediate American influences. The children themselves, as they grow up, often persuade their parents to move. As the native-born young people marry and establish homes of their own, they leave the colony in large numbers, and settle either in American neighborhoods or in what may be called semi-colonies of the second generation. For example, the Harlem Jewish district in New York is settled largely by young native-born Jews who have moved up there from the lower East Side. In Chicago there is a large Bohemian settlement of the same sort.

The young people often take their parents with them, or are followed by them later. Such second-generation settlements stand midway between the immigrant colony and dispersion through the community at large. When they include native and foreign-born people of different racial stocks, as they often do, they represent the cosmopolitan type of neighborhood. In this respect they are a transition stage between the one-race neighborhood of the foreign born and the neighborhood composed almost wholly of native born and known as "American."

As the result of these inner tendencies toward division and dissolution, most racial colonies would disappear with the passing of the foreign-born generation were it not for the fresh immigration through which they are continually replenished. On the other hand, were it not for the existence of the colony, the assimilation of large numbers of new immigrants would be far more difficult. In inducting such newly arrived immigrants into the life of America, the colony plays a vital part.

The absorption of fresh immigration may maintain or even increase the numbers within the colony, notwithstanding the constant outward movement. Such being the case, its foreign character may seem at first glance to be stationary or increasing. But on more careful analysis it appears that the colony is a dynamic organism, whose function it is first to adjust the immigrant to his new environment and then to graduate him or his children into the community at large.

These colony outworkings develop at different rates of speed and take somewhat different forms in different racial groups and under different local conditions. English-speaking immigrants, as might naturally be expected, scatter most quickly throughout the community. The Welsh and Irish, however, often develop colonies, while even Scotch and English immigrants, though interspersed with native Americans in residence, have their church and society centers, through which they maintain a more or less distinct group life of their own. The Scandinavians, particularly the Swedes, are quick to scatter and to learn English. This is also the tendency among the Greeks.

The extreme of colonization is probably to be found among Germans, Poles, and French Canadians. In their case the outward movement and the colony's dissolution take place comparatively slowly. Their Americanization must therefore proceed in larger measure through the inner forces of the group. All three of these races, but most pronouncedly the French Canadians, insist on the conservation of their native culture and traditions and emphasize the colony's stabilizing effect and its cultural contributions to America.

Examples previously cited show how the cultural activities of these groups, as well as their more directly adaptive activities, interrelate them in a natural and substantial way with the general community and the life of America. The immigrant group which is least attached to its own heritages and which is willing most speedily to discard all that has to do with its native culture and standards is not necessarily the group which makes the best Americans. On the contrary, other things being equal, a group which takes pride in the heritages which it brings to America is the sort which is most desirable. Not mere imitativeness and facility, but creative ability and stamina, are the qualities required for sound Americanism. Some of the immigrant groups whose mills grind slowest may in the end grind finest.

### 3. CONCLUSIONS AS TO METHODS

The study of which this volume forms a part has to do specifically with *methods* of Americanization. What general conclusions may now be drawn as to the methods which are most effectively applied through the medium of the neighborhood?

Throughout the foregoing discussion the aim has been to present actual facts, and to let these facts indicate the methods which are successful. Though in the main different methods have been considered in their larger aspects, and more as policies than in exhaustive detail, a good many details of procedure, as for example those mentioned in connection with the work of social centers and branch libraries, have been examined. Reiteration of such details at this point would be superfluous, nor would a mere summary be adequate. What is needed is to get down to those elements, in the various methods considered, which are so essential and so basic as to amount to *principles*.

In the light of the preceding discussion, it is submitted that three fundamental principles emerge as the foundation stones, upon which any successful neighborhood program of Americanization must rest. These principles, which may be called the A B C of Americanization, are as follows:

# AMERICA VIA THE NEIGHBORHOOD

A. Start with an adequate conception of Americanization;

B. Find out what the immigrants themselves are doing in this direction;

C. Correlate the program in view with the inherent forces and activities of the immigrant group.

### A. PARTICIPATION

However loosely and variously the term Americanization is used in its immediate application, in the last analysis it implies nothing less than taking part in and contributing to the common life of America. The essential tests by which such constructive participation is to be judged are loyalty to America, devotion to the American ideal of democracy, and the present application of that ideal in terms of democratic activity which is "*of* the people, *by* the people, and *for* the people."

Americanization thus understood is a process which begins as soon as participation in American life begins, which cannot be taught out of books or otherwise injected or bestowed, and which takes place only through and in pace with actual participation in community affairs. Furthermore, it is a process which, though presenting certain special problems in the immigrant's case, applies to native born as well as to foreign born. It is a great adventure in democracy in which native and immigrant Americans are equally engaged, and in which the effective Americanization of either is dependent upon and limited by that of the other.

## B. SELF-DETERMINATION

The question of what the immigrants themselves are doing in the direction of Americanization leads into the little explored field of organized neighborhood activities of immigrant groups.[1] The immigrant colonists of to-day organize to meet the problems which confront them in their new world in virtually the same way that the New England Colonists organized to meet the New World problems of their day.

The immigrant likewise exemplifies in practical ways those traditional qualities of initiative, self-reliance, and self-direction which we hold up as the chief characteristics of the typical American. Instead of allowing native Americans to provide for him as a dependent unable or unwilling to provide for himself, instead of being a burden or a parasite, the immigrant at once proceeds to meet his own needs in his own way and to take care of himself.

He does this by means of a great number and variety of organizations and activities. Though in the main these activities are carried on by each racial group within its own ranks and in its own language, their animating motives and tenden-

---

[1] Chapters ii to v.

cies are America-ward, and their ultimate effect is to interrelate the immigrant group with the surrounding community and with the common life and interests of America.

In Colonial times Dutch, French, and Spanish Colonists settled compactly in certain regions, organized closely among themselves, and for a time developed their communities along the lines of their own racial traditions and culture, but they eventually united with the predominating Anglo-Saxon element in common Americanism and equal patriotism.

The various immigrant groups which are colonizing in America to-day claim the same self-respecting rights and are passing through the same natural Americanizing process. They are working out their union with America in a way which is truly democratic, in that it is *of* them and *by* them, as well as for them and for America. The common assumption that immigrant colonies and group coherence prevent Americanization is a fallacy which is itself the most pernicious obstacle to real Americanization.

If American democracy is to be distributed throughout America, and not restricted to any one assumedly superior racial element or any one class, then every part of the population must function democratically and self-directingly, and thus contribute its maximum to the total democratic energy and resourcefulness of the nation. The various immigrant groups which are peopling America to-day are fulfilling this requirement in high degree. As pioneers they are constantly

refreshing our democracy and demonstrating its
efficacy anew.

## C. PARTNERSHIP

But much as the immigrants are doing themselves,
they cannot fully accomplish their Americanization alone and unaided. Americanization is
an undertaking in which both foreign born and
native born are mutually engaged. While each
does his respective part, both must also work
together. This is why the third foundation
stone, in any program for Americanizing the
immigrant, is to correlate that program with
what the immigrants themselves are doing, so
that native and foreign born really co-operate.

Speaking generally, the attitude toward the
immigrant of the social settlement, the neighborhood association, the school center, and various
other agencies of an assumedly neighborhood
character, is not thoroughly democratic, but
more or less philanthropic or paternalistic.
To a large degree such agencies are working
rather *for* the immigrant than *with* him.[1]

In consequence, the extent to which they succeed in getting a whole-hearted response from the
immigrant and in enlisting him in their activities
is limited. Such better results as are obtained
are due to a policy of meeting the immigrant
on his own ground and allowing him to share
in the enterprise rather than merely to accept
its benefits. The notable achievement of the

[1] Chapters vi to ix.

foreign-language division of the Liberty Loans was cited as demonstrating on a nation-wide scale the effectiveness of this policy.

Labor unions, co-operatives, and political organizations really take the immigrant into democratic partnership with the native American. Their activities have succeeded in enlisting the immigrant actively and in bringing native and foreign born together in close, harmonious and effective working relations and a common Americanism.[1]

This is because, first of all, the appeals which such forms of activity hold out to the immigrant are vital and practical. Labor unions and co-operatives have to do with his daily bread and the livelihood and well-being of himself and his family. Political organization has to do with the final and authoritative expression of democracy in terms of actual government. These appeals impress him as virile and adequate, and therefore he responds to them.

In the second place, labor unions, co-operatives, and political organizations are comparatively free from the elements of patronage, condescension, and uplift which estrange the immigrant from more distinctly philanthropic and paternalistic efforts. Owing largely to the numerical importance of the immigrant in the fields with which these self-dependent movements are concerned, they take him in on an even footing and make him a bona-fide partner.

They are based on an adequate conception of

[1] Chapters x to xii.

Americanization as actual participation. They recognize the natural lines of association of the immigrant groups by sanctioning organization on racial lines, but they correlate the kindred immigrant activities with the general American program by incorporating the racial organizations in the comprehensive American movements. These basic forms of activity therefore point the way to the most effective methods of Americanizing the immigrant. They demonstrate that the only methods which produce adequate results are those which *apply* democracy by actually taking the immigrant into *partnership*.

### COMMUNITY ORGANIZATION

There is a great deal of talk to-day about "community organization," and a good many more or less competing and conflicting schemes and programs are being zealously advocated. But withal, there is very little definition of just what community organization means, and very little in the way of tangible and durable results. There is plenty of promotion on the part of the "organizers," but for some reason this does not seem to produce much motion on the part of the communities which figure as the largely involuntary objects of all this benevolent effort.

Though this study has been concerned specifically with the immigrant, most of the agencies of which it has taken account do not restrict

461

their activities to the immigrant alone, but have to do with neighborhood and community problems in general. Such being the case, while the specific conclusions drawn here are confined to the effectiveness of these agencies in relation to immigrant groups, it is suggested that the facts which have been presented have a broader implication, and that the basic principles here involved determine the organization of any community, whether made up of foreign born or native born, or both.

Is not the real nub of community organization so to organize the local community that it will more and more function actively of itself, without the necessity of constant stimulation and subsidy from without? If there is no such motive power resident in the local community, then the task of its organization is endless and eventually futile. But if such inner power does exist, manifestly this inherent energy should be released and utilized.

Community organization may then be defined as the local vitalization of democracy, so that the neighborhood truly functions in ways which are "*of* the people, *by* the people, and *for* the people." Organization on this basis is final and lasting, because it rests on a solid foundation. The reason why most schemes of community organization are not accomplishing much is that they are attempts from without, and usually from above, in which the neighborhood itself has little or no part and to which therefore it fails to make any substantial response.

# THE OUTCOME

But while these outside schemes come and go, durable community organization is growing up within the neighborhood itself—organization which does not have to be forced, but which, on the contrary, to repeat the words that De Tocqueville applied to the township, is "so perfectly natural . . . that it seems to constitute itself."

The neighborhood is of course not the only basis for democratic organization. Such organization may follow lines of occupation, as in the case of trade-unions and professional and commercial associations, or lines of cultural interest, as in the case of artistic, scientific, and educational societies. But certainly the neighborhood is a fundamental basis. If neighborhoods the country over are not to run the affairs which are primarily their own, but are to be run by outsiders, whether "experts" or not, then, no matter how efficiently they may be run, democracy will be done for, and oligarchy, bureaucracy, or benevolent paternalism will take its place.

Not *pro*motive, but *auto*motive community organization will fulfill America's democratic ideal. Of such self-directing organization the *neighborhood* is a natural and vital nucleus.

# INDEX

# INDEX

# INDEX

473

PATTERSON SMITH REPRINT SERIES IN
CRIMINOLOGY, LAW ENFORCEMENT, AND SOCIAL PROBLEMS

PATTERSON SMITH REPRINT SERIES IN
CRIMINOLOGY, LAW ENFORCEMENT, AND SOCIAL PROBLEMS